(Continued from front flap)

license and supreme egotism is refuted
in these pages. Its essence as a credo of
humanist action and its insistence upon
ethical responsibility without religious
faith are vividly portrayed.

Included in this collection are:

Those Years: Existentialism 1943-1945—
JACQUES GUICHARNAUD

Sartre's Roads to Freedom—
HENRI PEYRE

Les Séquestrés d'Altona—
ORESTE PUCCIANI

*Humanistic Existentialism and
Contemporary Psychoanalysis*—
HAZEL E. BARNES

The Self-Inflicted Wound—
KENNETH DOUGLAS

Anguished Responsibility—
H. J. BLACKHAM

EDITH KERN, the editor, teaches French
literature at St. John's University, in
New York. She has also been Visiting
Professor of Comparative Literature at
the University of California, Los Angeles.
She received her doctorate at The Johns
Hopkins University and is a frequent
contributor to *Yale French Studies,
Contemporary Literature,* and *Modern
Drama.*

TWENTIETH CENTURY VIEWS

The aim of this series is to present the best
in contemporary critical opinion on major
authors, providing a twentieth century perspective on their changing status in an era
of profound revaluation.

Maynard Mack, *Series Editor*
Yale University

SARTRE

S A R T R E

A COLLECTION OF CRITICAL ESSAYS

Edited by

Edith Kern

A SPECTRUM BOOK

Prentice-Hall, Inc., *Englewood Cliffs, N.J.*

LIBRARY OF CONGRESS CATALOG CARD NO.: 62-17794

Printed in the United States of America

79111-C

Table of Contents

INTRODUCTION—*Edith Kern*   1

Preamble

    THOSE YEARS: EXISTENTIALISM 1943-1945—
    Jacques Guicharnaud   15

I. Fiction: The Novel

    THE DUPLICITY OF BEING—*Claude-Edmonde Magny*   21

    SARTRE'S *ROADS TO FREEDOM*—*Henri Peyre*   31

    THE SELF-INFLICTED WOUND—*Kenneth Douglas*   39

    JEAN-PAUL SARTRE: THE NOVELIST AND THE
    EXISTENTIALIST—*Edmund Wilson*   47

II. Fiction: The Theater

    THE STRUCTURE OF EXISTENCE: *THE FLIES*—
    Theophil Spoerri   54

    MAN AND HIS ACTS—*Jacques Guicharnaud*   62

    SARTRE'S STRUGGLE FOR EXISTENZ—*Eric Bentley*   73

    COMEDIAN AND MARTYR—*Robert Champigny*   80

    LES SÉQUESTRÉS D'ALTONA—*Oreste F. Pucciani*   92

III. Fiction: Style

    THE RHYTHM OF TIME—*Fredric Jameson*   104

IV. Literary Criticism

EXISTENTIALISM AND CRITICISM—*René Girard*   121

LITERATURE AND POETRY—*Guido Morpurgo-Tagliabue*   129

V. Philosophy

THE NEW EMPIRICISM—*John D. Wild*   136

EXISTENTIALISM AS A PHILOSOPHY—*John D. Wild*   142

VI. Existential Psychoanalysis

HUMANISTIC EXISTENTIALISM AND CONTEMPORARY PSYCHOANALYSIS—*Hazel E. Barnes*   149

VII. Politics

NEO-MARXISM AND *CRITICISM OF DIALECTICAL REASONING*—*René Marill-Albérès*   161

ANGUISHED RESPONSIBILITY—*H. J. Blackham*   166

Chronology of Important Dates   172

Notes on the Editor and Authors   173

Bibliography of Works by Sartre   175

Selected Critical Bibliography of Works on Sartre   177

SARTRE

Introduction

by Edith Kern

"Je leur ai laissé la vie entre les mains." ["I left my life in their hands."] This groan uttered by Garcin in Sartre's play *Huis-clos* [*No Exit*] must have come to the author's own lips many a time when he beheld his image as man and writer in the eyes of his contemporaries. Like Garcin, he must have felt the hellish torture of seeing himself objectified and transfixed by "the Look of the Other" that denied him those infinite possibilities of change which constitute human freedom. The impact of the Other on the Self which Sartre has explored with so much originality —philosophically in *L'Être et le néant* [*Being and Nothingness*] and dramatically in his entire fiction and particularly *No Exit*—must have been doubly apparent to him as the eyes of wartime Paris focused on him, the successful playwright. When his early plays *Les Mouches* [*The Flies*] (1943) and *No Exit* (1944) were staged, Sartre was by no means a newcomer to the literary scene. On the contrary, his novel *La Nausée* [*Nausea*] (1938), and his collection of short-stories *Le Mur* [*The Wall*] (1939), as well as his philosophical treatises, had met with considerable success. But their success could not match the sensational excitement that accompanied the production of *The Flies,* which seemed to carry a message of man's courage and responsibility to a Paris smoldering in a sense of defeat. Nor had Sartre's earlier achievements created anything like the sensation of solidarity in the face of common adversity that the audiences of *No Exit* experienced when they attended performances against a background of bombing and blackouts that held the hope of liberation but also the threat of death.

Torn from the quiet context of his life and work and thrust into the sudden glare of fame, Sartre appeared as the popularity-hunting "existentialist," "nauseated" by wartime conditions, a libertine advocating individual license. What remained in darkness was the man Sartre as he was known to his friends: a kind and patient man, habitually absorbed in thought. Nor did the philosopher come into view who, in *Being and Nothingness*, had developed a disciplined philosophical system; or the serious, imaginative author of *Nausea* and *The Wall*— stories permeated with the very thoughts that preoccupied him and which he considered expressive of the drama of modern philosophy. The sudden

1

glare of fame even blinded Sartre's critics to the fact that his philosophy, by its very nature, disdained to prescribe to other human beings the conduct of their lives and, rather, imposed upon each individual the full responsibility of choice and decision. Sartre's sudden notoriety kept concealed above all the moralist who, like some of his greatest predecessors, both Christian and non-Christian, was imbued with an awareness of man's solitude and responsibility in the world and who believed, like Rousseau, in the basic goodness of man. Moreover, many of his critics remained unaware of the fact that Sartre was largely following lines of thought already pursued by his own compatriot Gabriel Marcel and, in Germany, by such philosophers as Jaspers and Heidegger—prevailing indeed in all Western countries, except England and the United States. Unfortunately, it was this stereotyped and obliquely lighted image of Sartre that first crossed the Atlantic to the United States—only to suffer further from the fact that the first of Sartre's works to be translated was a hastily composed speech intended for a general audience. Published as a pamphlet, it bore the title *L'Existentialisme est un humanisme* [*Existentialism Is a Humanism*], which was translated as *Existentialism* and thereby acquired a significance hardly intended by the author.

But as critics in France and abroad have turned their gaze again and again upon Sartre, ever new aspects of that complex phenomenon, "Jean-Paul Sartre," have come to light and have led to significant appraisals and reappraisals of his work. It seems appropriate therefore to stop and pass in review some of the representative critical evaluations of Sartre's achievements in the fields of fiction: the novel, the theater, his style (Chapter I-III); literary criticism and biography (Chapter IV); philosophy (Chapter V); existential psychoanalysis (Chapter VI); and practical political thought (Chapter VII). Represented in this volume are authors in England, France, Italy, Switzerland, and the United States. Because of the vastness of the available material and the limitations imposed by space, only brief reference could be made to others—some of the greatest importance. Being by necessity contemporary with the author's writings, the evaluations in this volume are, of course, expressive of the sensibilities of our time. As such, they will, we hope, retain their significance, even if future events may show Sartre again in a different light and under different aspects.

It should be made clear first of all that, contrary to popular belief, Sartre never conferred upon himself the epithet "existentialist" which has come to be so inseparably attached to his name and work. The word was applied rather by Gabriel Marcel, and French journalists seized upon it eagerly as a convenient label for Sartre and his followers. To begin with, Sartre thought of himself as a phenomenologist, as is amply proved by the fact that he added to his fundamental work, *Being and Nothingness*, the subtitle *An Essay in Phenomenological Ontology*. Simone de Beauvoir relates in her memoirs an anecdote which clearly reveals that, at the beginning of 1943, the word *"existentialiste"* was still unknown to her. We may infer from this that it was at the same time also unknown to Sartre, with whom, as she candidly admits, her life *"a été étroitement liée"* and the manuscript of whose *Being and Nothingness* she had admittedly read and re-read. (At the time of her record the book was no doubt in the hands of the printer, because it was published that same year.) Simone de Beauvoir tells us that Sartre, having recently made the acquaintance of Jean Grenier, introduced him to her one day early in 1943 at the Café Flore—the meeting place of young Parisian intellectuals of the time. As Grenier talked about his intention to publish a volume on current philosophical thought in France, he turned to her with the question: "Et vous, madame, êtes-vous existentialiste?" ["And you. madam, are you an existentialist?"] Simone de Beauvoir recalls her embarrassment of the moment at not having known the meaning of the word. She had, of course, read Kierkegaard, and was familiar with the term *"existentielle"* as used in discussions of Heidegger's work, but the word *"existentialiste"* had not yet come to her attention. It had been only then put into circulation, she tells us, by Gabriel Marcel.

So it must have been in the course of the year 1943 and those years following it that Sartre was established as the existentialist writer *par excellence*. Although first objecting to such labeling of his person and thought, Sartre soon resigned himself to it and himself adopted the epithet. Had he not realized in *Being and Nothingness* that "the being of an existent is never to reveal itself completely" and that man was not justified in assuming the image he held of himself to be closer to reality than that which Others beheld? Had he not, therefore, to accept as reality the way in which he revealed himself to the Other—be that ever so fragmentary and incomplete? The freedom left to him was that of not conforming to the mold Others had prepared for him. Thus we find Sartre, by 1946, blatantly displaying the word "existentialism" in the title of his pamphlet *L'Existentialisme est un humanisme*. We find Simone de Beauvoir outlining in an article, published at about the same time in *Les Temps modernes*,[1] the "existentialist way" of capturing metaphysical reality in the dramatic moment of experience, maintaining that "existentialism" often chooses to express itself through fiction—mainly novel or play—and citing Gabriel Marcel, Jean-Paul Sartre, and Albert Camus as representative "existentialist writers." It may have been at that time also that the designation "existentialist" came to be used even in connection with Heideggerian philosophy in France—thus supplanting *"existentielle"* which it resembled so much.

Of course, both words derive from the Kierkegaardian phrase "existential dialectic." In its more recent form the word still betrays this origin. But the form merely conceals the changes that have actually taken

---

[1] "Littérature et métaphysique," I, April 1946, pp. 1153-63.

place underneath the apparent unchangeability. In 1947 the well-known French philosopher Jean Wahl reviewed briefly before his fellow philosophers in the Club Maintenant in Paris the history of existentialism. During the discussion, in which Berdyaev, Gurvitch, Koyré, Gandillac, Marcel, and Lévinas participated, it was held that in any formal philosophy or doctrine, "existence"—in the Kierkegaardian sense—was bound to vanish. For Kierkegaard's quarrel was precisely with all formal philosophy: he had objected to Hegel's intellectualization of life and had maintained that it is only in subjectivity that man can know existence. In this sense neither Heidegger nor Sartre, having each developed a formal doctrine, could be considered truly "existential" thinkers, and only Heidegger's somewhat esoteric lyric-philosophical writings and Sartre's fiction could pass the test. Sartre's plays and novels, therefore, must be considered as independent expressions of philosophy and not as mere echoes of the ideas developed in *Being and Nothingness*. Only recently Sartre has emphasized this fact in an interview with Madeleine Chapsal, thus encouraging us to find in his fiction those views on ethics and human relationships that are not included in his philosophical works.

But whether in terms of the history of philosophy Sartre fully deserves the appellation "existentialist" and whether it was bestowed upon him with or without his consent, are moot questions. We may blithely assume that since the middle Forties the terms "existentialist" and "existentialism" have been filled with the meaning inherent in either Sartrean or Heideggerian philosophy. At the Club Maintenant, Jean Wahl gave —with the approval of his fellow philosophers—the following rules of thumb to distinguish between existentialist and non-existentialist philosophers:

> If we say: "Man is in this world, a world limited by death and experienced in anguish; is aware of himself as essentially anxious; is burdened by his solitude within the horizon of his temporality"; then we recognize the accents of Heideggerian philosophy. If we say: "Man, by opposition to the 'In-itself,' is the 'For-itself,' is never at rest, and strives in vain towards a union of the 'In-itself' and the 'For-itself'"; then we are speaking in the manner of Sartrean existentialism. If we say: "I am a thinking thing," as Descartes said; or, "The real things are Ideas," as Plato said; or, "The Ego accompanies all our representations," as Kant said; then we are moving in a sphere which is no longer that of the philosophy of existence.[2]

Thus Sartre's philosophy is plainly established as "existentialism," in spite of these philosophers' awareness of the term's ambiguity in this sense. In adopting the term they merely showed their acceptance of the

---

[2] Jean Wahl, *A Short History of Existentialism*, translated by F. Williams and S. Maron (New York: Philosophical Library, 1949), pp. 31-32. For an explanation of the terms "In-itself" and "For-itself," see Chapter V of this volume.

fact that paradox and ambiguity are at the very heart of existential thinking. It is not accidental that Simone de Beauvoir has entitled her book
on existential ethics *The Ethics of Ambiguity,* and has reminded us that
the basis of Kierkegaard's opposition to Hegel and to philosophy per se
was his affirmation of the "irreducible character of ambiguity" inherent
in human existence: Man is the word become flesh; mind and matter;
the finite moment of the infinite; opaque inertness and translucent,
energetic intelligence; immanence and transcendence.

Heidegger has probably found the most hauntingly poetic manner of
expressing this ambiguity, in the formula *Dasein.* In this ordinary German word signifying *existence,* Heidegger has found concealed the very
essence of human-ness. *Dasein,* which, when broken down into its
linguistic components, simply means "being there," has come to mean
through Heidegger's perceptive exploitation of linguistic relationships,
the "there" of Being or the "here and now" of Being. In human existence
Being is, as it were localized and temporalized. Man is the "here and
now" of Being, for through man alone does Being disclose itself: without man Being would remain innocent of differentiation and phenomenality. Man or *Dasein* is, in Heideggerian terms, the "openness"
of Being. It is its *lumen naturale* through which Being comes to light in
its manifoldness and acquires meaning—within man's horizons of place
and time. Through *Dasein* the world becomes man's world. But since
man is a part of Being—its "here and now"—he cannot be an outside
observer of Being, and no subject-object relationship can exist between
man and Being. Man as the *Da* of *Sein,* the "here and now" of Being,
can neither create it subjectively nor look at it objectively. To live
authentically man must let Being come to light through him—let it
speak through him. He is the *per-sona,* that through which Being speaks.
Because he is the "here and now" of Being he distinguishes himself from
all other forms of existence, conditioning in a historic-materialistic
sense the way in which Being reveals itself. Man is thus always *Being-in-
the-world* as opposed to all else which is merely Being-in-the-midst-of-the-
world.

The terms "subject" and "object" have, in fact, been rejected by
Heidegger as metaphysical anachronisms which insinuated themselves
into occidental thought by way of "logic and grammar" and whose
validity must be challenged.[3] It has since been challenged, as is well
known, by modern poetry and by all those who have turned to Chinese
Zen to find there an attitude totally averse to the Western assumption
that "reality has an intrinsic structural correspondence with the nominal
language structure we use." [4] A similar annihilation of the subject-object
dichotomy has, of course, previously been experienced by poets. It is

---

[3] Martin Heidegger, *Über den Humanismus* (Frankfurt: Vittorio Klostermann, 1947),
pp. 17, 35.
[4] "The Appeal of Zen," *Times Literary Supplement,* Dec. 29, 1961, p. 926.

not at all surprising, therefore, to find Heidegger quoting in his own correspondence a passage from a letter which Mallarmé wrote to a friend almost a hundred years earlier. Written in May 1867, the letter states: "C'est t'apprendre que je suis maintenant impersonnel, et non plus Stéphane, que tu as connu, mais une aptitude qu'a l'univers spirituel à se voir et à se développer à travers ce que fut moi." [5] ["This is to tell you that I am now impersonal, no longer Stéphane, whom you have known, but an aptitude which the spiritual universe possesses to perceive and develop itself by way of that which was my Self."] The poet is not a spectator of the world but the *per-sona* of Being. As a consequence, even language is no longer structured on a logical subject-object relationship but can speak through image and symbol, which ignore this dichotomy.

If such Heideggerian conceptions deserve discussion here, it is because they proved of foremost interest to Sartre. Man's Being-in-the-world became one of the most fundamental concepts of Sartrean philosophy and has usurped his fiction, his literary criticism, his views on writers, and even those on psychoanalysis. We learn from Simone de Beauvoir that Sartre had been reading the works of Heidegger (in the original as well as in the Corbin translation) since the late Thirties, finding in them food for his own thoughts and an echo of his own endeavor to recapture philosophically "the reality of the world." [6] Many entries in Simone de Beauvoir's wartime diary show that the problem of reconciling subjectivism and objectivity came up over and over again in their conversations during those rare hours that Sartre could spend on furlough in Paris. In April 1940 Simone de Beauvoir recorded in her diary a conversation on this topic and the admiration which Sartre felt for Saint-Exupéry's *Wind, Sand, and Stars,* because it seemed to represent the most arresting and convincing illustration of Heideggerian thought. Sartre felt that, in describing the world of the pilot, Saint-Exupéry had arrived at a Heideggerian conception of existence which transcended both subjectivism and false objectivity. To Saint-Exupéry's pilot the airplane had become an organ of perception and the reader a witness to the metamorphosis of earth and sky which the pilot experienced through his plane and in the process of manipulating it. New truths concerning distance and the relationship of forms were thus revealed through new techniques and new tools—all expressive of Being.[7] Saint-Exupéry's pilot was precisely Being-in-the-world, the *Da* of *Sein* where Being came to light.

Sartre's brilliant philosophical essay *The Transcendence of the Ego* (1936-1937) gives evidence of his early preoccupation with the traditional

[5] Quoted by Egon Vietta, *Die Seinsfrage bei Martin Heidegger* (Stuttgart, 1950), p. 39. See also Mallarmé, *Propos sur la poésie,* ed. Mondor (Monaco, 1946), p. 78.

[6] Simone de Beauvoir, *La Force de l'âge* (Paris: Gallimard, 1960), p. 364.

[7] *Ibid.,* p. 447.

subject-object conception and his concern about its philosophical and psychological inadequacy. In an effort to transcend this traditional conception, Sartre presents human consciousness as an absolute consciousness, purified of any *I*. "This absolute consciousness," Sartre concludes, "when it is purified of the *I*, no longer has anything of the subject." [8] Yet, as a first condition of existence, it establishes an interdependence between my *me*—which is-in-the-world—and the world. In this manner the *me* has not been created by the world, nor has the *me* created the world: they are both "objects for absolute, impersonal consciousness, and it is by virtue of this consciousness that they are connected." Such a view of existence makes the *me* co-existent and contemporaneous with the world and endows it with the same transcendence and opacity as any other phenomenon in the world, so that it never reveals itself completely. The psychological and psychoanalytic implications of such observations are only too obvious. (See Chapter VI.) Even Sartre's fictional heroes appear forever as that lucidity which is trying to bring to light a *me* that is Being-in-the-world.

Sometimes this *me* appears to be the promise of self-fulfillment, as when Orestes, the protagonist of *The Flies,* counters Electra's frightened inquiry as to where he will take her with the proud reply: "I don't know; toward ourselves. Beyond the rivers and mountains there are an Orestes and an Electra who are waiting for us. We must search for them patiently." (II,3) Sometimes his lucidity reveals to the Sartrean hero but "thoughts, thoughts on thoughts, thoughts on thoughts of thoughts" from which his *me* ultimately emerges "rotten ad infinitum," as in the case of Mathieu in *L'Âge de raison* [*The Age of Reason*] and that of Roquentin in *Nausea* before him. At other times his pursuit of the *me* proves him to be "nothing"—like the actor Kean in the play by that name: "I took myself for Kean, who took himself for Hamlet, who took himself for Fortinbras." The hero's lucid consciousness may even haunt his *me*—this Being-in-the-world—in an effort to detect whether the reasons for an act committed or to be committed are the "real reasons." Such is the torture experienced by Garcin in *No Exit* as well as by Hugo in *Les Mains sales* [*Dirty Hands*]. A lucidity trying to bring to light his *me*—this is in fact the haunting and hunted Sartrean Intellectual whom Victor Brombert has so perceptively analyzed in his book on *The Intellectual Hero.*[9]

In *Being and Nothingness*, whose period of gestation must have largely coincided with the discussion of Heidegger's Being-in-the-world that Sartre and Beauvoir engaged in, the problem is investigated from still

---

[8] Jean-Paul Sartre, *The Transcendence of the Ego,* translated by F. Williams and R. Kirkpatrick (New York: Noonday Press, 1957), p. 106.

[9] "Sartre and the Existentialist Novel: The Intellectual as 'Impossible' Hero," *The Intellectual Hero: Studies in the French Novel 1880-1955* (Philadelphia: Lippincott, 1961).

another angle. "My body," Sartre writes here, "is co-existensive with the
world, spread across all things, and at the same time it is condensed into
this single point." [10] To this body capable of seeing, smelling, feeling,
and hearing, the world manifests itself in an infinity of ways, though
only in one way at a time. Yet these various appearances of the world
are not to be considered subjective and psychological: they are considered by Sartre as deriving from the nature of things and determined by
human consciousness in the world.[11] Human consciousness becomes a
center in relation to which they arrange themselves in certain perspectives.

Corresponding to this view, Sartre's short stories and novels abound in
descriptions that make us equally conscious of the autonomy inherent in
things and man's sensitivity at their center experiencing and revealing it.
We have but to think of the Public Garden in *Nausea* which suddenly
and unexpectedly "smiles" a Sunday smile at Roquentin:

> I went out and walked through the streets as usual . . . and then suddenly,
> as I opened the gate to the park, I had the impression that something was
> winking at me. The park was deserted and bare. But . . . I wished I knew
> how to say it, the garden did not have its ordinary appearance, it was smil-
> ing at me. I remained a moment leaning against the gate and then, sud-
> denly, I understood that it was Sunday. It was there upon the trees and the
> lawns like a delicate smile.

In his novels, especially *Le Sursis* [*The Reprieve*] (second volume of
the trilogy *Les Chemins de la liberté* [*Roads to Freedom*]), Sartre has
given this philosophical view of the world its most appropriate artistic
expression. There we may briefly glimpse the universe of Ivich, on her
way to Paris on bombed and deserted roads; that of Lola, aging enter-
tainer whom the war deprived of her young lover; or that of Daniel,
feeling the muddy water of the river rising within him as he is about to
drown his cats. In *The Reprieve* an infinity of universes parades before
our eyes, each as detached and lonely as the human being at its center.
An infinity of universes comes into focus, showing objects, places, and
events only for the brief span of time that the human consciousness at
their center lends them its lucidity and a certain order. Then they vanish,
leaving us with the impression that the world of the novel is one of
chaos and that there is no communication between man and man:

> These four walls and this woman on the bed were but accidents without
> importance, one of those inconsistent aspects of the night. Mathieu was
> everywhere as far as the night reached, from the most northern border of the

[10] Jean-Paul Sartre, *Being and Nothingness,* translated by Hazel E. Barnes (New York:
Philosophical Library, 1956), p. 318.
[11] *Ibid.,* p. 317.

country to the Mediterranean. He was with all of it. He looked at Irene with all the eyes of the night: she was but a minute light in the blackness.

The conception of man as Being-in-the-world has also affected Sartre's theories on literature, his criticism. In a discussion on the postwar writer, he has accused novelists of previous centuries of having presented us with a view of the world as if from a window, something merely perceived through the eye and not truly experienced: *"Nous ne sommes pas dedans."* [12] ["We are not inside it."]

Again he praises Saint-Exupéry among contemporary writers for having shown man as Being-in-the-world: man revealing Being while participating in Being. He compares Saint-Exupéry in this respect to the sculptor Giacometti, who also transcended, in Sartre's view, the limitations of subjective idealism as well as those of false objectivity and realism.[13]

It would be quite wrong, however, to give the impression that Sartre merely adopted and adapted the Heideggerian reflections on man's Being-in-the-world. Rather, he used Heidegger's concept of *Dasein* as a point of departure for his own ontological observations, his own descriptions of the conditions under which there may be a world and human reality. These are, of course, described in detail in Chapter V of this volume. What interests us here is the particularly ingenious conception of Nothingness which differentiates the Sartrean world from that of Heidegger. The German philosopher, like the mystic, sees the world, or all-that-is, rise from the abyss of Nothingness into which man is plunged through anguish and dread. Sartre, in a much more humanistic manner, conceives of Nothingness as the prerogative of man's consciousness of Self in the world. Instead of one all-embracing Nothingness, he conceives of many nothingnesses that permeate existence. Consciousness, he holds with Husserl, is always consciousness *of* something. It must, therefore, reveal something which it is not. First rising within man, it reveals to him his Self and the relationship of that Self with other phenomena in the world. At the same time it reveals itself as not being that Self or those phenomena which it reveals. Thus it always represents a momentary rift, a distancing which divides Being into that which it is and that which it is not: an In-itself and a For-itself. This distancing, of which only man is capable, is "nihilating" (*"néantisation"*) and results in Nothingness. Sartre may say, as a consequence, that man brought Nothingness into the world, but by the same token he has "created" the world.

Unfortunately, Sartre's ingenious emphasis on Nothingness in man's perception of the world has often been misunderstood as being a moral and ethical Nihilism. This misinterpretation was, no doubt, facilitated

[12] Jean-Paul Sartre, "Qu'est-ce que la littérature?" *Situations II* (Paris: Gallimard, 1948), pp. 263-65.
[13] Simone de Beauvoir, *La Force de l'âge*, p. 502.

by Sartre's own shift of emphasis from a purely philosophical to a more moralistic plane. We see the translucency and total impersonality of consciousness, as stressed in *The Transcendence of the Ego,* changing more and more into an individual consciousness which implies individual responsibility. In *Being and Nothingness,* the For-itself, which is consciousness, is presented as being anchored in facticity and historicity through the In-itself, without which it cannot exist (since it has to be conscious of something). Though it is nothingness, it is the "nihilation of an individual and particular In-itself and not a being in general."[14]

> The concrete consciousness rises in situation, and it is a unique, individualized consciousness *of* this situation and (of) itself in situation. It is to this concrete consciousness that the self is present, and all the concrete characteristics of consciousness have their correlatives in the totality of the self. The self is individual; it is the individual completion of the self which haunts the For-itself.[15]

> It is in its effort to choose itself as a personal self that the For-itself sustains in existence certain social and abstract characteritics which make of it a man (or a woman) . . . [and] in this sense each For-itself is responsible in its being for the existence of the human race.[16]

This trend towards individualization and humanization in Sartre's philosophy has been clearly perceived by Heidegger, who takes issue with it in a letter entitled *Über den Humanismus [On Humanism],* originally written to Jean Beaufret and later published in a booklet, but unfortunately not yet available in English translation and therefore little known. This letter, clearly a reply to Sartre's *L'Existentialisme est un humanisme,* criticizes Sartre for having stated "we are precisely on a plane where there are only men" and prefers the proposition: "We are precisely on a plane where there is mainly Being." Heidegger asserts that for him *Being* and *the plane* are one and the same thing. For *il y a l'Être* (in German *es gibt Sein*) means that *Being is a given.*[17] Being is simply there, and it is man's essence to reveal Being. This is where his responsibility begins and ends.

Existentialism has established the "authenticity of man's existence" as its most important ethical tenet.[18] Heidegger's *Dasein* achieves such authenticity when it is most genuinely the *Da* of *Sein* and thus has become most genuinely the *per-sona* of Being—that through which Being manifests itself. On the other hand, Sartre's authenticity not only consists in faithful revelation of Being but also makes it the task of the For-itself, which has brought the "why" into the world, to supply the answers and the "wherefor." Human consciousness, having led man through Nausea

---

[14] *Being and Nothingness,* p. 618.   [15] *Ibid.,* p. 91.
[16] *Ibid.,* p. 520.   [17] *Op. cit.,* p. 22.
[18] See also Marjorie Grene, "Authenticity: An Existential Virtue," *Ethics,* LXII, pp. 266-74.

to an awareness of his superfluity, must give itself and the world a reason for being. Man, maintains Simone de Beauvoir in her *Ethics of Ambiguity*,[19] must assume his place in the heart of destiny and, in Kantian manner, assume responsibility for all men. To live authentically he must be aware of his freedom and responsibility of choice—above all of the original choice of his life. Such freedom cannot authorize license because it would thereby deprive any other For-itself of its freedom. Although Sartre declares that man is a "useless passion," trying in vain to bring about a synthesis of the For-itself with the In-itself, man can exist authentically only in living thus passionately. Like Goethe's Faust, man can be "saved," if he strives with all his heart. The Sartrean hero, therefore, instead of indulging in Nihilism, feels himself challenged to heroic existence, like Orestes in *The Flies* or Mathieu at the end of *La Mort dans l'âme* [*Troubled Sleep*]. Though he is Being-in-the-world and thereby defined to some extent in a materialistic-historical sense, man is predestined in neither a Jansenistic (or Calvinistic) nor a Freudian way. Sartre's views, instead of being nihilistic, represent thus an affirmation of man and his responsibilities in the world.

It is true that, in his fiction, Sartre has often chosen indirect ways of pointing towards authenticity and an affirmative acceptance of life, as Claude-Edmonde Magny has clearly shown in her penetrating discussion of *Nausea,* below. Such a negative approach is perhaps most strikingly represented by *No Exit*. It is because he condemned their lack of authenticity that the author put the three characters of the play into the stuffy drawing room which is but a modern version of Hell. The crimes they committed against society are outrageous, but, ironically, society never took any notice of these crimes. Estelle, the nymphomaniac who killed her extramarital offspring, was never found out by either society or her own husband: she died of pneumonia. Inès—who in her burning desire to make others suffer had broken up her brother's marriage, seduced her sister-in-law, and then convinced her that she was responsible for her husband's death (although he died in an accident)— was killed, not for her sins, but because her sister-in-law one night in despair turned on the gas. Garcin, the idealist-pacifist, was shot as a deserter—not for having sadistically tortured his wife by parading his female conquests before her. What we learn from them in the course of their gruesome revelations is that they were dead before they had physically died. For each one had surrendered his freedom of choosing his life. Inès had accepted as a fact that she was born with a certain "character," that all was arranged without her doing, that, from the start, she had been *"une femme condamnée,"* a perverse creature. Estelle had all her life only played a rôle and had watched herself play that rôle before the mirror. The part she played was that of the sweet, sensi-

[19] Simone de Beauvoir, *The Ethics of Ambiguity* (New York: Philosophical Library, 1948), p. 12.

tive young woman who sacrificed her own happiness and married a rich old man to save the life of her sick brother. She lived in a world of make believe never facing reality. Garcin, once the idealist, had long forgotten his idealism and used his intellect only the better to reason away his responsibilities. It is because they have never been "alive" and have never been able to assume their freedom as human beings that the three cannot leave Hell when its doors unexpectedly open. It is because, dead or alive, they cannot live authentically, that their lives are in the hands of Others and that, deprived of the possibility of change, they are tortured by each other's unblinking, merciless stare.

If Sartre's concern here is mainly on a plane of individual philosophy and morality, his shift to one of social scope was soon to follow, largely brought about by the challenging events of the war years. By February 1940 Simone de Beauvoir felt impelled to note in her diary an important change of which she and Sartre had become aware within themselves. Sartre had come to feel that he could no longer remain aloof from political involvement. The concept of "authenticity" at which he had arrived demanded that he "assume" his "situation" in the world, and he could do so only by transcending it and engaging in action. Simone de Beauvoir found herself in full agreement, and the deliberations of the two friends were followed by Sartre's engagement in political activities. Though the very concept of existential authenticity prevented him from adhering to any rigid party-line,[20] it led him directly towards his view of literature as *"engagée."* He began to think of speaking and prose-writing as forms of action—an attitude clearly expressed in *Les Temps modernes,* which he founded and has edited since 1945. From being a writer of pure philosophy and literature, Sartre thus became another link in the long chain of French moralists.

> Like La Rochefoucauld he analyzes human conduct in order to fashion a system for judging it. Like Pascal he insists on the *justification or non-justification of acts and poses the essential problem of their value* when judged in terms of man's fate rigidly and harshly defined.[21]

Now this Sartrean For-itself, which assumes moral responsibility and conceives of writing above all as moral action, could not possibly have the same relationship to language as Heidegger's *Dasein,* from which it was developed. To both philosophers language is essential because without it man could not perform his fundamental task of revealing Being. But to *Dasein* language is not merely a tool. It rather carries within itself so much of Being that only the most subtle and perceptive human being can fully grasp it. Thus to Heidegger the *word* is imbued with

---

[20] *The Ethics of Ambiguity,* pp. 20-22. See also Chap. VII in this volume.
[21] René Marill-Albérès, *Jean-Paul Sartre: Philosopher Without Faith,* translated by Wade Baskin (New York: Philosophical Library, 1961), p. 9.

primordial wisdom. Like Mallarmé and Joyce he has found such wisdom concealed in the etymon and the pun and, like them, he has tried to cleanse language from the dullness of everyday usage and restore it to its pristine splendor. His conception of language is thus that of the poet, to whom only the image can express the full mystery of Being and fully reveal the world because it transcends grammar and logic. To Sartre, on the other hand, the truly authentic For-itself is that of the prose writer who uses language as a means of communication and "names" the world. "Naming" in the Sartrean sense has the significance which it holds in many ancient myths where language is thought to have brought order into primordial chaos. Man is like the Adam of Creation giving a name to all that God has made and thereby making it part of his own world.[22] Thus a word dropped into the vagueness of man's relationship to things and other human beings may suddenly crystallize a certain aspect of the situation and almost magically change it.[23] It would at the same time reveal the situation. Clarity of speech is necessary, in Sartre's view, for such disclosing of reality. Hence his rejection of the poetic image from engaged writing. To the Sartre of "Qu'est-ce que la littérature?" language is above all translucent consciousness, appealing to the translucent consciousness of the Other: the reader. For it is only because of the reader, to whom it may represent a challenge, that the work of literature comes to life. Hence Sartre's concern, similar to that of Brecht, for the audience. Hence his avoidance in his plays of the language of the absurd in spite of the fact that he considers absurdity and irrationality part of the human condition.[24]

In more recent years, however, Sartre seems to have had his doubts about the effectiveness of writing as political action. He has expressed himself in an interview with Madeleine Chapsal in accents similar to those of Swift's Gulliver, when he said "I cannot learn that my book hath produced one single effect according to my intentions."[25] He has concerned himself deeply with such writers as Mallarmé and Flaubert, for whom writing had no reason other than that of constructing their cosmography of the world. He has pointed out, in fact, that these writers were truly *"engagés"* because literature had meant everything to them and therefore their language resounded on all levels of man and society. At the same time he has reminded us in recent interviews that he has never considered it the task of the dramatist to expound political ideas, unless he could translate them into myths.[26] Thus he has lately come to define writing rather as a deep-seated need of man for a purification

[22] Ernst Cassirer, *Language and Myth,* translated by Susanne K. Langer (New York: Dover Publications, Inc., 1946), pp. 71-81.
[23] "Qu'est-ce que la littérature?," pp. 64, 70, 73.
[24] Cf. Martin Esslin, *The Theatre of the Absurd* (New York: Doubleday, 1961), p. xix.
[25] Madeleine Chapsal, *Les Écrivains en présence* (Paris, 1960), pp. 210-20.
[26] Kenneth Tynan, "Jean-Paul Sartre," *Zeit,* XXIX, July 8, 14, 1961, p. 8.

of experience which life does not permit. Only in literary purification
can tragedy be lived tragically and pleasure pleasurably. Again, then,
it is human consciousness and reason that lend meaning to a world
which would otherwise be absurd and distill from it the hardness of
ideas and rules for which Roquentin longed at the end of *Nausea*.

"What all people want, some without being aware of it," said Sartre
in his interview with Madeleine Chapsal, "is to be witness to their time,
their lives and, above all, themselves." For man essentially is the witness,
the judge, the Other. Roquentin, though aware of the futility of the
writer as a teller of tales, must nevertheless tell us how he arrived at the
recognition of this futility. Man's intelligence hovers about the world
of things and other men, revealing Being in its tangible and intangible
form, physically and morally. Without him Being would remain innocent
of differentiation. But he is in turn the object of the Other who, as his
witness and judge, objectifies him. In *Nausea* the man in the blue cape
may arouse in the little girl's eyes a reaction of fascination and horror as
he stares at her, only to lose his power over her as he himself feels
observed and judged. A Look may torture and condemn, as do the
lidless eyes of the three characters in *No Exit*. It may also confirm
existence, as in *Les Séquestrés d'Altona* [*The Condemned of Altona*],
when the eyes of Frantz, who considers himself "the witness of all men"
and "of history," reveal to Johanna that she is beautiful. In *The Reprieve*, Mathieu, feeling himself observed by Irene, is reduced to "a
particle in suspense within a glance." Irene, on the other hand, turns
into a lifeless China doll as soon as her glance loses its intensity. Witness
and being witnessed, man is forever experiencing and re-experiencing the
Fall from innocence, the *"chûte originaire."* But though Sartrean man—
as he looks and is being looked at—forever loses his Paradise, he may,
if he lives authentically, gain a world.

NOTE: The *Bibliography of Works by Sartre* at the conclusion of this volume provides a list of English translations of his works, as well as of the original French editions. Page references in the articles that follow refer to these editions.

Preamble

Those Years:
Existentialism 1943-1945

by Jacques Guicharnaud

I have been asked to be subjective, on the grounds that in 1944 I was in my twentieth year, that I frequented the Café de Flore and, for various reasons, was often in contact with Sartre and the existentialist "group." Often I shall say *we:* "We were sitting outside the Flore. . . . Sartre told us. . . ." This *we* obviously needs definition. In the first place it means myself, or what I remember about myself, revised by the intervening ten years[1] of sometimes tangential development; and it means some of my friends, what I remember about them or imagined I knew. It is an abstract *we.* It is historical; and a handy category for imposing a significance that transcends personal experience on these souvenirs of a time that, by a rather considerable margin, transcended me.

*　　*　　*

Our earliest existentialist "apprenticeship" was spent, in the main, in reading Kafka, Sartre's *Nausea,* and *The Stranger* by Albert Camus. In these works we found (more readily than in Pascal, for we were in-

"Those Years: Existentialism 1943-1945." From *Yale French Studies,* No. 16 (Winter 1955-1956). Reprinted here by permission of the author and *Yale French Studies.* The pages reprinted here are from the original article, which was translated by Kevin Neilson.

[1] The article was written in the summer of 1955.

fidels) the great metaphors that rendered intelligible for us our own lot, made up of solitude and of a complex of slavery and freedom. This coming to consciousness can be achieved only through anguish—and although this may not have been experienced for the first time, now we could give it a name and understand it better.

One cannot begin one's philosophical education at the end, and even less can wisdom be forced on one from the outside. Each man on his own account has to relive the philosopher's progress. At a particular moment in history, for young people of a particular station, the first step, the becoming aware of the actual state of things, must be despair. Anguish and despair were certainly better than thoughtlessness. We were overly happy (if I may put it thus) at having found the writings and the men able to express us, so that our attitude perhaps was not free of a certain pose, of a little snobbery. At all events, it had nothing in common with the spectacular manifestations of romantic despair. Sartre and Simone de Beauvoir, whom we were beginning to frequent, and later Albert Camus, with their seriousness and their rejection of all scandal and frivolity, scarcely invited us to take that path.

They invited us, indeed, to very little. They were not "masters" on the prowl for disciples. We sought them out. Refusing to betray their own time by a flight or refuge into inoffensive literature, they knew that we like others were the representatives of the time; they were less anxious to guide us than to express us, and were convinced that by expressing us and exhorting us to express ourselves (for we all more or less prided ourselves on writing), they would assist in the burgeoning of our freedom.

The tone of the meetings and conversations . . . could not exactly be characterized as tender. The violence of the era, and what was at stake in these discussions, namely our lives or, at least, our consciences, hardly encouraged that. Nevertheless, from more than ten years' distance, I cannot help feeling a sort of tenderness as I recall the immediate setting and the savor of this turning-point in our lives. For example, the smoky warmth of the Café de Flore on certain winter afternoons. Sartre and Simone de Beauvoir usually sat at the back, toward the right. With pipe or cigarettes, glass of tea or spirits, paper and pen, they wrote on (*Being and Nothingness, She Came to Stay* [*L'Invitée* by Simone de Beauvoir]). They were undisturbed there, and warm. One of us would enter, shake hands, chat with them for a moment and then settle down at another table, usually to write also. In the late afternoon Camus, coming from his work at Gallimard's, put in an appearance. Or, perhaps, one of us showed up with a manuscript under his arm: short stories, the first pages of a novel. The thing was read during the next few days by Sartre and Simone de Beauvoir, and duly criticized. If it deserved it, it was passed on to Camus. Throughout these years I can't recollect any of the three having refused substantial criticism and abundant literary counsel to any young author of good faith who asked for their opinion.

Of course, all this had rather the air of a "conventicle." But unlike some other conventicles, this one did not resemble a tolerated house, and even less an ivory tower. Above all, the journalists and other out- siders who have satirized the group failed to record, either from igno- rance or in deliberate misrepresentation, the cordiality that prevailed. "Despair" does not necessarily imply bitterness and a "difficult charac- ter." At times despair and hatred are necessities, or at least realities, there is no sense in closing one's eyes to them; there is no sense, either, in yielding to them: one lives *with* them. Sartre, in any case, with his entire lucidity and his violence, and in the sincerity of his personal drama, has always seemed to me a "good-humored" man. The real Sartre bears no resemblance to the atrabilious and sordid character which cer- tain papers have seen fit to depict. In this connection, here is an anecdote. One evening as with Jean Genet I walked along the banks of the Seine, still quite dazzled by the NRF crowd I was getting to know, I was called to order by Genet, who found my naïveté irritating. After hurling vehe- ment diatribes at some of the establishment's great names, he summed up: "Fundamentally, among all French writers there are only two I really respect: Cocteau because he is intelligent, and Sartre because he is kind."

Some of the thoughtless laugh to hear speak of Sartre's seductiveness. Perhaps that is not the right word. Let us say that he attached us to him by his patent kindness, by the clarity of his articulation, by his refusal of any polite compromise in argument, by the call that went out from him to what we really were, to what our solid education as civilized young intellectuals forced us to hide. After my first meeting with Sartre (it was in a little café behind the Lycée Condorcet—a friend, a former pupil of Sartre's, had taken me along) I was bursting with problems. Everything had become important, lighting a cigarette, stirring a cup of coffee, using certain words and intonations. The world had become an immense trap for catching crimes. I had discovered the uneasy conscience in connection with little things. Sartre had talked on, in the little café, quite unaware of all this; it was my friend who had sized me up shrewdly and judged his shot well . . . I like to think that this individual experience is typical. To employ a term that Sartre himself would detest, he played for some of us the part of an "awakener." "The world is yours," he seemed to say. This did not mean that we should undertake to ensure its continued existence on the lines laid down by our elders, in the hypocrisy of the clear conscience and of the ex- ploitation of Man, camouflaged as fidelity to the traditions of bour- geois humanism. We understood, on the contrary, that the only way to achieve this kind of continued creation of the world was to change it. The majority thought such a procedure ridiculous: those, that is, who lived in accord with a philosophy determined in advance. There were two sections: the bourgeoisie, whether collaborationist or resistant, which (and this quite sufficiently demonstrates the abstractness of its attitude) had chosen one side or the other *for the selfsame reasons;* and the Marxist proletariat, supplemented by some intellectuals who long before had been enfeoffed and enrolled in a universe where these trivial questions could be solved by the utterance of slogans.

By word of mouth, before the Liberation, and subsequently in the newspapers, the Marxist Left indulged in a vigorous criticism of the existentialists, even in the days of "unity of action against the Nazi invader." That distressed us, at the time: for like these people we too placed our hopes in a better earth. The indignation voiced by the Right, which after its wartime divisions was once more united in reaction, always delighted us. To be dragged through the mud by certain papers is, if not a mark of distinction, at least the indication that one is on the track of a few truths. Pious souls took pleasure—as indeed they still do —in dissecting the incoherence, the flaws and certain sleights-of-hand to be found in the Sartrean "system." Apart from the fact that no system can withstand, from beginning to end, a relentless criticism of detail, the dishonesty of these criticisms becomes patent when one considers that (1) they were made by people who, quite frequently, were moved to ecstasy by the "system" of Maurras and his acolytes, either fully realizing (and then they were contemptible) or unaware (and then they were dupes) that Maurras' views were based on an astonishing misreading of history; (2) at the very moment that Europe was undergoing the most gigantic attempt at enslavement, it was criminally frivolous to blame a philosophy that put the concept of liberty in the forefront for confusing Cartesian liberty and political freedom and for giving too little weight to heredity, and to blame its begetter because too often, in his literary works, he used such words as *"merde"* and *"con."*

For liberty is the root of the matter. As a general notion it was perhaps hard to grasp, even for intellectuals: we began to take excessive liberties with it in our philosophy papers, at the Sorbonne or in *Première Supérieure.* Some of our teachers condemned the excessive use we were making of it. It's true: on paper we juggled too freely with such words as "anguish," *"Dasein,"* "nothingness," "liberty," "commitment." But it's no fluke, after all, that they could so readily enter our speech: they aroused in us the consciousness of what we were and of what we might be. And reduced to an over-simple definition, but accurate enough for young bourgeois of eighteen or twenty, Sartre's *"Soyez libres"* resounded with a note quite different from the *"Fais ce que voudras"* of Rabelais' Abbey of Theleme.

This makes sufficiently clear how Sartre had brought philosophy down to earth for us. I envy those of us who were his pupils at the Lycée Condorcet or elsewhere. Many indeed have claimed to "have brought philosophy down to earth." They succeeded but ill: they touch earth but they abandon philosophy, and all ends in a pseudo-positivism, an imbecile

drooling that exalts the illusions of the convenient to the rank of a value.
Sartre, . . . Merleau-Ponty, and Simone de Beauvoir, both in their
purely literary works and in their "phenomenological" essays or studies,
have made our world and the circumstances of our lives intelligible to us.

I repeat: we became horribly entangled in the subtleties of phenomenology, we said plenty of silly things, we reveled in argument—in school,
in the cafés, during our "surprise parties." We could refer our disputes
to Sartre, who never refused to explain (after all, he was a teacher), and
to whom we perhaps rendered a service by compelling him to clarify
for himself certain notions and crucial points in his argumentation.
These "supplementary classes" did not destroy but rounded out the
teaching we received elsewhere, at the Sorbonne or in the preparatory
classes for the *"Grandes Écoles."* Some of our teachers had adopted a
certain mark of dignity: I remember one of them who closed the class-
room door himself and then turned to us. "Once this door is shut," he
said, "we are free. Truth is a prisoner along *with* us." And then he went
on to execute, in all its perfection, the death leap of an *explication de
texte* on Théophile Gautier's "Symphonie en blanc majeur," for example. One can too easily forget that, with his preliminary remark, he
risked Fresnes and the concentration camp. But when all is said and done
it was Sartre who, by his private conversation, enabled us to see in the
proper perspective this sort of courage—and Gautier also. More generally, the world ceased to be absurd because we knew it was absurd, and
in what way. Food shortages, the disappearance of our Jewish friends
and of those in the Resistance, the broadcasts of Radio Paris and the
BBC, our own behavior, our surprise parties under the menace of aerial
bombardment, they all acquired a meaning: tears and sentimental out-
pourings are an acceptance of the absurd, whereas the intellectual
identification of the absurd leads to rebellion.

. . . What we discovered in the course of those years is this, that the
words *greatness, patriotism, citizen, Man, humanism* (and with them, of
course, *work, family, fatherland*) are terribly equivocal, and that a man
is not justified by the "names" of these characteristics recognized as his,
for the name is the height of abstraction.

We knew well the meaning of *virtus* in Latin; yet, without admitting
it to ourselves, we had no idea what *Man* signified. By taking us as we
were, and going beyond both classical humanism and anthropology,
existentialism became for some of us the only possible bridge between
our thoughtlessness, which our milieu had assiduously fostered, and our
entering the world. Thanks to this "philosophy," and to those who had
founded it in France or had adopted it, we became conscious of the
position we occupied and of its possibilities. Whether we availed ourselves of them or not, on each one of us rested the responsibility. Yet
nonetheless, and quite apart from the question of our individual deeds,
for many of us those particular years were a time of purity. No doubt

we had bumped into the problems of retarded adolescence that mark the young bourgeois intellectual. But our fresh attacks of puberty and the minor setbacks of our love-life were readily disposed of, to the extent that we succeeded in realizing that the world we lived in and were a part of had other worries, and could not allow itself the luxury of yearning over an adolescent's blackheads.

On June 6, 1944, I was to meet Sartre on the terrace of the Brasserie Lip, at Saint-Germain-des-Prés. He didn't show up that morning: the Allies had just disembarked in Normandy.

Each of us lived through that following summer as his convictions, possibilities, vocation, and destiny permitted. . . .

In the months that followed the Liberation, the "group" came together once more, impoverished, enriched, and a stage farther on. We lived under the sign of happiness, or at least of that which betokened an extraordinary thirst for happiness. The final victory of the democracies was in sight, we were dazzled by the prospects of freedom suddenly presented us, the world was ours. The intellectual world celebrated the triumph of the writers of the Resistance.

In today's world, that summons to a clear consciousness, which Sartre and his philosophy voiced in 1943, is still valid. Let it not be said that he has hit on nothing new for, even were this true, he would still have been the only one to give it utterance at that time, and to express it in terms we could understand. Today, the evolution of his thinking, of his activity, and of his group continues to hold the forefront of our interest. It is more important and more vital to know and grasp why Sartre adopts one course or another than to mull over the fancies of Mlle Sagan or the latest metamorphosis of Jules Romains. Those pious souls whose essential mission it seems to be to unload their feelings of guilt upon others will accuse us of dwelling in the allegiance of our adolescent years. To which it is easy to rejoin that so far we have seen no reason to change allegiance, and that quite objectively it can only be said that the world, in the last decade, has set nothing before us that would make such a change possible.

I

Fiction: The Novel

The Duplicity of Being

by Claude-Edmonde Magny

It was Sartre's misfortune to have declared the amount of freedom which an author leaves to his characters the mark of true art. Ever since he did so, in an article on Mauriac—and a remarkable one at that—critics have judged him by this very precept. They have tried to find in this problem of freedom the unifying principle of his work—thus expecting an obscure philosophical term to throw light on literary endeavor quite sufficient unto itself. This means misunderstanding the contribution which art—and literature in particular—can make to the problem of freedom. Art and literature oblige us to present freedom concretely, directly, and without the mediation of any readymade "philosophical" categories or, more precisely, social concepts, which current usage forces upon philosophers and of which they have only too often considered themselves the guardians.

What precisely becomes of this concept of freedom at a time when the theory of conditioned reflexes has voided all the traditional arguments for or against the existence of "psychological" determinism and when, on the other hand, the novel (that of Proust or D. H. Lawrence, not

"The Duplicity of Being." From *Les Sandales d'Empédocle, Essai sur les limites de la littérature* by Claude-Edmonde Magny. Copyright 1945 by Editions de la Baconnière, Boudry (Suisse). Translated and reprinted by permission of Editions de la Baconnière. The pages printed here are from the chapter "Sartre ou la duplicité de l'Être: Ascèse et mythomanie." They were translated by James O. Morgan.

to speak of Faulkner or John Dos Passos) seems to manage triumphantly without the Victorian and Louis-Philippian notions of novelistic "characters" on the order of those of Balzac, Meredith, or Thackeray? That is the question we would like to ask our novelists.

We shall try to show that the traditional opposition, freedom-determinism, at least as far as it relates to our actions, must be transcended. Sartre's novelistic work may be considered a move in that direction, for it destroys the notion of a necessity external to ourselves and a stability inherent in things. It also definitely abandons the idea of endowing those beings which it presents to us with a specific "character" as the mainspring of all their actions, recognizing rather as the basis of their existence a choice even more far-reaching than that mythical choice of which Plato speaks in the tenth book of *The Republic*.

It would seem then, at once, that Sartre, the critic of Mauriac, did not simply establish as a universal rule what Sartre the novelist was practicing. What Sartre the novelist has tried to establish through his characters is perhaps—if we wish to put it that way—a certain fundamental "freedom" which they all possess. That freedom, however, is quite different from the one whose absence he regrets in the characters of Mauriac. It has nothing in common with what one usually calls freedom: the power to decide (like Buridan's ass) whether to act or not to act or to choose one or the other action. If Antoine Roquentin and the Pierre of *The Room* have "made a choice," it is less with regard to a specific *act* (one can hardly even speak of an action or a plot in *Nausea* or *The Room*) than with regard to a certain way of life, an attitude towards things, an almost metaphysical choice. They have chosen, for instance, between resisting certain impressions, rejecting them (the price at which sane people daily maintain their sanity)—and letting themselves be invaded and almost submerged by them (though borne by them as on a wave) in the hope of discovering their meaning and thereby attaining a truth surpassing that of normal man. They have chosen what we shall call—pejoratively, it would seem at first—"cheating." This abandonment to certain impressions, this manner of letting oneself sink to the depth of nausea or madness would be impossible without a certain compliance, at least initially—were it for no other reason than that these impressions do such violence to our social habits as must necessitate the consent of our will. Because of the deliberate, "willed" and therefore suspect, almost disquieting quality of this initial choice, we say that the characters of Sartre "cheat." One would have to turn to the Russian novel, to Dostoevsky, to find something comparable: an equally radical choice between the unconscious and madness, a choice which, as much as a deliberate crime or sin, separates the "cheaters" from other men: the Pharisees or those who live smugly or brutishly—all those whom Sartre calls *"salauds."*

The first thing "cheating" requires of us is a renunciation of our "personality," that is, our lucid consciousness and our "will," if we call "will" that semiconscious force which, while imposing continuity on our actions, makes us form connected series of thoughts. The first step consists in letting our "I" dissolve itself; in allowing our thoughts to think themselves within us, without our controlling them; in saying no longer "I," for instance (p. 227),[1] much less "I think," but "something thinks within me"; in being no longer anything but "a little suffering of the town square"; all this even if we must at first buy this impersonality of our thoughts at the price of their precision and the possibility even of communicating them.

> *In the past* [Roquentin says towards the beginning of *Nausea*], *even a long time after she had left me, I thought of Anny. Now I no longer think about anyone; I never even bother to find words.* Something flows within me more or less quickly, *I fix nothing, I let it flow. Most of the time, for lack of attaching themselves to words, my thoughts remain hazy. They outline vague and pleasing forms, then are engulfed:* I forget them immediately. (p. 15)

Then he realizes the impossibility which this will mean of telling about the simplest matters; of telling neat and precise stories, for instance, like those he intends to tell the young people around him:

> *When one lives alone one no longer even knows what it means to tell: The plausible disappears along with one's friends. . . .* But, as if to make up for it, the implausible, all that cannot be seen in cafés, is not lacking.

One sees here what first disappears from thought: the envelope of social concepts which made it communicable, capable of being expressed in words and which at the same time ventured to mask for us the profound reality, enshrined behind the screen of all-too-human concepts. It is then that the "cheater's" social framework crumbles, his integration in a family, a profession, a group of friends and relations—that barrier which usually separates and protects even the most defenseless of men from Nothingness and Nausea. The journal of Antoine Roquentin can only be that of a semi-indolent bachelor, of a *"grand type roux"* who loiters all day long on café benches and lives at a hotel, who even lacks that conventional refuge: a home. It might carry for subtitle that of one of Kafka's fragments, *"Das Unglück des Junggesellen"* [The Misfortune of the Bachelor].

Such "cheating" not only requires that we renounce saying "I," it even means renouncing our "past." For what we call our past is not a veritable sequence of experiences which we once had and whose reality has irremediably vanished, but only their mediocre translation into the

---

[1] For the convenience of the reader, page references are to the translation of *Nausea* by Lloyd Alexander (New York: New Directions, 1959), although the phrasings in the present text do not follow it. The italics are those of the author.

language of the herd for the benefit of other men. There is a sort of mythomania, another kind of "cheating," which consists in telling oneself and others the story of one's life in the form of interesting *adventures* while it is made up of only gratuitous *events,* disconnected, without significance, and leading nowhere.

> *This is what I thought: for the most inane event to become an adventure it must—and that is sufficient—be told. That is what fools people: a man is always a teller of tales, he lives surrounded by his stories and the stories of others, he sees all that happens to him through them; and he tries to live his life as if he were telling about it.* (p. 56)

In other words, he tries to establish between these diverse happenings a fictitious (because totally intellectual) bond, whereas the true feeling of adventure is an imponderable that cannot be expressed conceptually, a state of grace as Roquentin experienced it at the end of that "Sunday in Bouville" ["Mudtown"] (pp. 77-78).

But such is only the negative aspect of "cheating." Like the ascesis which moral and religious systems have always prescribed, this depersonalization and stripping away of all social elements are not undertaken for their own sake. They are justified only because they serve as preparatory to something else. They permit us a contact with certain aspects of reality which we might otherwise never know. As a result of living alone, said Roquentin in the passage we have cited, one ends up losing sight of the plausible: "but, as if to make up for it, the implausible is not lacking." The essential of "cheating" is its value of *revelation.* We must divest ourselves of the social integration of our life and thought, because only then will we be able to see those things that do not exist for the *"salauds."* Thus a certain aspect of the streets of Paris appears only to those who, by vocation or destiny, go to bed late and drag themselves through the streets interminably until dawn. The others will never know anything but the reassuring aspects: the stores, the lighted shop windows, the dense crowds of passersby—but not the solitude, the inhumanity. They will know nothing of the aspect things reassume as soon as they are alone.

The novel *Nausea* in its entirety is dedicated to the description of that objective reality, exterior to us, which can be attained through "cheating." The novel tries to make us accept it and admit that it holds an essential aspect of reality. At the bottom of the experience of "nausea" is the sudden revelation that *things can be almost anything*—that they are not essentially stable, permanent, and immutable as we had believed. The apparent stability which they offer to our view is illusory and may disappear from one moment to another: in fact, if things do not change it is because of their indolence or ours (cf. p. 106).

Recognition of this truth starts with sudden transformations of things.

One day we discover that a certain object, which until then we believed to be well defined and to have certain precise and recognizable characteristics, can appear under the aspect of another which is conceptually as different as can be.

> This enormous belly turned upward, bloody, inflated, bloated, with all its dead legs, this belly floating in this box, in the gray sky, is not a bench. It might just as well be a dead ass for instance, bloated with water and floating adrift, belly in the air, in a large gray river, a river in flood. . . . (p. 169)[2]

At such moments social concepts and words seem to be merely placed upon the surface of things. As soon as we open our eyes a little wider they vanish, leaving us alone with nameless things and at their mercy, without defense against them (cf. p. 169). Then we realize that whatever is stable in existence was put there by us, that we have foisted it upon existence. We realize that by necessity all will crumble some day and abandon us: the barriers we have set up between the objects and ourselves, all the refuges we have built—the walls, the towns, the physical laws, the framework of time and space, the libraries with the reassuring certainty they convey to us that everything which happens—even miracles —happens according to certain laws (cf. pp. 105-106). This is what came to pass on that day of the fog in Bouville: the first revelation of the cosmic range of Nausea.

If one continues to keep one's eyes open, one realizes that one cannot even speak of "things" any longer. That would still be a human concept, a new effort to name what is nameless. For, in reality, there is only existence: something absolutely gratuitous, totally contingent, which is there (one does not very well know why) because of a fundamental absurdity, and whose presence is unasked for. Yet something which is contingent, not in the manner of a pure act, the fiat of some creator who might assert himself proudly, magnificently, as if saying "It is I" without deigning to recognize a law other than his own pleasure, his own desire for a moment of self-affirmation. Existence is something which exists—indolently, limply, with a kind of emptiness—something which cannot help existing.

Nausea, then, is the disgust we experience in the face of that total absence of necessity, either interior or exterior, and the freedom which characterizes existence. This disgust soon changes to horror and dread

---

[2] What is being described is a bench in a streetcar. We should be aware of the fact that this description is made in such a way, I believe, as to make it impossible for anyone not anticipating it to recognize the bench until the object is named and labeled. This procedure is similar to Proust's or Elstir's, except that it is oriented differently— not toward beauty but toward ugliness. Sartre is not after poetry, after something which overwhelms and delights us or puts us in a state of grace; he is after something monstrous that disheartens and horrifies us. But the value of revelation is the same in both cases.

when we discover the ultimate aspect of the world which is, by the way, the immediate outcome of this absence of all necessity; when we discover the capacity for indefinite, lawless proliferation which things carry within them—that tendency to multiply like cells of a cancerous tissue, like bacilli of a colony of microbes, without necessity or reason, simply because the initial impulse was given. Existence, no more than Being, can keep from multiplying and invading all and everything. This is the apocalyptic nightmare of Antoine upon his return from Paris, when he sees the towns invaded by vegetation, the last refuges of man submerged in the rising tide of things existing. "Things" suddenly begin to change their aspect, eyes multiply on faces, and even organisms abandon their familiar shape. Yet all this is nothing new or strange. It has all been *there,* in fact. For these changes without shape or law, which are henceforth possible, always have been essentially inherent in the world of existence which we have before us—though we may not have deigned to recognize them.

Sartre succeeds, by various means, in making us accept this vision of the world, which is so far removed from the ordinary. Sometimes it is a literary device within the novel that leads us gradually toward the vision of Antoine, a certain structuring of the events, a certain order in which experiences follow each other. Sometimes he establishes the value of "cheating" as a means of attaining the deepest reality of "things" through a negative approach. He may present the pitiable spectacle of those who "do not cheat" and even deliberately refuse to do so . . . He may also show the misery of those who dare not go all the way with their "cheating" and who, before having reached the ultimate experience, become afraid and take refuge in one of the many substitutes for "cheating": inane mythomania, for instance. The inner nothingness which is theirs serves to justify the "cheating" of the others. In that respect Sartre's entire work, including his critical essays,[3] abets the negative approach of *Nausea* and thus complements our analysis.

One can distinguish in the novel several "turning points" which establish the objective value of Nausea. Several changes of attitude are required of the reader with regard to the events reported to him. Correlatively, by the way, with each one of these changes the content of the experience becomes clearer. At first Antoine has a whole series of rather confused experiences. There is, for instance, that of the pebble whose significance is not clear to him and even less capable of being formulated. Each one of these experiences is very short: Nausea makes its appearance like lightning which vanishes at once—and even Antoine cannot attribute any value to what has happened. He asks himself simply whether he is not beginning to lose his mind. The first step toward objectivity is constituted by the recognition of an analogous experience in someone

---

[3] Especially those on John Dos Passos and Giraudoux.

else. It takes place on that evening "Chez Camille" between "Monsieur Achille" and Doctor Rogé (pp. 89-96). In the analysis of the reasons which make "Monsieur Achille" participate—even if ever so humbly and dimly—in the same experience as Antoine's while the Doctor is excluded from it, one may recognize the classical proceeding from a proposition toward truth through the intermediary of "universal consent." In the course of the conversation of the two men, wherein their visions of the world are inadvertently juxtaposed, it becomes gradually apparent to us that "Monsieur Achille" is right—even if he is not aware of it, even if the Doctor considers him an "old fool" and he himself accepts the verdict in as much as all appearances speak against him. If the Doctor misses the experience of Nausea, it is because of indolence and cowardice, because all his life he has entrenched himself comfortably behind "experience"—one of those myths invented by social man to help him never admit anything new and thereby lend stability to whatever may happen (p. 95). All his life he had labeled as "insane" or "morbid" anything unusual or unpleasant so as not to have to think seriously about it, in the manner of all the *"salauds."*

Now, feeling himself old, depleted, and dying, he entrenches himself more than ever behind experience, seeking refuge in the memory of the past—a delirious, comforting compensating (p. 96). In this sense one might even say that he too "cheats." But it is a stupid, petty way of "cheating"—or rather, "counterfeit cheating," since it refuses to see what is and tries to find for itself illusory refuges from existence without even knowing that they are refuges. With the Doctor, therefore, the first representative of this indefinite variety of *"salauds"* makes its appearance. The Museum of Bouville is to offer us a complete gallery of them, their "natural history," whose sclerosis and inner emptiness we have to be shown in order to understand why Antoine's experience, in spite of its contact with Reality, cannot be universal. Thus the philosopher who propounds a system must first explain the genesis of the error of those who do not think like him.

Another dialectical turning point in the novel is the day of the fog in Bouville. For the first time Nausea appears there is a *cosmic experience,* collective, almost universal, which none can escape because it is inscribed in things. On the day of the fog Antoine feels Nausea hovering over the entire town: it is vaguely sensed by all the town's inhabitants: the hooded character in the square, the Self-Taught Man, the Readers in the Municipal Library—instead of being merely as heretofore Roquentin's awareness of the failure of a certain mechanism within him and of the strange things that happen to him now each day (for instance his sudden inexplicable disgust at the sight of a pebble or a glass of beer of quite innocent appearance). It is evidently necessary to consent to this anguish in order to become fully conscious of Nausea. One must not retreat into the Municipal Library with its four book-lined walls, which is simply another way of saying that one must not try, in fact, to find refuge behind the reassuring habits with which our tribe has provided us since childhood, from the "object lessons" of elementary school which persuade us that an "object" is a well-defined entity possessing certain precise characteristics—that it is "this" and not something else—up to the chemistry manuals which assure us that sulphur melts at a precisely determined temperature. Compared to the "cheating" which brings us face to face with the fundamental absurdity of existence, its irrationality and lawlessness—that is, face to face with Nothingness itself—the thawing of our habits of spatial and social thinking and the renunciation of readymade frames of reference advocated by Bergsonism merely seem a gentle little joke, a harmless diversion for Members of the Institute.

If one wanted, however, to "classify" Nausea, so as to subdue it and make it harmless, one might present it as the terminal point of the evolution of man's thought. There would be first of all magical thinking, for example that of the child or of primitive man. In the realm of such thinking objects remain stable, as long as that seems desirable. But they are also capable of being modified at the whim of our desires, provided we have the key, know the hidden spring, the magic word that has the power to change them. At the bottom of such magic thinking there always lies a disquietude: we feel that things might possibly begin to change some day against our will. What if some malevolent spirit wanted them to change, or some stronger enemy who had succeeded in obtaining our magic word? But such fear would not yet be the supreme horror of Nausea because this change of things would still be brought about by an exercise of the will, generally human or at least conceived on the model of our own and therefore eminently understandable. The worst imaginable would be that change might come about because things themselves want to change. Thus the fear of a transformation not bound by law and totally gratuitous is pushed aside and back into the shadows of our unconscious.

To exorcise this fear completely we need, it seems, science and technology. The best assurance against change is, in fact, familiarity with the laws of change. Then it will no longer even appear as change but merely as multiple aspects assumed by a basic identity. There would at any rate be nothing disquieting about it. In Bouville the Municipal Library, testifying as it does to human knowledge, is the safest refuge, the strongest citadel, even if sometimes—as on the day of the fog—the waves of Nausea come to beat against its walls everywhere. It is to the stability of chemical elements, to the constancy of physical laws and human regulations, that we turn for protection against the gratuitousness of pure existence.

But at this point reflection, epistemology, and philosophy ruin everything. They desert us. They almost betray us by pointing out that this stability and this constancy are only approximate and, as if figments of our desire,[4] in existence only as long as—insisting on discipline—we keep them under close surveillance, feeling sure that they dare not change as long as we are present. But who knows what may happen as soon as our backs are turned (pp. 107-108)? That is why Antoine Roquentin is filled with nostalgia for Anny. It is not simply a desire for the presence of a human being or longing for the woman loved. It is nostalgia for her tightly-closed universe sealed off with draperies and myths—that magic universe where everything has a specific meaning, not always known but always known to *exist* and apt to change only when the required gesture is made. Since science has not succeeded in satisfying the exigencies of our reason or in definitively concealing from us the presence of Nausea, we turn toward the world of magic as the sole salvation, and hope to acquire that power over Things which—though irrational, and perhaps because of this very irrationality—will measure up to their essential absurdity.

This is the meaning which, in the entire context of the book; must be seen in Antoine's attempt to "recover" Anny: his going to see her in Paris; the failure of his attempt; his being thrown back, upon his own return, into the universe of Nausea—the only one where there is henceforth any place for him, since he has broken with the world of the "*salauds*" [5] and since the world of magic is now closed to him. He is doubly condemned to life in that universe. In the first place, the loss of Anny has finally delivered him to the material solitude of the bachelor which symbolizes and accentuates the intellectual solitude of the clearsighted man and leaves him no hope for escape from his perpetual ruminating and his daily contact with Nausea. But he is condemned to it above all because the doors of the magic universe that only Anny had the power to create for him and where she alone could make him enter are henceforth closed to him. One sees now why it is immediately after his return from Paris that he clearly perceives the universality of Nausea and man's inability truly to escape Existence. Every refuge is vain: neither nature nor cities offer sufficient protection against existence. The cities conceal it from us in the most effective manner (but only if we pass rather quickly between the walls of their houses without lingering in the streets), because Mineral is the least disquieting of all existents, the one which seems the most stable, the least swarming, the least inclined to consume everything. But if man were to relax even for a moment his efforts to defend against Vegetation the cities he has built, they would at once be submerged in the mounting flood of existence.

One might compare the situation of Antoine at this point of the novel

---

[4] If Sartre were writing a philosophical essay and not a "novel," he would obviously be able here to support his thesis with the logic of "intentionality," an epistemology like that of Meyerson, and with most of the results of contemporary physics.

[5] The conscious rupture is accomplished at the end of Roquentin's visit to the Museum of Bouville with his "*Adieu, salauds.*"

with that of Eve in "The Room." [6] Eve also needs Pierre to introduce her
into the only universe that seems desirable to her. But she has not discovered Nausea. There is only within her a vague repugnance against
the universe of "normal people," based on an intellectual refusal to
accept it as authentic. What she seeks to flee from in "the room" is the
world of the *"salauds"* rather than existence. There is a striking parallel-
ism between the world which Anny carries with her (or rather carried
with her before she gave up finding refuge in it herself) and the universe
of "the room," equally "closed" and hung with curtains, with "never
enough blackness," and furnished by paranoia as is Anny's world by
mythomania. Even the supreme horror of "the room," the passage of
"the statues," takes on predictable form and happens at an almost fixed
hour . . . For there are laws governing this universe—absurd though
they may appear. But the streets of Bouville on the day of the fog
offered no refuge from Nausea. . . .

Madness then appears, after magic and scientific technology, as the
third stage in the evolution of thought. Or rather: man faced with
Nausea has these alternatives: philosophy or "metaphysics" (in Heidegger's sense of the word)—that is, lucid recognition of the absurdity of
existence—or madness, the desperate effort to return to the world of
magic and deny absurdity in the name of a superior universe constructed
by dint of arbitrariness and cheating.

[6] "La Chambre," one of the short stories in the collection *Le Mur.*

Sartre's *Roads to Freedom*

by Henri Peyre

Three volumes of *Les Chemins de la liberté* [*The Roads to Freedom*] have appeared, the first two, *L'Âge de raison* [*The Age of Reason*] and *Le Sursis* [*The Reprieve*], in French in 1945, the third, *La Mort dans l'âme*, in 1949. They have all been translated, the first two by Eric Sutton[1] and the third by Gerard Hopkins under the title *Troubled Sleep*.[2] While they met with considerable success, especially in Europe, it is our conviction that the superb skill of the author and their immense significance as sheer literary works have been underrated by many hasty or hostile reviewers. Two easy escapes were offered to critics, who could not remain unaware of Sartre's immense importance in world letters: one was to brand him as immoral and pessimistic, whereas no great writer has perhaps been more concerned with the formulation of moral values. His outlook on life has been called, by a very lucid critic, Oleg Koefoed, from a Protestant, earnest, and "bourgeois" country, Denmark, "the most rashly optimistic humanism which our generation has produced." The other was to acknowledge Sartre's triumph as a dramatist (and it is indeed dazzling),[3] but to add in the same breath that, as a novelist, he was a failure. Our conviction is that not only *La Nausée* but *Les Chemins de la liberté* tower above most European fiction of the years 1935-55.

Even in his hatred of the flesh and in his cruder pages, Sartre has

[1] New York: Alfred A. Knopf, 1947.   [2] New York: Alfred A. Knopf, 1951.

[3] Even so, a great many cultured American readers and students, admitting that the two early dramas by Sartre were great achievements, will treat with condescension *Morts sans sépulture*, which is in no sense a sensational melodrama but a masterly study of pride, as one of the masks of bad faith, in the tortured resistance fighters. They pour out their scorn upon *La Putain respectueuse*, in which the Americans, who, since Tocqueville remarked upon it, have always been mortified at being misunderstood in Europe, have insisted in seeing a crude treatment of the Negro problem. Sartre intended nothing of the kind. The prostitute, Lizzie, and the innocent Negro are, in the eyes of the author, the true villains of the play. They lack the courage to revolt, to assume their responsibilities. They bow to prejudices through sentimentality, inadequate intellectual force, and the same fear of freedom that crushed Electra's early passionate revolt in *Les Mouches*.

remained a moralist and, as the French say, *un grand timide,* whose
psychoanalysis would doubtless reveal him as an unusually sensitive
orphan, hurt, like Baudelaire and Hamlet, by his mother's second marriage and wounded in his early idealization of women by his lack of
facile grace and of superficial "good looks." The sound and the fury
raised by some outraged Pharisees about Sartre's unromantic delineation
of love have too easily blinded some readers to the highly perspicacious
analysis of love and of sexuality in his works. The pages on love, desire,
hatred, and sadism (pp. 431 and following) in *L'Être et le néant* go very
deep and take for granted the truth that man is originally and fundamentally a sexual being, and aware of it, just as he is the only animal
with the awareness that he will die (or so we claim). Love must be free,
that is, without tyranny or sadism. The lover cries:

> My existence is, because it is called for. In so far as I assume it, it becomes
> pure generosity. I am because I give myself lavishly. . . . Instead of feeling
> ourselves as superfluous [*de trop*], we now experience that our existence is
> prolonged and willed in its slightest details by an absolute freedom that, at
> the same time, it conditions, and that we want to deserve through our own
> freedom. In this lies the deepest element of our joy in loving, when it
> exists: that we feel justified in existing.

It is well-nigh impossible to summarize Sartre's novel, because its
center is to be found neither in the plot or plots nor in the characters in
the traditional sense. The protagonist is, once again, a professor, as was
the case in the very early story written and published by Sartre at the age
of eighteen, "L'Ange du morbide." Ever since he had broken a beautiful
ancient vase at the age of seven as a gesture toward freedom and then,
upon reading Spinoza at twenty-one, had decided to be in nature "not
like a subject, but like an empire within an empire," reversing Spinoza's
formula, Mathieu had been yearning for freedom. But he is no man of
action or of determination. He has little will power, and he analyzes and
ponders every problem, displaying his own flabbiness pitilessly. The
others, however, respect him and cannot conceal their awe in the presence
of a philosophy teacher who attends all their parties, lives unconven-
tionally like them, but all the while pursues elusive freedom.

He has had a mistress, Marcelle, for several years. She appears in the
book as not particularly attractive and as unusually sedate and weak-
willed. She is now pregnant and, having few illusions about her lover's
passion for remaining unattached, free from responsibility, and available
for the visitation of freedom devoutly wished for by him, she is hardly
surprised when he advises her to have an abortion. Mathieu, however, is
disturbed by his act and by the little creature whom he will thus keep
from ever existing. He silences his scruples and gets the money needed
for a first-class clandestine "operation" from his disciple Boris, who steals

it from his mistress. But he is nonplussed when a friend of his, Daniel, offers to marry Marcelle and father the child.

Mathieu wallows in bad faith and unauthenticity, merely enjoying a mockery of freedom. Daniel lives in worse falsehood still: he is a homosexual who has not been able to accept himself for what he is. A concealed shame, hence a tormenting hatred for himself and for others, rules his every act. He is the ideal sadomasochist, who looks in vain for his own redemption in his "generous" offer to Marcelle, who cowardly accepts it. Lola, a singer, a passionate and tragic woman whose mellow ripeness fills her with a desperate fear of losing her very young lover Boris, and Ivich, also of Russian origin, an intelligent, peevish, unpredictable girl, not far remote from Xavière in Simone de Beauvoir's *L'Invitée* (*She Came to Stay*), are the other women portrayed. Mathieu feels attracted by Ivich, emulates her semimystical and masochistic gesture when, at a party, she pierces her hand with a knife, and is fascinated by her adolescent coldness, yet he refuses her when at last she offers herself to him. Boris, Ivich's brother, an admiring student of Mathieu, is a caricature of the disciple, like the famulus of Goethe's *Faust,* but a caricature delineated with warmth by Sartre; he has more ebullience and more naturalness than most of the other characters in the volume.

The actors in the dramatic fresco of *L'Âge de raison* seem to wade hopelessly through the marshes of the prewar world. Only one of them, the Communist Brunet, has resolutely decided for *engagement,* for abdication of any further choice through affiliation with the Communist party and support of the Spanish republicans. Mathieu, as he himself confesses, sedulously tills the inner garden of his freedom, mistaking availability to any future whatever for freedom, awaiting, like Orestes in *Les Mouches* [*The Flies*], the ideal free act, his own freely elected deed, which would dispel his dreary complacence in his wasted Parisian years. He is now thirty-four; he has kept shy of political ties, of ideological affiliations, of patriotic *élans,* of any velleities of reforming the world— and, of course, of marriage. But, as Dr. Johnson said long ago and as Kafka has echoed, if marriage has many pains, celibacy has few joys. Mathieu is aware of his own desiccation, and, having read Hegel on the unhappy conscience, he has diagnosed the gnawing worms in him: bad faith and cowardice.

Le Sursis, which displayed Sartre's virtuosity in handling, better than John Dos Passos himself, the simultaneous technique of *Manhattan Transfer* and *U.S.A.,* is astonishingly clever. The reader wonders whether Sartre, like Picasso—Sartre and he have the same cool mastery in handling the new and the unpredictable, the same tantalizing knack for carrying off successfully tightrope acrobatics—has not starved his genius to feed his talent and his greed for experimenting. But Sartre's attempt was not that of the effete traditional novelist, laboriously building up characters whose dreary continuity seems unaffected by the momentous events in which they are immersed. He has vehemently repudiated the convenient faith in a stable, universal human nature, entertained by the classical writers of France, and has stressed man's perpetually fluid behavior.

His purpose was to embrace the variegated and discordant unity of Western Europe in the tragic week of September 1938, which preceded the surrender of Chamberlain and Daladier at Munich. Few of those who lived through those days and nights of anxiety and shame and saw the abject intellectual dishonesty of men who deluded themselves into believing they had achieved peace in our time will refuse to proclaim the truth and the power of Sartre's portrayal. Unanimism is at play here, far more felicitously than anywhere in Romains' works; the actors or the puppets in the tragicomedy of Europe are delineated with a concrete vigor and a skill in vivid dialogue that make many of the pretentiously symbolic and cerebral novels of the present time appear unreal and sham.

Daniel has hardly changed since the crisis in the first volume in which he attempted to drown his cats before his contemplated suicide, then toyed with the idea of mutilating himself so as to be free forever from his pederastic urges, and finally justified himself in his own eyes through playing the archangel for Marcelle. He will emerge fully in the third volume, when the reign of evil has spread over France with the defeat. And heroism may well save him, too, when, in the fourth volume, Sartre portrays the resistance to the German occupiers. Charles, a paralytic from Berck, evacuated under gruesome conditions with a whole trainload of invalids, "rising" to a disgusting and yet pathetic copulation with another human wreck, is a bold and powerful character. The adolescent, Philippe, even Mathieu's sister-in-law at Juan-les-Pins, and other episodic characters compel belief, as do the boisterously comic adventures of the illiterate shepherd from Prades, Gros-Louis. The humble fellow will never understand what the mobilization was all about or why he was buffeted by a fate personified by malicious men, greedy prostitutes, and the blind machinery of the army. But he rings truer than any heroes of Maupassant or of Courteline, and he provides the proof, if one were needed, that Sartre can depict people far removed from professors, phenomenological introspectives, and idlers of Montparnasse cafés.

The hydra of war reaching over men, aghast and powerless, enables Mathieu to cast a backward glance, ironically bitter, at his vain search for a false freedom. He had thought he could treasure up his leisure, his comfort, and his refusal of all family, party, and other social bonds. But, like a sponge, life had perfidiously absorbed the slimy semblance of freedom he had cultivated. In a classical meditation on the Pont-Neuf, at the end of *Le Sursis*, he realizes his error. His liberty had been there all along, at hand; he was *it*. It does not descend upon one like an illumina-

tion of delight, a tongue of fire. Freedom does not come laden with comforting presents; it is grave and massive, "a plenitude." "Freedom is
exile and I am condemned to be free."

War is only delayed by the reprieve of Munich, and, when it comes,
Mathieu will not turn overnight into a flamboyant warrior. The path to
freedom and perhaps to heroism is an arduous one. (Sartre, remembering
Gide's and Mauriac's warnings about the impossibility of portraying
noble feelings and saints, must be pondering lengthily his fourth volume,
now overdue.) *La Mort dans l'âme* still resorts to the devices of simul-
taneity bewilderingly used in *Le Sursis.* But there is more continuity
within each chapter, and more concessions are thus made to the reader's
laziness. Moreover, while Munich impressed Western Europeans as Sartre
depicts it, as a senseless shake-up of all illusions, in which placid and
selfish beings like Mathieu were nothing but peas suddenly mashed up
in the crushing of a big can, the defeat of France stressed again the
barriers behind which countries sought to convince themselves that the
wretched fate of France could in no case be theirs. A Spanish republican
in New York, who represents the attitude of some of the European
refugees in America, is aware that the events of June 1940 meant defeat
for all liberals and for civilization, yet he sees in the oppression of
France a punishment for her betrayal of the Spanish republicans and
the Czechs. Boris has become a determined fighter. Mathieu has witnessed, as a participant, the disorderly retreat. He now stirs up other
French soldiers to reorganize and to shoot the approaching Germans. It
will be of no avail and he knows it; the armistice is then being signed.
But through the ordeal of fire he will emerge a new man.

Sartre has been accused of lacking warmth and sensibility. But sensibility need not be declamatory and does not necessarily lie at the opposite
pole to the superb intelligence, one of the broadest since Goethe and
Renan, which marks the existentialist leader. Though cold and insensi-
tive, the man who wrote "La République du silence," "Paris sous l'occupation" in the third volume of *Situations,* the impassioned evocations
of torture and injustice in "Qu'est-ce que la littérature?" and the chapters
in the third volume of *Les Chemins de la liberté* devoted to the Communist Brunet, bolstering up the morale of his companions in a German
prison camp, has produced some of the most moving passages in modern
fiction. (Sartre had a firsthand acquaintance with prison camps in 1940-
1941, until he was released because of his deficient eyesight; he then
engaged in the resistance movement.) We do not believe there is anything
more telling, more restrained and, since the word must be used in spite
of Sartre's *pudeur,* more noble in spirit in the abundant literature devoted by the French to the ordeal of captivity.

Sartre's fiction is original on many counts. First of all, his mastery of
the language is extraordinary. And few significant works of our age, since

Joyce and Mallarmé, can afford to ignore the problems and the pitfalls of language. The flashes of poetry in prose, which illuminate the novels of Malraux and of Giono, are absent from Sartrean fiction. Metaphors are scarce, but they are precise, convincing, and sharply delineated. Sheer adornments are spurned by him, as well as the music of prose. But the great moments when the characters, suddenly aware of their existence or of their nascent freedom, seem to be favored with a gift of second sight are impregnated with a severe and precise beauty, not unlike that of Stendhal, without his fondness for dreams. Above all, Sartre's mastery is conspicuous in some of his dialogues, in an interior monologue purified of much of the irrelevancy and insignificance of the genre, and in his unorthodox use of the spoken language. With less artificiality than Céline or than Queneau, Sartre has successfully broken with the romantic illusion that interposes a pretty screen of words between the reader and the scene represented. His language welcomes slang, profanity, and obscenity. It catches up with the least conventional spoken language, as written words had not done for a whole century, in spite of Wordsworth's rebellion against poetic diction and of Hugo's *mettant un bonnet rouge au vieux dictionnaire*. Not only does it thus translate an individual, specific, and concrete reality without betraying it and without imprisoning it in abstract categories, it revivifies French through integrating into the written style all the fluid and picturesque, or malodorous, wealth of the language of the common people.

Then, in spite of many assertions to the contrary, Sartrean fiction avoids most of the dangers of philosophical literature, and it gains, in our opinion, far more than it loses, in paralleling an arresting philosophy. Sartre's early novel, *Défaite,* written in his teens and destroyed for lack of a publisher, his early story, "L'Ange du morbide," and even *La Nausée* seem to indicate that he was, even in terms of chronology, a literary artist before he was a philosopher. Whatever philosophy there is in his fiction and in his plays is not artificially and didactically placed there, as might be said to have been the case with Balzac and Tolstoy, and even more so with Bourget and Romains. He creates and endows with autonomous life his own universe. The main postulates of Sartre's philosophy are to a certain extent present in his fiction. But they are no longer assertions dialectically presented; they are lived situations. There are no essences, and therefore no types, no general categories, no universal human nature, no harmonious consistency in man. There is no determinism, and man is not to be "explained" ponderously by all the shackles that bind him to his environment and to his past. Freedom alone, slowly and painfully conquered, can constitute an exit from a world that would otherwise be a purposeless, loveless, derelict abode of viscousness and cowardice.

The novels of Sartre thus stand in reaction both to naturalism and to intellectual analysis. Existentialism as conceived by Sartre, despite some superficial similarities with the stories of men adrift, dear to Zola and the early Huysmans, despite the dreary humiliation of sex lengthily described by the same writers in *Pot-Bouille* and elsewhere, is a revulsion from the materialistic and deterministic novel of Zola, Maupassant, Dreiser, even of Hardy and Heinrich Mann, to the extent that they might be called naturalists. For Sartre, man is not determined by heredity and environment, and only to a very limited extent by his past. He himself is his own Prometheus, as Michelet would have put it. He always remains unpredictable, free to break with what he has been and to elect a new path. Within each of Sartre's characters there is indeterminacy and the possibility of accomplishing a new action, which will stand totally unconnected with previous actions and inconsistent with other features of the characters as they had previously appeared. In a revealing interview, granted on November 24, 1945, to Mme Dominique Aury and published in *Les Lettres françaises,* Sartre declared:

> Every one of my characters, after having done anything may still do anything whatever. . . . I never calculate whether the act is credible according to previous ones, but I take the situation and a freedom chained in situation. . . . In Zola, everything obeys the strictest determinism. His books are written in the past, while my characters have a future. . . . With Mathieu, for example, the situation which he slowly created for himself is of consequence. He is bound hand and foot by his mistress and by his culture. He himself forged his own links. He is much too clearsighted for psychoanalysis to be of any usefulness to him; this is moreover true for all intellectuals. . . . He is still waiting for God, I mean for something outside him to beckon to him. But he will only have the cause which he will have decided to be his own.

Proustian analysis is treated with no less severity, and Mauriac's technique of leading his heroes by a leash to God comes up for even harsher criticism. Such analysis appears to Sartre as the luxury of a select leisure class, trained in self-contemplation and cherishing every nuance of its enjoyment of nature, of food, of art and of the delicious "reciprocal torture" of love. It went as far as it could go with Proust, Joyce, and Mann; it perhaps even became lost in a blind alley. But this analytical literature no longer fully answered the demands of a new and less cultured public and of a generation that had endured the material and spiritual agonies of World War II and German concentration camps. Many young men discovered that Dostoevsky, Malraux, and Faulkner had a truer ring for them. The French, who had hitherto constituted the ideal audience for the novel of analysis, went over to the side of the unanalytical novel of action and violence translated from the American. Sartre proclaimed how significant to him and to his generation the discovery of Dos Passos, Hemingway, and Faulkner has proved.[4] His own novels tend to set off the

---

[4] *The Atlantic Monthly,* August, 1946.

truths that man perceives when he least expects them and when a new quality in objects is suddenly revealed to him.[5]

Lastly, much has been written—often glibly—on the pessimism of existentialist fiction. There is far more pessimism in Thomas Mann's stories of decreptitude and of the inevitable unbalance of genius, in Cesare Pavese's and in Alberto Moravia's novels, indeed in almost all modern Italian literature, and in three-fourths of American letters, Mark Twain and John Dos Passos not excepted, and William Faulkner himself included in spite of his official speeches, than there is in recent French literature. There was infinitely more obsession with decadence and death in Flaubert and his contemporaries, between 1850 and 1870, than there has been in our own age.

[5] Similarly, in a remarkable manifesto, "Forgers of Myth: The Young Playwrights of France," *Theatre Arts,* June 1946, Sartre declared that, for the existentialist dramatist, "man is not to be defined as a 'reasoning animal' or as a 'social' one, but as a free being, entirely indeterminate, who must choose his own being when confronted with certain necessities. . . . We wish to put on the stage certain situations which throw light on the main aspects of the condition of man and to have the spectators participate in the free choice which man makes in these situations."

The Self-Inflicted Wound

by Kenneth Douglas

If this paper had taken for its theme not self-mutilation but the allied topic of self-punishment, one character in *Les Chemins de la liberté* would have merited a thorough examination: Daniel, the guilt-tortured homosexual who is further afflicted by the failure of others to loathe him as he demands and needs to be loathed. He might say with Baudelaire: "When I have come to inspire universal horror and revulsion, I shall have attained solitude." For Marcelle, he is the "archangel." To his disgust, the concierge's little girl leaves violets at his door. Mathieu cannot dislike him even when Daniel reveals a wallet stuffed with thousand-franc notes although, claiming to be "broke," he has turned down Mathieu's request for a loan. But Daniel also fails himself. He arrives at the river's bank with his three cherished cats, Scipion, Poppée, Malvina, yet cannot go through with his plan to drown them. "For each man kills the thing he loves"—our thirster after penance, since he lacks the resolve to incarnate that bitter truth, also robs himself of the suffering which the execution would have brought.

As a self-mutilator, Daniel is scarcely more impressive. He projects and carries out the preliminaries for, not punishment merely, but the drastic cure suggested in the Gospels ("if thine eye offend thee, pluck it out"). The only result is that he scares himself. Previously, he *had* used his razor to behead a pimple on his chin. The notion of gashing his face was rejected, it would still be a human face and have some meaning for other men. At long last Daniel makes the discovery of the existence of God, of that irreducible Other who sees us as we are, in our essence and in our accidentia. In the meantime, he hits on the ingenious idea of marrying Marcelle, the no longer terribly young nor terribly adored, pregnant mistress of Mathieu. That will be a heavy sentence for a man of his predilections and aversions. Adieu, Daniel.

Subsequent developments lend an exceptional interest to a comparison made on two occasions in Sartre's first novel, *La Nausée,* which was

"The Self-Inflicted Wound." (Original title: "Sartre and the Self-Inflicted Wound.") From *Yale French Studies,* No. 9 (1952). Reprinted by permission of the author and *Yale French Studies.*

published in 1938. Lucie, the maid of the hotel, transfigured by *chagrin d'amour,* is described (p. 44) as standing with outstretched arms "as if she were awaiting the stigmata." The absurd "self-taught man" and provincial humanist proclaims his entire happiness (p. 152) and stretches out his hands palms upward "as though he were about to receive the stigmata"—very soon, indeed, he will undergo a kind of martyrdom. Between the two usages of this comparison there occurs an actual case of "stigmatization"—quite apart, however, from any religious connotation. Roquentin, the narrator and central figure of *La Nausée,* has been submerged by groundswells of a novel sensation profoundly disturbing in its universality, the sensation namely of the nauseous quality of every existing thing and of the totality of things. That is why he has begun to record his experiences, so that he may understand and, it may be, exorcize this all-enveloping horror. At this point (pp. 131-33) Roquentin has arrived at the distressing realization of his limbs and body and taste as existing, hence nauseous. More than that, he comes to see that these and all other existents are constituted, in their phenomenality, by the relentless and unbiddable travailing of his own consciousness. And he rings a change on the "I think, therefore I am" of Descartes: "At this very moment—it's frightful—if I exist, *it is because* I find it loathsome to exist."

Mathieu, in the *Chemins de la Liberté* (1945), will define the sensation of existing as "drinking oneself without any thirst." Here (p. 133) Roquentin has the same experience of his personal existence, and he attempts to escape from it.

> My saliva is sweetish, my body lukewarm; I feel insipid. My penknife is on the table. I open it. Why not? In any case it would change things a bit. I place my left hand on the writing pad and dispatch a good knifethrust into the palm. It was too nervous a movement; the blade slipped and inflicted only a surface wound. It's bleeding. What of it? What difference has that made? All the same I am glad to see, on the white paper and amidst the lines I have just finished writing, this little pool of blood which at last has ceased to be me. Four lines on a sheet of white paper and a bloodstain, that will be a pleasant memory. . . .

In spite of this bold deed the world rolls on as before:

> Will I bind up my hand? I hesitate. I look at the monotonous little trickle of blood. Now it's congealing. It's over. My skin looks rusty round the wound. Underneath the skin all that's left is a trivial little feeling like all the others, or perhaps more insipid still.

Roquentin is trying to elucidate the significance of this nauseousness which adheres to all things or as which all things manifest themselves. He is not looking for the motivations of his present acts nor seeking to psychoanalyze himself. The interpretation of his present, if that is required, must be our own. It is clear that the desire for self-punishment plays little part here (unlike the stabbing of the thigh with which Gide's Lafcadio regularly disciplined himself). This thrust of the penknife aims at changing things. What it would change is their nauseousness: the quality experienced when a human being becomes aware that every real thing is contingent, is logically and also more generally speaking unjustifiable, that in all its pullulating thusness it bursts the dikes of any happy little conceptual scheme. It is superfluous, or excessive, it is *de trop*—and the real world, unless the aspect of it under consideration be "nihilized" in order to advance some human undertaking, will swamp in the immeasurable our pretention to be "measure of all things." That claim can be justified only so long as man continues to measure and, having measured, to construct.

That portion of contingency which the penknife-thrust would nihilize is Roquentin's own body. Let us list a few related expressions: the body as contingency, as a facticity imposed on the individual, a mere givenness in whose creation he has had no share. By sticking the penknife into his hand, Roquentin in a sense (in a sense only, and certainly not absolutely—but psychoanalytic investigations have shown what pathetic subterfuges and bad puns we humans employ in our struggle to attain equilibrium) redeems his body, founds it, gives it to himself. If we are willing to concede a sexual and sadomasochistic resonance to the act, it becomes even more clear that Roquentin, the lover who possesses himself, beloved who is self-penetrated, has reached a stage that is, as Valéry no doubt would have called it, "rather divine." Except that this "stage" is a fleeting illusion, dissipated in the moment of actualization. Man's basic, self-contradictory aim, Sartre repeatedly avers in *L'Être et le néant,* is to be his own foundation, *ens causa sui,* to reach the satisfying fullness and self-identity of the object, while yet remaining sufficiently distinguished from this self to be conscious of it. In a word, his ultimate and unattainable longing is to become God. He would realize in his own consciousness the relations which hold good only between the Three Persons of the Trinity.

This, then, is at the root of Roquentin's self-mutilation—of what may be called his narcissism—for he seeks his own body's redemption, and no one else is involved.

The next example we come upon in Sartre's fiction is intrapersonal and more complicated. Ivich begins it, that intensely irritating chit of twenty who arouses an incomprehensible and pure devotion in the breast of Mathieu, the thirty-four-year-old central figure of *L'Âge de raison,* first volume of *Les Chemins de la liberté.* Fearing to learn on the morrow that she has failed in the university entrance examination, she drinks freely and incurs the disapproval of a woman at an adjacent table in the night club. To avenge herself ("I want to see if she can stand the sight of blood") she seizes the horrible Basque knife her brother has just acquired and gashes her own hand diagonally across the palm. Yet she refuses to go to the washroom and insults Mathieu, whom already she had accused of decency, reasonableness, and other shocking crimes. Mathieu, pale with fury, takes the knife and with a masculine thrust drives it into his hand. "You see," he tells Ivich, "anybody at all can do it" (p. 200). While aware how childish this is, the gesture pleases him all the same, for it is as if he had thumbed his nose not only at Ivich but at all the others who in the previous twenty-four or forty-eight hours had gravely indicated that he was on the wrong road. Ivich at all events was moved, and while they waited for the washroom attendant to return with bandages and iodine, she pressed her wounded hand against his—in blood brotherhood, as she explained. But this intimate bond did not survive their next meeting.

To treat as a symbol some element of a literary work is to venture on the alluring seas of analogy. Such voyages might well prove interminable, were it not for the blessed brevity of human existence and the even prompter mercy of an editor's "regrets." Nevertheless I shall risk providing grounds for a charge of irrelevance. "It glitters like a diamond," Ivich had declared, just before her self-wounding. What? "This very instant. It is circular, it is suspended in the void like a little diamond, I am eternal." And Mathieu, afterwards, reflected on this with joy.

> He was happy, he wasn't thinking anything about himself any more, he felt as if he were sitting on a bench outside: outside, outside the dancing joint, outside his own life. He smiled. . . .

So that here we have a similar attitude to Pétrus Borel's, when that minor French romantic arranged for himself to be portrayed turning a dagger against his bosom, over the inscription *"Soy que soy."* I am that I am— an affirmation of plenitude of being, rightfully to be uttered by God alone. The aged and crazy Jonathan Swift, too, according to André Breton in the preface to his *Anthologie de l'humour noir,* had the habit of staring at his reflection in the mirror and muttering: "I am that I am," and the servants made haste to put away the knives. For a human being may imagine that by choosing the form and instant of his own death he most nearly becomes that "which religions call God" (*L'Être et le néant,* p. 708), that impossible object which would yet be conscious of itself. The solitary death envisaged by Borel and perhaps by Swift is not *de rigueur* for this order of thought, and the mock twin-suicide of Ivich and Mathieu yields to the genuine suicide of Villiers de l'Isle-Adam's Axel and his beloved, in the domain of literature, and in actual life to the suicide of Heinrich von Kleist and his fiancée. There have been many others. Whether accompanied or alone, the self-slaughterers play both the active and the passive role, and so improve upon the passively awaited destiny of Edgar Allan Poe, as Mallarmé proclaimed it in that magnificent opening line: "As into Himself at last eternity changes him":

Tel qu'en Lui-même enfin l'éternité le change.

The time has fortunately not yet come, with respect to Sartre, for indiscreet biographical probings. We must be content to observe that not only in Sartre's writings is this self-wounding a recurrent theme: there is a parallel incident in the first and outstanding novel by Simone de Beauvoir, *L'Invitée* . . . [*She Came to Stay*, 1943]. Xavière is a girl of much the same age as Ivich with the same infuriating little ways, similar appearance, and similar situation in life, since she also fears an enforced return to her parents in the provinces. While sitting in a night club Xavière deliberately burns her hand with a cigarette butt. She later explains, and there is no reason to question her partial truthfulness, that she wished to punish herself for a silly sentimental gesture. But the action, even when performed a second time, has none of the matter-of-factness of Lafcadio's self-disciplining. Beforehand, Xavière had been following with passionate absorption the movements of a Spanish dancer. Then, unobserved by her companions, she had somehow shaken off this fascination. Françoise witnesses the actual burning, however:

Xavière pressed the red glow against her skin and her lips curved upwards in a suddenly etched smile; it was an intimate, lonely smile like a madwoman's, the voluptuous, tortured smile of a woman in an erotic transport, one could scarcely bear to watch it. . . .

When Xavière repeated the action, Françoise

had a movement of revulsion. It was not only her flesh which rebelled, she felt that she was being assaulted in a deeper and more irremediable fashion, at the very core of her being. Behind this convulsive leer some danger was lurking. . . . There was something there which greedily clutched at itself, which existed for itself with an absolute certainty; not even in thought could one come near it, at the instant of attaining the goal the thought became evanescent: this was no object that could be grasped, it was a ceaseless upward-streaming and a ceaseless eluding transparent for itself alone and for ever impenetrable. One could but circle around it in an eternal exclusion.

Xavière herself declared that there was "something voluptuous about a burn," and Françoise continued to be haunted by "this tortured, ecstatic countenance the memory of which made her shudder" (all these quotations come from pp. 293-95). Thus self-punishment with the aim of self-correction is not the whole story for Xavière, any more no doubt than it was or is for the flagellants of counter-reformatory Spain and present-day Mexico. The divergencies between Xavière's behavior and that of Ivich are too obvious to need stressing. The greater intensity of emotion is experienced by Xavière, although she finds and desires no associate. She also brutally drags Françoise to the edge of a metaphysical, not a purely biological abyss, whereas the middle-aged woman upset and "routed" by Ivich's exhibitionism can scarcely be thought to have penetrated deeper than the biological level. What should not be overlooked, however, is the common reference, on the part of Sartre and Beauvoir, to *circularity* and *eternity*. The divagation concerning Swift, suicide pacts, and Borel is an attempt to reveal the ultimate significance which here may pulse discreetly within these terms: the desire to be *ens causa sui*, foundation of one's own being, even—should no other way be discoverable—at the cost of transforming oneself into the slayer and the slain.

As he lives through the French defeat of 1940, Mathieu—he too had told Marcelle [*L'Âge de raison,* p. 18] that he wanted to found himself, to be self-given, *"ne me tenir que de moi-même"*—recalls with displeasure his self-mutilation in the night club: "gestures, gestures, little annihilations, where does that get you, I thought that was freedom, he yawned" (*La Mort dans l'âme,* 1949, p. 135; and another reference, p. 153). He even began to tell it to his comrades, the handful of soldiers with whom he had freely chosen, amidst the chaos of the total collapse of the French armies, to resist the advancing Germans and almost certainly to die. But he stopped, probably out of shame.

A slight accident had brought it once more into his mind. He had cut his thumb while trying to open a can of food for the last meal before the end. Someone notices the cut, another produces gauze and binds up Mathieu's thumb. The incident, which no exhibitionism had defiled, helped to make of this last meal a communion meal.

With this threefold recall of the self-pierced hand and the healthy contrast of the accidental minor wound, Sartre had not yet exhausted his interest in the gesture. His most recent play, *Le Diable et le bon Dieu* (1951), may be considered finally to consecrate it. Goetz, leader of mercenaries, a bastard and bitterly aware of his exclusion from a hierarchized society founded on primogeniture and legitimate birth, has consciously done evil, in deliberate defiance of God. Having been convinced, however, that the good is incomparably more difficult of realization, he casts off evil and faces the new challenge of the good. He finds indeed that to do good is desperately hard. When his former mistress Catherine, dying and plagued with visions of demons and hell-fire, is brought to him, he prays that the burden of her sins may be transferred to his own shoulders. Let gangrene, leprosy, or some other sudden affliction strike him, as a visible testimony that she has been purged of sin. He prays to receive the stigmata. At last in desperation, as Catherine's voice grows weaker, he takes his dagger and pierces his two hands and his side. Catherine dies in peace, and Goetz calls on all his rebellious followers to accept the evidence of the miracle. And since a wangled miracle is too useful a device to be allowed to slumber, Goetz from time to time reawakens his wounds.

Now, surely, the end has been reached, and an effective exorcization finally performed on a deed whose repeated appearance in Sartre's works kindles the suspicion that it reflects a personal, ill-digested experience. Roquentin's penknife-stab was wedged between and separated from two seemingly casual references to stigmatization—and to actual or future suffering. In Goetz the trivial gesture is ennobled, it has become merged with the imposition of the stigmata and with participation in the sufferings of others.

There is a progression in these self-woundings. Roquentin, isolated as he is from others, performed the action narcissistically: whatever the benefit he may have hoped to gain, no one else is involved. Mathieu imitated Ivich, the deed was done with Ivich, and as a result a momentary comradeship arose between them. Goetz did it neither *alone* nor *with* but *for,* for a woman during her death agony.

The progression continues. These stigmata of Goetz's were not a sign from Heaven, but self-imposed. While they enabled a woman to die in peace, repeated exploitation of the "miracle" exemplifies the law of diminishing returns: it ceases to impress. "Ceases to impress"—could it be that this expression correctly characterizes Sartre's present attitude to the motif of the self-inflicted hand-wound? Goetz at all events outgrows it, and passes on to a more adult enterprise. Having clearly acted in God's stead upon that occasion, he realizes some time later that all the decisions and value-judgments he had attributed to God bear in effect his own stamp, are his own doing and positing.

Another very different and yet related evolution can now be discerned within Sartre's work—unless "overcoming of a barrier" should be a more accurate description. This concerns the relationship of one man and one woman, and demonstrates that the sensibility of Sartre can function with profit also in a less specialized context. Roquentin was greatly attracted to a certain Anny, and looked forward to seeing her again, for he very much needed her aid. But their reunion serves to show only that each of them has, at bottom, taken the same wrong turning. They can do nothing for one another. In "La Chambre," a short story written during the 1930's, Eve's self-sacrificing love is unavailing: she is cut off from her husband Pierre by the latter's grave and worsening insanity. Mathieu frequents Marcelle from force of habit, the liaison has gone dead for both of them. Nor does he succeed in establishing anything approaching a genuine understanding with Ivich, apart from the fleeting moment dealt with here. Only Mathieu's transitory association with Irène (*Le Sursis,* second volume of *Les Chemins . . .*) seems to suggest that misunderstanding and the sense of being judged are not unavoidable between lovers, that camaraderie is possible. *Les Mouches,* Sartre's first play, depicts the growth of a very genuine affection between Orestes and the sister Electra whom he sees for the first time since their childhood. But he is unable to save her from the wiles of Jupiter; she slips back into the old unhealthy pattern of remorse and expiation.

The basic situations treated in the later plays offer little scope for the unfolding of a mature relation between man and woman (the Jessica of *Les Mains sales,* although married, is of an Ivichian unripeness and remains incorrigibly and irresponsibly frivolous). But *Le Diable et le bon Dieu,* with its vast dimensions and numerous characters, allows the love of Goetz and Hilda to occupy an important though subordinate place. It is perhaps significant, and fits in with the helplessness or awkwardness vis-à-vis women which sometimes paralyzed Roquentin and Mathieu, that Hilda had long enjoyed the love of the poor folk whom Goetz was never able to win for himself; similarly, while Goetz is slowly assembling the experiences which eventually will lead him to realize God's nonentity, Hilda without splitting any theological hairs had long ceased to busy herself with God. Gretchen, having gone on ahead of Faust, was able to welcome him to the heavenly mansions—Hilda stood solidly on the earth before ever Goetz agreed to come down to it, and there it is that she welcomes him. For men, one of the less obviously fraudulent "Eternal Others" with whom they may struggle to unite is woman, either as wife, as Aspasia, or as Muse. While still enmeshed in the toils of religion, Goetz could already say to Hilda:

> . . . you are warmth, you are light *and you are not myself,* it's insufferable! I do not understand how we can form two, and I would I could become you while yet remaining myself.

To attain maturity, Goetz like Mathieu must cease to play with dagger and self-inflicted wounds, those sterile and childish simulacra of union with another or with oneself or of self-destruction as self-creation. They must strive for a union not of the imagination but in reality, on this earth. Mathieu finds it, shortly before perishing, with a few like-minded comrades. Goetz finds it with Hilda. His last word to her is, before he accepts the role of peasant military leader in which she will help to sustain him: "You are myself. We shall be alone together." *Seuls ensemble.* Sartre's conviction and concern might be worse expressed than by this stoutly welded, tersest of paradoxes.

Jean-Paul Sartre: The Novelist
and the Existentialist

by Edmund Wilson

The Age of Reason is the first novel of Jean-Paul Sartre's to be translated into English. It is the first installment of a trilogy under the general
title *The Roads to Freedom,* of which the second installment in translation has been announced for the fall. *The Age of Reason* deals with a
group of young people in Paris—*lycée* teachers and students, Bohemians
and night-club entertainers—in the summer of 1938. The second novel,
The Reprieve, which has already appeared in French, carries the same
characters along but works them into a more populous picture of what
was going on in France during the days of the Munich Conference. The
third volume, *The Last Chance,*[1] has not yet been published in French,
so it is impossible at the present time to judge the work as a whole or even
to know precisely what the author is aiming at.

The Age of Reason, however, stands by itself as a story. Sartre displays
here the same skill at creating suspense and at manipulating the interac-
tions of characters that we have already seen in his plays. His main
theme is simply the odyssey of an ill-paid *lycée* teacher who does not
want to marry his pregnant mistress and who is trying to raise the relatively large fee required for a competent abortion; but though the
author makes this provide a long narrative, in which we follow the hero's
every move and in which every conversation is reported in its banal entirety, he stimulates considerable excitement, holds our attention from
beginning to end and engineers an unexpected dénouement which has
both moral point and dramatic effectiveness. The incidents are mostly
sordid, but, if you don't mind this, entertaining. The characters are well
observed and conscientiously and intelligently studied, so that the book
makes an interesting document on the quality and morale of the French

"Jean-Paul Sartre: The Novelist and the Existentialist." From *Classics and Com-
mercials: A Literary Chronicle of the Forties* by Edmund Wilson (New York: Farrar,
Straus and Cudahy). Copyright 1950 by Edmund Wilson. Reprinted by permission of
the author.

[1] There are now to be four volumes instead of three. The third, *La Mort dans l'âme,*
has appeared in French. 1950.

just before their great capitulation. An American reader is struck by the close similarity of these young people, with their irresponsible love affairs, their half-hearted intellectual allegiances, and their long drinking conversations, to the same kind of men and girls at the same period in the United States—just as the novel has itself much in common with certain novels that these young people produced. I do not believe, however, that this is the result of imitation by Sartre of the contemporary American novelists whom he is known to admire so much. It is rather that such young people everywhere have come to be more alike, so that the originals for Sartre's Parisians must have been far less specifically Parisian than the Parisians of Balzac or Flaubert or Anatole France or Proust.

It is true, besides, that the writing of the book shows few of the traditional traits that we have been used to in French fiction. It tells the story with a "functional" efficiency, but it is colorless, relaxed, rather flat. It loses little in the English translation, not merely because the translator knows his business, but also because Sartre's style does not put upon him any very severe strain. The conversation is mainly conducted in a monotonous colloquialism of catch-words, where some expression like *"C'est marrant"* does duty for as many emotions as our own ever-recurring "terrific"; and for this Mr. Eric Sutton has been able to find a ready equivalent in a jargon basically British with a liberal admixture of Americanisms.

Of Sartre's imaginative work, I have read, besides this novel, only his plays and a few of his short stories. On this showing, I get the impression of a talent rather like that of John Steinbeck. Like Steinbeck, Sartre is a writer of undeniably exceptional gifts: on the one hand, a fluent inventor, who can always make something interesting happen, and, on the other, a serious student of life, with a good deal of public spirit. Yet he somehow does not seem quite first-rate. A play of Sartre's, for example, such as his recent *Morts sans sépulture*—which is, I suppose, his best drama so far—affects me rather like *Grapes of Wrath*. Here he has exploited with both cleverness and conviction the ordeal of the French Resistance, as Steinbeck has done that of the sharecroppers; but what you get are a virtuosity of realism and a rhetoric of moral passion which make you feel not merely that the fiction is a dramatic heightening of life but that the literary fantasy takes place on a plane that does not have any real connection with the actual human experience which it is pretending to represent.

I have approached *The Age of Reason* purposely from the point of view of its merits as a novel without reference to the existentialist philosophy of which Sartre is one of the principal exponents and which the story is supposed to embody. But, with the publication, also, of a translation of a lecture of Sartre's called *Existentialism* and a pamphlet called *What Is Existentialism?* by William Barrett, this demands consideration, too. It should, however, be said that neither of these discussions of the subject provides for the ordinary person the best possible key to Sartre's ideas. The Barrett essay, though very able, is mainly an exposition of the ideas of Martin Heidegger, a contemporary German philosopher, from whom Sartre took some of his prime assumptions, and it presupposes on the part of the reader a certain familiarity with the technical language of philosophy. The lecture by Sartre himself has the special object of defending existentialism against charges which have been brought against it by the Communists, so that it emphasizes certain aspects of the theory without attempting to state its fundamental principles. It would have been well if the publisher had included a translation of the article called *Présentation,* in which Sartre explained his position in the first number of his magazine, *Les Temps modernes* (October 1, 1945), and which gives the best popular account I have seen of what this literary school is up to. I can also recommend especially a short summary of the history of existentialist thought and of its political and social implications—*Existentialism: A New Trend in Philosophy*—contributed by Paul Kecskemeti, a former U.P. foreign correspondent who is also a trained philosopher, to the March 1947 issue of a magazine called *Modern Review* (published in New York by the American Labor Conference on International Affairs). This study has the unusual merit of not getting so deeply enmeshed in the metaphysical background of existentialism that it fails to focus clearly on the picture of mankind on the earth which is the most important thing to grasp in a doctrine that is nothing if not realistic.

What is this picture, then? In Sartre's version—to skip altogether the structure of philosophical reasoning on which it is made to rest and which Sartre has set forth at length in a book called *L'Être et le néant*—it places man in a world without God (though not all existentialists are atheists), in which all the moral values are developed by man himself. Human nature is not permanent and invariable: it is whatever man himself makes it, and it changes from age to age. Man is free, beyond certain limits, to choose what he is to be and do. His life has significance solely in its relation to the lives of others—in his actions or refrainings from action: to use a favorite phrase of Sartre's, the individual must "engage himself."

Now, this conception of man's situation may appear to the nonreligious reader, if he has also the "historical" point of view, precisely what he has always assumed, and may cause him to conclude with surprise that he was already an existentialist without knowing it. To a Marxist, when he has further discovered that Sartre assigns human beings to the categories of the social classes almost as relentlessly as Marx, it will be evident that Sartre has borrowed from Marxism, and he may ask in what way existentialism is an improvement over Marxism. In a debate between Sartre and a Marxist, a record of which follows the printed lecture, the Marxist actually scores rather heavily. The one advantage, it seems to me, that the doctrine of Sartre has is that it does away with Dialetical Ma-

terialism and its disguised theological content. There is for Sartre no
dialectical process which will carry you straight to salvation if you get
on the proletarian train. He sides with the proletariat, but intellectual or
proletarian has to put up his own battle, with the odds looking rather
against him. Yet Sartre does insist like a Marxist that every member of
modern society belongs to a social class, and that "every one of his feelings, as well as every other form of his psychological life, is revelatory of
his social situation." This molding of the individual by class—and
Sartre allows also for the effects of "origin," "milieu," nationality, and
sexual constitution—produces the limitation on freedom which I mentioned in passing above. One finds oneself in a situation which one did
not make for oneself, but, given that situation, one can choose various
ways of behaving in it. The bourgeois—with whom Sartre is particularly
concerned—can either go along with his class or rebel against it and try
to get away from it. The Marxist may inquire how this differs from the
classical Marxist formulation that "men make their own history, but
. . . do not choose the circumstances for themselves," and how Sartre's
practical doctrine of man realizing himself through action differs from
Marx's conception of testing our ideas through action. To the writer, the
conception of a wholly free will seems as naïve as the contrary conception
of a wholly mechanistic determinism, and it is surely hardly less naïve
to declare, as Sartre appears to do, that we are determined up to a certain
point, but that beyond that we can exercise choice. If Marx and Engels, in
exploring these problems, are somewhat less schoolmasterishly clear than
Sartre, they seem to me, in their tentative way, to give a more recognizable
picture than he does of what happens when what we take for the will
tries to act on what we take for the world, and of the relation between
man and his environment.

But the existentialist philosophy of Sartre is the reflection of a different
age from that which stimulated the activist materialism of Marx, and it
has the immense advantages of sincerity and human sympathy over the
very peculiar version of Marxism, totalitarian and imperialistic, now ex-
ported by the Soviet Union. Let us see it in its historical setting. Mr.
Kecskemeti has shown in his essay how the neo-Kantian idealism of the
pre-1914 period in Germany, which "admirably expressed the average
German's awe in the presence of every kind of expert and official," had to
give way, after the first German defeat, which shook this faith in specialized authority, to an effort to find principles of morality in the study
of human conduct itself. So, eventually, the Germans got Heidegger.
In the same way, Kecskemeti says, the defeat of the French in 1940 deprived them of all they had leaned on: they had at one stroke lost both
their great traditions—the tradition of the French Revolution, which
collapsed with the Third Republic, and the monarchist-Catholic tradition, which, through Pétain, had sold them out to the invaders. It is
characteristic of the French that the destruction of French institutions

should have seemed to them a catastrophe as complete as the Flood and caused them to evolve a philosophy which assumes that the predicament of the patriotic Frenchmen oppressed by the German occupation represented the condition of all mankind. They felt imperatively the duty to resist, with no certainty of proving effective, and they had, as Albert Camus has said, to formulate for themselves a doctrine which would "reconcile negative thought and the possibility of affirmative action." Hence the emphasis on the individual—since the Resistance was always an effort of scattered men and women—so different from the emphasis of Marx on the importance of collective action at a time when a great working-class movement was looming and gathering strength. Hence, also, the suffocating atmosphere of corruption, degradation, and depression which is a feature of Sartre's work and for which the French Communists, hopped up by the Kremlin to the cocksureness of propaganda, are in the habit of showering him with scorn. But such reproaches have no real validity, either artistic or moral: this atmosphere is Sartre's subject, and he has not allowed it to drug his intelligence or his conscience. It is the climate of the Occupation, and the chief literary achievement of Sartre is to have dramatized the moral poisoning of a France humiliated and helpless, in which people, brooding guiltily or blaming someone else, squabbled horribly, betrayed one another or performed acts of desperate heroism. For, says Sartre, though you cannot appeal to God, you have always a margin of freedom: you can submit, you can kill yourself or you can sell your life dear by resisting. Where this freedom is now to lead Frenchmen since the Germans have been driven out, I do not think that Sartre has yet made clear. Though anti-bourgeois and pro-working-class, he is evidently not an orthodox Communist of the kind who takes his directives from Moscow. One has a little the feeling about him that his basic point of view has been forged, as his material has been supplied, so completely under pressure of the pain and constraint of the collapse and the Occupation that he may readapt himself to the temper of any new period.

And now how does *The Age of Reason* point the morals of Existentialist principles? Well, if you already know something of the subject, you will recognize some of its concepts turning up in the reflections of the hero as he drearily walks through the Paris streets. And the conflict of classes is there: a seceder from the bourgeoisie, we see this hero, Mathieu, revolving in a lonely orbit but experiencing gravitational pulls from a successful lawyer brother who represents the bourgeoisie, an old friend who has become a Communist and represents the proletariat, and a young girl of Russian émigré parents who represents the old nobility. It is not, however, this central character, so far as this volume takes him, who "engages himself" by a choice: his choices are all of the negative kind. It is the sexual invert Daniel, a neurotic and disconcerting personality, who, exercising free will, resists his suicidal impulses and performs, unexpectedly and for devious reasons, a responsible and morally positive act. Here the difficult "situation" is a matter not of social class but of biological dislocation; and the triumph of Daniel's decision is to be measured by the gravity of his handicap.

Yet it is difficult to see how *The Age of Reason* can have been very profoundly affected by Sartre's existentialist theory. In such a production of his as his play *Les Mouches,* the dramatist turns academic and rather destroys the illusion by making the characters argue his doctrine; but this novel might perfectly have been written if Sartre had never worked up existentialism. It does differ from the picture of life presented by the embittered French naturalists after the French defeat of 1871, whose characters were invariably seen as caught in traps of heredity and circumstance and rarely allowed to escape—though Sartre's mood, as in his play *Huis-clos (No Exit),* is sometimes quite close to theirs. But this book does not essentially differ from the novels of other post-naturalistic writers, such as Malraux, Dos Passos, and Hemingway, for whom the international socialist movement has opened a door to hope and provided a stimulus to action that were unknown to such a Frenchman as Maupassant or to the Americans who paralleled his pessimism. In Sartre, as in these other writers, you have a study of the mixture in man's nature of moral strength and weakness, and a conviction that, although the individual may not win the stakes he is playing for, his effort will not be lost.

Since *Partisan Review* has published, in the same series as Mr. Barrett's pamphlet, a translation of one of Sartre's long articles, *Portrait of the Anti-Semite,* one should say something about his activity as a journalist. These essays that he contributes to his *Temps modernes* seem to me among the most interesting work of their kind that has appeared during the current slump in serious periodical writing. In this field, Sartre can be compared only with George Orwell in England; we have nobody so good over here. Mr. Barrett, in an article on Sartre, has complained that he ignores, in his *Portrait,* the Freudian springs of anti-Semitism. It is true that Sartre makes no attempt to explain this phenomenon historically in its political and social connections; but he does pursue with merciless insight at least one of the psychological factors involved: the need of small frustrated people to fake up some inalienable warrant for considering themselves superior to somebody. Sartre's whole essay, in fact, pretends to be nothing else than an elaborate development of this theme. It is no scientific inquiry but an exercise in classical irony, which might almost have been written, we reflect, by one of the more mordant eighteenth century Encyclopedists. *The Age of Reason* of Sartre's novel is the intellectual maturity of the hero, but the phrase recalls also a period with which Sartre has a good deal in common. In penetrating these enormous editorials that mix comment on current affairs with a philosophy which, whatever its deficiencies, is always clearly and firmly expressed, we are surprised and reassured to find ourselves chewing on something which we might have feared the French had lost. For it is Sartre's great strength in his time that he has managed to remain quite uninfected by the Cocteau-esque Parisian chichi of the interval between the wars. If Existentialism has become, like surrealism, something of a *mouvement à exporter,* no one has probed so shrewdly as Sartre, in one of his articles in *Les Temps modernes,* the recent attempts of the French to distract the attention of the world from their political and military discredit by exploiting the glory of their writers, or pointed out so boldly the abuses to which this practice may lead. If he sometimes has the air of pontificating, it is probably almost impossible for a French literary man whose influence is being felt to refrain from playing the role of *chef d'école.* And Sartre, bourgeois and provincial, has succeeded in preserving for the French qualities which they very much need and which it is cheering to see still flourish: an industry, an outspokenness, and a common sense which are the virtues of a prosaic intelligence and a canny and practical character. This does not, perhaps, necessarily make Sartre a top-flight writer, but, in these articles of *Les Temps modernes,* it does provide some very good reading.

August 2, 1947

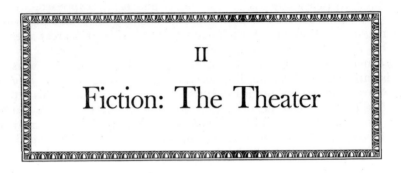

II

Fiction: The Theater

The Structure of Existence: *The Flies*

by Theophil Spoerri

In 1943, Sartre's first drama, *The Flies,* was staged in Paris under the very eyes of the occupying powers. It is a modern *Oresteia* which formulates the age-old problem of freedom in a bold and modern way.

To the freedom of the individual, represented by Orestes, who is at first unencumbered and untouched by destiny, is opposed the leaden submissiveness of the masses. For fifteen years Argos has been suffering under the immense pressure of guilt. Aegisthus knew how to elevate the murder of Agamemnon to a sort of national guilt. All are responsible, all equally guilty, and all have to atone. Atonement, however, means penitent submission to the authority of the rulers and the gods. In order to keep the contrition of the masses at the proper pitch, the king has introduced the Day of the Dead. Each year, in the presence of the royal family, the populace assembles in front of the mountain cave that leads into the underworld. Upon a signal of the highpriest, the black rock that blocks the entrance is rolled away. Through this open gorge the dead stream out into the town—invisible but dismally oppressive, like a clayey, sticky mass. Each inhabitant must house for one day and one night his dead: a woman the man she deceived, parents their mistreated children,

"The Structure of Existence: *The Flies*," from *Die Struktur der Existenz* by Theophil Spoerri. Copyright 1951 by R. Römer, Speer-Verlag, Zürich 7/44. Reprinted by permission of the publisher. The pages translated here represent part of the chapter "Die verfehlten Strukturen: Jean-Paul Sartre und der Existentialismus."

and creditors the debtors whom they drove to suicide. Remorse is re-awakened and kept alive all year long by swarms of flies that rapidly multiply in the humid, sticky air of this city of corpses which broods in the cruel sun. One single human being in Argos remains unbroken and secretly nourishes in her heart hatred and scorn for the oppressors. This is Electra, who is treated like a slave, but suffers every humiliation steadfastly, as she waits for the avenger.

In the first scene, Orestes appears as an independent traveler who, accompanied by his tutor, visits the town. His tutor is a well-educated man with rosy cheeks who prides himself on having brought up his pupil as a nonbeliever without love or hatred. One wonders in what way the pupil will fall under the spell of the town. Orestes' transformation is the basic theme of the play. The decisive turn of events occurs after the dreadful obsequies have ended. Orestes, who has pretended to be a certain Philebos from Corinth, is advised by Electra not to abandon his universe of levity. But he wants to be a human being who "belongs somewhere." He knows that his freedom can gain significance only through deeds, his own deed. In his insecurity he asks for a sign from the gods: if they really do not require of him anything but "resignation and common submission," they should give him a signal. The answer comes with unexpected promptness. Jupiter, hidden in the background, murmurs some magic formula and suddenly a light hovers about the dark rock. Electra has to laugh at the success of the pious prayer. But Orestes' eyes are opened: "So that is what it means to be good," he says staring at the light, "to bow down obediently. Always to say, 'I beg your pardon,' and 'I thank you,' that's it. That's what is good. That's what they think is good. . . ." And now suddenly all is changed. The mild young man becomes the son of Agamemnon who cannot rest until he has murdered Aegisthus and Clytemnestra. But Electra is frightened by this transformation, and the moment she hears her dying mother cry, her inner strength gives way. She cannot follow Orestes on his manly road to freedom. She abandons him. With the outcry "I repent, I repent," she throws herself at the feet of Jupiter and creeps back into the divinely protected community of men of bad conscience. But Orestes, defying the gods until the very end, takes his guilt upon himself without remorse and, pursued by the furies, sets out on his road to freedom.

It is revealing to note to what extent the *dramatis personae* represent various kinds of failure in and imbalance of the structure of their human existence.

One of the basic motifs of the play, which imposes itself from the start, is an irresistible *desire for realization,* a thirst for incarnation. Orestes, who had breathed the rarified air of an intellectual upbringing, passionately seeks the proximity of sensuous life and things.

The growing concreteness of things, which results from the repeated contrasting of his attitudes of detached spectator and passionate participant, is only the exterior mark of the *stabilization of personality* expressed in Orestes, the central character. It is in his clash with the other characters, shaped by external forces and lost in paralysis, that the free man, who shapes himself from within, emerges ever more distinctly. All others are in one way or another unbalanced in the structure of their existence—too light or too heavy. In contrast to the unanchored freedom of the intellectual and the bewildered vexations of the bigoted masses, Orestes finds the road to total existence through a voluntary acceptance of guilt and destiny.

The very contrast with the *false spirituality* of the tutor is a drama in itself. How different is the attitude of these two people toward Jupiter! The tutor is metaphysically blind; Orestes has an unerring feeling for the presence of mystery.

Because of this we sense the *false other-worldliness* of Jupiter. There is certainly a profound problem involved here, bewildering to many. Jupiter's appearance on the stage is often thought to be perturbing, if not sacrilegious. But it is fundamental to the dialectics of history that false other-worldiness and false this-worldliness should provoke and condition each other. Sartre makes Jupiter appear in a strangely ambiguous light. The jovial Jupiter with his magic tricks and theatrical effects calculated to impress the masses is at the same time the tragic god who, in an effort to create order among men, must stage his eternal dance before them. The conversation with this dictator echoes at times the Dostoevskian episode of the Grand Inquisitor. It is only fitting that this ambivalent Jupiter, in a melodrama which is both grandiose and ridiculous, should have to propagandize his own creative greatness through a loudspeaker. He is caught, so to speak, in his own machinations. Jupiter appears here as the god of the stars, the planets, ebb and tide, of all things that are prearranged and that depend on causality and natural laws. If we think of him elsewhere as being uncomfortably close, kneeling as it were upon man's soul, arbitrarily rummaging about within it and playing on the psychological levers of fear and remorse—in fact, he proves his mastery in this art when he finally succeeds in overpowering the soul of Electra—he appears to us here as a soulless, entirely extraneous robot. One is reminded of Goethe's line: "Could he be god who acts but from without?"

Man, this fugitive from nature, cannot close his ears to "the stony voice of the things that accuse him." He is himself a part of nature and remains subservient to it. But just at this point, where he feels himself most strongly bound, Orestes utters his strongest repudiation of Jupiter: "You should not have created me free."—"I have given you freedom so that you may serve me," replies Jupiter. Whereupon the proudly submissive Orestes replies: "Perhaps. But it has turned against you, and for this neither of us is responsible."

The character of Orestes detaches itself even more vividly when contrasted with that of Electra. One might ask why Electra, who in Giraudoux's most successful play still appears as pure, strong, and incorruptible, in the end breaks down and is untrue to herself in Sartre's play. For the writer of *The Flies* even Electra remains trapped in one-sidedness. She embodies *false, overexcited humanity*. In her hatred of her mother and Aegisthus and in her defiance of Jupiter she shows a woman's eccentricity and lack of measure, just as she shows a woman's weakness and loss of composure at the moment of her mother's death. She is too close to things and to people. Her lack of distance and perspective is revealed in her dream of happiness: she wants to learn from Orestes whether, in Corinth, boys and girls may walk about together freely, and it is such happiness that she speaks of when she addresses the bewildered masses. One might say that Electra represents here the traditional weakness of woman as men like to imagine it. She needs others so that she may lean upon them in love and hatred. Electra has consumed her individual existence in human relationships of too narrow a scope and has found realization only in her dreams. She has become, by denying herself, a helpless thing. Hence she falls prey to the psychological manipulations of Jupiter. In wanting to free the masses through "beauty," she represents a stage of development that Sartre has already surpassed. But just because of that the writer needs her, so that the new solution brought about by Orestes may stand out, more sharply silhouetted. The more vivid and human she is in her femininity, the more powerful and irresistible must the deliberative act of the male appear, in its defiance of all human bonds and natural limitations. Here, too, something like a law of equilibrium seems to be at work, just as in the case of the false transcendence of Jupiter. Electra is too close, whereas Orestes is at too great a distance; she is too feminine, he too masculine. Immediately after the deed has been done, Orestes keeps insisting on the fact that he has done *his* deed, but the world darkens for Electra. She no longer sees Orestes; the flies become larger and larger until they appear at last as the furies, dancing their hellish dance about the fearful soul of Electra.

In their contrasting attitudes toward the ruling pair, the difference between Orestes and Electra becomes completely evident. Just as it would have been unthinkable for Orestes to spit into the face of the wooden Jupiter as Electra does, so he could never have remained satisfied with Electra's static defiance of Aegisthus and Clytemnestra. He sees them as they really are: living corpses whose nothingness he must demonstrate, as it were, by destroying them physically. Aegisthus and Clytemnestra seem but to represent the petrified counterpart of the contrast between Orestes and Electra. They are in their own way prisoners of their deed. The queen has no regrets that Agamemnon, "the old goat," was murdered, but the murder was for her a mere emotive explosion, and by this one deed her whole life was spent in vain. Electra becomes, as Clytemnestra prophesied from the start, the precise mirror image of her mother. Nor is Aegisthus able to accept the burden of his deed. Jupiter says to him: "The deed of Orestes is hateful to me, but I love yours, because it was murder dumb and without consciousness, murder as antiquity knows it, comparable to a natural catastrophe rather than a human undertaking." Thus the dictatorship resulting from this murder has no human greatness. It is something sullen and inescapable. It is not rooted in a future living order, but in a past petrified in death. Bad conscience has arrested time. Men fearfully cling to their past. At that dead moment the tyrant gets a hold on them. But he himself is a dead tool in the hand of the highest dictator, "the god of the flies and death."

The *symbol of the flies* condenses into one image all that is uncanny in the play, all that is atmospherically oppressive. In this swarm, feeding on carrion and decay, are condensed all the murky secretions of the soul, all anguish, remorse, and scrupulousness left unassimilated—all the guilt one would wish to repress but of which one cannot rid oneself because it clings to man like a sticky mass. The theme of the flies is marvelously and dreadfully embodied in the idiot at the beginning of the play.

We are face to face here with a ghastly vision characteristic of all of Sartre's writing and thinking. In his great philosophical work, *Being and Nothingness,* he entitles one of his last chapters "Existential Psychoanalysis." What he has in mind is a psychological clarification of thingness, and the example he discusses at length is that of the viscous. He demonstrates that the viscous is a state intermediate between liquid and solid. Life considered in itself—an aggregation as it were—is for him just such a viscous mass. It is still flowing but begins to solidify. It has the resistance of some clodlike object, yet it cannot be seized. It is disgustingly ambivalent. Such is the manner in which reality appears to a man who no longer flows freely, who can no longer move from within, whose blood no longer pulsates freshly, and in whom the sap of life slowly thickens. Whatever happens to him coagulates and inescapably approaches fixity. It enters the realm of the dead. All life appears merely as decay. The slimy existence, this "pitch-like filth," as Erich Brock has called it in his perceptive essay "Philosophy in the Literary Work of Jean-Paul Sartre" (*Neue Züricher Zeitung,* October 7, 1944), is for Sartre the basic form of existence. On this decaying soil vermin swarm and larvae fatten, which develop into flies.

It is important to realize the similarity which exists here between Sartre and André Malraux, who in his first novel, *La Voie royale,* described the basic form of reality as the swamp-life of the jungle, the fermentation of formlessness, the rank intertwining of plants, and the swarming of insects. And his latest work, *La Lutte avec l'ange,* shows the same picture in a gassed landscape on the Russian front during the First World War, where all plants have become a decaying, poisonous black mass. Malraux, too, escapes through action from this apocalyptic bogging down of existence. "He no longer walked in muck but on a plane," he says of a revolutionary in *La Condition humaine.*

But here the difference between Malraux and Sartre reveals itself. Whereas in Malraux's work the liberating act brings about the beginning of a visible communion, Orestes remains alone. In this last isolation of the mind, the abstract side of Sartre's world becomes apparent. The much talked about *cerebrality* of the playwright here receives, however, its inherent explanation. It is simply the counterpart of the viscosity and density of life. To the degree that life is sticky and resinous, mind is hard and brittle. The too intimate femininity of reality (Sartre speaks of pitch-like existence as a "revanche douceâtre et féminine"), finds its counterpart in the too remote male mind. The responsibility remains with the mind. "If it lets itself be shaped by the world, it thickens and coagulates," says Sartre in *Being and Nothingness,* and this means cowardly resignation: "une démission de la réalité humaine en faveur du monde." If mind cannot keep step with life, if it does not set life in motion and is not filled with life, then life stagnates and mind loses its power to change the world. It remains isolated like Sartre in his study.

This is what lends the play its desperate, brittle ring and moves the spectator most deeply. Here the structural law of Sartrean writing comes through. Just as the world of viscosity appears in such images as heads burst open, faces "like squashed raspberries," putrified eyes, the beard of Aegisthus which runs like "a legion of spiders from ear to ear," so does the world of the solidified mind appear in metallic or mineral images, which evoke abstractions. Ideas are "beautiful and hard as steel," Clytemnestra says of guilt that it is "dark and pure like a black crystal," Jupiter speaks of the harmony of the spheres as an "énorme chant de grâces minérales."

This cool breath of abstractions which wafts toward us from the language of Sartre enables us to sense also what is specifically French in this play: the ruthlessly cruel clarity which stops short of no horror and continues to a point of self-immolation. Here the poet is most strongly involved. The nihilistic trend of thought can here also be best understood. To a mind which thinks in Cartesian geometrical terms, which fixes all life in concepts that have the brittle clarity of crystal, a slow organic flow is unthinkable. Movement is split into a series of static snapshots. Becoming is like a leap into the empty spaces between solidified phases of development. The French language can designate the transcendent force of life only as Not-Being, Nothingness.

Many obstacles that confront the writer—the pressure of dictatorship, the growing reification of the bourgeois-capitalistic society, the logical fossilization of Cartesian thought and of the French language, the loneliness and passivity of the philosopher limited to his study, and of the man who feels that he is cut off from the fullness of life—all these

obstacles are visibly concretized at the end of the play. The denouement
leaves the spectator bewildered. One would like to know what happens
to Electra, to the burghers of Argos, to Orestes himself. He has destroyed
the old order, defeated the old Jupiter, and freed the town of the flies
and its tyrant, but what of the new order, the new community, the new
beliefs? To this the spectator who wants readymade solutions is given no
satisfactory answer.

How easy it would have been for Sartre to unite the burghers of Argos
at the conclusion in a male chorus singing a hymn to freedom! What
applause the audience would have bestowed upon him in return for
such consolation and encouragement!

It is clear, however, that Sartre did not wish to present such a solution. He did not wish to do so because he could not do so. He did not
try to jump over his own shadow in unjustifiable anticipations. But at
the very point where obstacles seem insuperable, his true strength shows
itself.

The dramatic tension is dissolved, apparently, with the murder of the
tyrant. Admittedly the play becomes more and more problematical after
that. But the inherent tension appears all the more clearly. To shake
off the foreign yoke is only the external aspect of the desire for freedom.
Its inner sense is that man, in the midst of the world, discovers himself.
That is the real theme of the play. Orestes is transformed into himself.
The anonymous tourist of the opening scenes now bears his own name
and accomplishes his family's destiny. All of Argos, with its guilt and its
flies, now rests upon his shoulders. He will forever see before him the
eyes of his mother as they grew wide with the fear of death. He will
forget nothing, will omit nothing. Thus he strides through the open
gate of the temple into the future.

In the words he addresses to the mourning Electra the transcendent
impact of this movement is felt:

> My dearest, it is true, I have taken all from you and have given you
> nothing—except my crime. But it is a tremendous present. Do you think
> it does not burden my soul like lead? We were too light, Electra: now our
> feet sink into the earth like the wheels of a wagon into the ruts. Come, let
> us move away and walk with heavy tread, bent underneath our precious
> load. You will give me your hand and we shall leave. . . .
>
> ELECTRA: Where to?
>
> ORESTES: I do not know; toward ourselves. Beyond the rivers and the
> mountains there are an Orestes and an Electra waiting for us. We shall have
> to search for them patiently.

Here a *transcendence of a special kind* makes itself felt. It bears no
resemblance to the other-worldiness of Jupiter (to which one might
oppose the phrase of Ernst Jünger in his *Blätter und Stein*: "What use
transcendence to him to whom there is nothing which is not transcend-

ent?"). This is transcendence realized in the immanence of the world, of man, and of the community. As false other-worldliness and false this-worldliness betray themselves through their mutual dissociation, so true transcendence reveals itself through its coinciding with the pure immanence of human relationships. The two highest commandments are identical: the love of God and the love of your neighbor, and the *humana civilitas* agrees in its tangible outline precisely with what the Holy Scriptures refer to as the *Kingdom of God.* With the same transcendental desire with which he seeks his Self ("de l'autre côté des fleuves") Orestes seeks also his neighbor: "Electra! My sister, dearest Electra! My only love, only sweetness of my life, do not leave me alone, stay with me."

And his love includes also the burghers of Argos who wanted to kill him: "I frighten you, and yet, oh you people, I love you, and it was for your sake that I killed." The association of "loving" and "killing" seems strange but it reveals precisely the *ultimate secret of Sartrean form.* Against the rigid limitations that surround him everywhere, there is no other means of remaining within the movement of life and love, except by a breakthrough. Mind can express itself only in opposition, in the wild explosion, the sudden lightning flash. Because of that the action does not move smoothly but progresses in fits and starts. What is novel occurs in the crash of the thunderbolt. The word *éclair* is a favorite word of the writer: "Freedom," Orestes says, "has struck me like lightning."

The more difficult the obstacle to be overcome, the more sundered is the world which has to be reunited, the more does strength have to prove itself. Sartre appears to us like a man imprisoned in a house of glass. He pushes his head through the wall, unconcerned whether he hurts himself fatally—provided that he thereby opens a way to freedom.

Man and His Acts

by Jacques Guicharnaud

Starting from the principle that man is alone before man and the fact that such a situation is understandable or conceivable only in terms of action, Sartre and Camus have tried to create a type of theater in which the concrete representation of life and their own philosophical concepts are absolutely inseparable. Given their basic philosophical positions, the dialogue is indissolubly linked to physical *acts*. The plays are crammed with action or the expectation of action. Whether the play takes the form of an historical drama (Sartre's *Le Diable et le bon Dieu*),[1] an allegory (Camus' *L'État de siège*), a kind of semidetective story (Sartre's *Les Mains sales*, Camus' *Le Malentendu*, even Sartre's *Nekrassov*), or a series of debates (Sartre's *Huis-clos*, Camus' *Les Justes*), the spectator is held by the expectation of rebounds, the promise of extreme and definitive acts, the surprise of certain dramatic effects, and the double question: What's going to happen? How will it turn out? Sometimes both writers do end by creating a rush of physical happenings that border on the unreal. Camus' *Caligula*, for instance, might seem like an arbitrary catalogue of acts of cruelty and madness. Hence the adjective "melodramatic" as applied by some critics to their plays.

As treated by Sartre and Camus, physical action, generally violent, takes on a new value in that their basic philosophy consists in destroying the importance traditionally accorded to motives. What really counts are not the reasons for an act but the act itself, its present significance, and the significance it gives to the characters and the world. In other words, the search for the psychological causality of an act is either shown to be vain or replaced by an investigation of the act's significance.

This does not mean a total rejection of motives. Although explanations may be reduced to a minimum, they are indeed necessary, for the acts are not gratuitous. . . . Yet the motive is only very briefly pre-

[1] For English translations of these plays see Bibliography.

sented and in such terms that it seems more metaphysical than psychological. . . .

Even in a retrospective play like Sartre's *Huis-clos,* in which the acts are in the past and the characters try to evaluate them, emphasis is not put on discovering why, through what determinism of the world and men, the characters happened to commit their crimes. When they try, as Garcin occasionally does, they fail to reach any conclusion. The subject of the play is a study of the different ways in which men "bear" their acts. When any psychological causality is brought in, it is only as an *a posteriori* rationalization of the characters themselves. It is no more than a present state of consciousness. The same is true for *Les Mains sales,* in which the long flash back that makes up the greater part of the play contributes nothing more than plain facts, and no explanation. The meaning of Hoederer's murder is given only in the present and through Hugo's decision. In *Les Séquestrés d'Altona* as well, the hero is so tortured by the possible historical *significance* of his monstrous war crimes that he takes refuge in madness.

It has often been pointed out that Giraudoux's characters have hardly any pasts and are completely open to their futures. With a very different vision of the world, Sartre and Camus present much the same attitude. What counts for them is the project an act represents or its meaning in the present—a meaning which changes according to the agent's choices and the interpretation of other people. Of course for the existentialists, a concrete situation requires that a certain *nature* be taken into account. In general, no existentialist ever dreamed of denying given elements such as a man's body, sex, age, social class, temperament. And that weight, along with a consciousness of it and the effort made to objectify it or reject it, is inseparable from the subject of *Les Mains sales, Le Diable et le bon Dieu,* or *Les Séquestrés d'Altona.* To use the existentialist vocabulary, all freedom is *en situation;* but as Sartre and Camus want to bring out the irreducible element that distinguishes man from the rest of the world, their interest lies more in its manifestations and creations than in the mechanism of "natures" or "essences," which are considered as secondary. Such emphasis in theater means a complete reversal of the treatment of action. Acts are no longer considered as products but as inventions.

Therefore an act is seen as a creation, almost as unique and irreplaceable as a signed work of art, and at the same time as both a source of drama and drama itself, not only at the moment it is committed—when it implies a struggle and a choice—but even afterwards, in man's effort to clarify the relationship between it and himself. Sartre's characters' frequent use of the expression "my act" emphasizes the idea of its being both an outer object and a reciprocal bond between man and what he does. His plays are investigations of the different relations of man to his acts, whether he tries to rid himself of them (which is impossible,

whence Estelle's painful tragedy of bad faith in *Huis-clos,* Frantz's escape
into madness in *Les Séquestrés d'Altona,* and the judge's Pontius-Pilatism
in *L'État de siège*) or completely assumes them. Without denying all the
excuses that science gives for his behavior, man is considered in the
perspective of the formula: In any case, whatever I do, *I* am the one
who does it.

If the formula is taken as a central point, the existentialist theater
opens out around it and examines the ethical and political extensions
it implies. Men are considered as having no excuses, as from the start it
has been accepted that man is thus distinguished from the rest of the
world.

As a result, the play's intensity depends largely on the seriousness of
the acts committed. Everyday acts, taken one after the other, can be
successfully used in the novel, as in Sartre's *La Nausée.* But dramatic
economy demands that the weight of dilution be replaced by the shock
of concentration, and the effect is produced through a violent or monstrous act. Indeed we are back to the ancient, Shakespearean, or classical
conception of exemplary and extreme acts. If it is true that every act
brings man's very being into question, murder, where even an illusion
of reparation is impossible, is the best means of bringing it into play.
Moreover Sartre and Camus, in the belief that great violence is a sign of
the times, use murder in all its forms. As death is the situation par excellence for bringing man's being into question, whether the tragedy be
private or collective, to kill or be killed is the symbol of man's greatest
problem.

The more horrible the act, the more the individual, who always acts
alone, begins to "question." Malraux, in *La Condition humaine,* had
already described the solitude and anguish involved in murder. Sartre
and Camus bring the greatest violence and the deepest solitude together
in their situations. Solitude in this case is what separates the would-be
murderer from the arguments in favor of the murder. For instance, in
Les Mains sales Hugo begins to like Hoederer whom he wants to kill
for political reasons; and Kaliayev, in *Les Justes,* had decided to throw a
bomb at the Grand Duke until he saw children in the carriage. Emphasis
is put on the isolation of each individual in his action or his suffering,
in a vision of the world where, to use Roquentin's terms in *La Nausée,*
there is obviously no "communion of souls"—for, as he says, "I have not
fallen so low." My suffering is *my* suffering just as my murder, even in
the case of collective action, is *my* murder.

The isolation of man in action is often symbolized by the choice of
heroes whose basic situations are exceptional. Orestes' background has
made him a stranger to all the cities in Greece (*Les Mouches*); Hugo is
a young bourgeois in the Communist party (*Les Mains sales*); Goetz is
a military leader and a bastard born of a nobleman and a peasant (*Le
Diable et le bon Dieu*); Lizzie is a prostitute on the fringe of American

society (*La Putain respectueuse*); Nekrassov is an adventurer (*Nekrassov*); Kean is a great actor (*Kean*); Caligula is an emperor (*Caligula*); Kaliayev is a poet (*Les Justes*).

Often there are more specific reasons for the choice of certain characters. In *Les Mains sales,* for example, Sartre was speaking directly to the young bourgeois Franchmen attracted by Communism at the time. But in general, the characters' exceptional situations are meant to express, in the form of a hyperbolic metaphor, the similar agony of any man faced with himself. They are not meant to imply that humanity is naturally divided into heroes and the superfluous rest of mankind.

The agony here is metaphysical. Although the hero may be acting out of passion or in the name of a value, what suddenly strikes him is the bare fact of his own existence and the dizzying vacuum of the nothingness it implies. Whether the hero be Sartre's Garcin, Goetz, Hugo, or Camus' Caligula, his hopeless discovery is that the world is absurd and his acts the unjustified creations of his freedom.

"You are no more than the sum of your acts," says Inez to Garcin in *Huis-clos.* The traditional idea that man commits such or such act because he is thus and so, is replaced with its opposite; by committing such or such act, man makes himself thus and so. Nothingness to start with, man spends his life giving himself an essence made up of all his acts. And it is through acting that he becomes conscious of original nothingness. The anguish that grips him is provoked by that nothingness, that absence of justification, and the metaphysical responsibility which makes him the creator of his own essence. The idea is alien to many minds. It is uncomfortable, to start with. But more important it eliminates the notion of human nature, a fundamental concept in Western thought, and treats human destiny in itself as meaningless and useless agitation, in other words, absurd. The dramatic hero also finds it difficult to accept, and the conflict between his awareness of the absurd and his need for justification constitutes the strongest dramatic tension in Sartre's and Camus' works.

Once the hero accepts the idea—if he does—a second dramatic conflict becomes apparent: what is he to do now? The choice is simple. Either he can fall back into blindness and bad faith, that is, into a belief in reasons, eternal essences, the value of established orders, human or divine, with a meaning given in advance; or he can assume his acts and his life, fully aware of the world's absurdity, and accept the crushing responsibility of giving the world a meaning that comes from himself alone.

In his first play, *Les Mouches,* Sartre showed the transition from frivolous freedom to the discovery of terrifying metaphysical freedom. He also showed that the discovery is unbearable (Electra's collapse) and at the same time how, unbearable as it may be, man can save himself and others when he assumes his act, as Orestes did.

Orestes is an apprentice as . . . [is] Goetz in *Le Diable et le bon Dieu*. Except that Orestes is in the privileged position of not being from anywhere and participating in nothing. When Jupiter tells him about the crimes of Clytemnestra and Aegisthus, he answers: ". . . I couldn't care less. I'm not from here" (Act I, scene 1). A bit later, when he begins to dream about the lives of men who are anchored in one place, with their possessions and their worries, he feels a touch of regret but continues all the same to congratulate himself on what he calls his "freedom": "Thank God I am free. Oh! How free I am. And what a superb absence is my soul" (Act I, scene 2). There Sartre, with the help of the Greek myth, skipped a certain number of stages. His hero is already outside the blind conformity of collective behavior.

Having begun life with the illusion of disengagement taught him by his cosmopolitan pedagogue, Orestes, at the cost of a great struggle and a double murder, succeeds in creating the "royal way" that leads him to assume his own acts. In addition to his pedagogue's impossible frivolity, he has to avoid two temptations: the attitude of the oppressed social group, convinced that their oppression is in the order of things, and its correlative, the alliance with a divine order, symbolized by the terrifying and grotesque figure of Jupiter. In other words, he must avoid the freedom of the "spider's web that floats ten feet above the earth at the mercy of the wind" (Act I, scene 2), as well as the human and divine traps that transform man into something determined, into "stone" (Act III, scene 2). By murdering his mother and her lover, Orestes discovers that an act is nothing more than an enormous and obscene presence, a parasite of man, both exterior and possessive. Orestes is the hero who understands that the act is his and only his. He also understands that it has outer consequences: a tyrant's death frees the oppressed people, whose bondage stemmed only from the tyrant. But as far as the act itself is concerned, only the agent can determine its weight, only the agent bears the burden. *Les Mouches* is a sumptuous metaphor intended to show men that responsibility is not synonymous with guilt, that the world of men is made up of the impact of actions, whose meaning comes only from the men who committed or suffered them. The play also indicates that the plague (and here we partially rejoin Camus) exists only to the extent that men accept it. The plague is in fact no more than the imposition of responsibility on others from the outside, and man has the power to counter that act with a contrary act.

This point of view has brought true overtones of tragedy to the theater of Sartre and Camus. Their heroes love life. They have no particular desire to die, nor do they seek any glorification in death. But they prefer death to a degradation of the man within them. They fall from a high state in that, whether emperors or proud terrorists, they are reduced to suicide, prison, and physical or moral torture. And the catastrophe is always accompanied by an awareness which makes them superior to that which crushes them. However their awareness does not imply the recognition of a superior order but rather a recognition of man as the one and only value.

On that level, Sartre's and Camus' plays can be divided into two categories: those in which emphasis is put on the agony itself (*Le Malentendu, Huis-clos*) and those in which both writers, succumbing to a kind of proselytism, seem to want to prove that the only way of really being a man among men is to assert one's freedom by rebelling against established orders, mere masks of the absurd (*L'État de siège, Les Mouches*). . . . Yet in both cases, whether the action is effective or only a desperate protest, the basic tragedy and heroism are the same. And the writers' intentions were the same: to bring out, from behind the false face of humanity, man's true condition.

Here the return to man excludes a tableau of everyday life and mediocrity. Men are not truly men in their petty and niggardly daily acts but rather at the moment the idea of man is heroically brought into question through themselves. Consequently when everyday banalities are suggested, it is only to emphasize their *inauthenticité*, that is, their power to dehumanize the individual by blinding him to his own freedom. The portrayal of beings and situations at their most ordinary and average constitutes a complete misunderstanding of humanism. Sartre's and Camus' humanism makes a distinction between a false humanity, which doubtless merits being portrayed but not as the true definition of man, and a true humanity, which in the world today can be found in any individual at moments of great crisis or in extreme situations. At such times man really wonders what he is. What counts is the portrayal of man, stripped of his pettiness and "the most man possible"—that is, not positively defined but rather suspended between possible definitions. For man can be defined as being outside any definition and at the same time bewilderingly in search of one. The best means of concretely expressing that point of view is the portrayal of characters caught in a paroxysm of situations and acts.

While both the existentialists' and Camus' way of considering the relation between man and his acts is profoundly dramatic in itself, the addition of a supplementary element, bearing also on the basic philosophy, makes the plays of Sartre and Camus not only dramatic but theatrical as well.

In the three chapters devoted to Albert Camus' theater in her recent book, *Camus,* Germaine Brée comes back time and again to the theme of the play within the play and the characters' own staging of it. . . .

Sartre also seems to have had a similar theatrical vision in most of his plays. The characters in *Huis-clos* act out precisely the drama expected of them by the powers of Hell; Goetz is the stage director of Good and Evil in *Le Diable et le bon Dieu;* Jupiter and Aegisthus organize the collective spectacle of men and the universe in *Les Mouches;* the leading characters in *Nekrassov* and *La Putain respectueuse* are made to play parts written in advance by the powers of this world; and the problems of the actor himself are portrayed in *Kean,* an adaptation of Alexandre Dumas' play.

On the whole, such references to a theater of life give an especially theatrical savor to the works of Sartre and Camus. Their devices are somewhat comparable to those of Cocteau and Anouilh but the implications and significance are different. Rather than provide a solution to life by living "as if," the use of an imposed scenario or a play within the play is meant to furnish a means for action. The job of the stage director consists in assigning a place and a function to everyone and everything in relation to a given end and a plan of the whole. Defined as part of a whole, things and individual beings must sacrifice their spontaneity and freedom. The tension thus created generally results in an explosion of the elements outside the game or of anyone who freely refuses to enter in. Sometimes the stage director's order wins (*La Putain respectueuse*); most often the unpredictability of the absurd (*Le Malentendu*) or of freedom (*Les Mouches, Les Mains sales, Le Diable et le bon Dieu, L'État de siège*) reduces man's scenarios and the metaphoric scenarios of the gods to nothing; and on occasion the individual or private self, the person who answers for his own fears, loves, etc., stands out at the height of the action as isolated and separated from the over-all plan (*Les Justes, Morts sans sépulture*).

The great directors are the oppressors, the liberators, and the experimenters. Jupiter and Aegisthus, the Plague, the American senator, and in certain respects the Communist party, belong to the first category; the revolutionaries and Martha in relation to herself, to the second; Caligula and Goetz, to the third. In other words this particular form of second degree theater, as compared to that found in other works, is not presented as an aesthetic solution of the absurd, but as a metaphor of the oppressive order as well as the necessary means to explode its lies and injustices. Whether mask or anti-mask, it takes the form of a scenario written in advance and, through a necessary antithesis, evokes the themes of freedom and contingency. Anouilh also used the device in *Antigone, L'Alouette,* and other plays in which the heroes refuse to play the game of a scenario written in advance. But Anouilh's solution lies in the play itself, in the very theatricalism of the conflict, whereas in Sartre and Camus theatrical creation is always a means, never a reconciliatory end.
. . . The basic conflict is threefold: the comedy of a world of illusions (false justification) as opposed to the theater or anti-theater of those who seek the absolute, and both opposed to the plain fact of existence as it is lived or to be lived, both individually and collectively. In Camus, existence as such is expressed more or less allegorically in the character Cheréa in *Caligula* and the Mediterranean richness of certain images in

L'État de siège and *Le Malentendu*. Sartre expresses it less poetically in Hoederer's vitality and relation to objects in *Les Mains sales,* Hilda's love in *Le Diable et le bon Dieu,* and *Nekrassov*'s gaiety. But as it is most often outside the play, it can only be alluded to. Man's unchanging tragedy lies both in the search for it and in the tension between the first two elements of the conflict.

Despite great similarities in basic philosophy and theatrical vision, Sartre and Camus differ profoundly on the aesthetic level, just as in a comparable way *La Nausée* differs from *L'Étranger,* or *La Peste* from *Les Chemins de la liberté.*

Sartre's dramatic universe is nearer to realism or traditional naturalism. Eric Bentley[1] points out the fact that *Huis-clos* is essentially Strindbergian in tone and a drawing-room comedy in form. And indeed three boulevard melodramas can easily be made out of each of the three characters' lives: a frivolous young lady who killed her child, a rather nasty Lesbian who led her friend to suicide, a pacifistic journalist who deserted in time of war—all phychological dramas with social implications and perfect material for a "well-made" play. Even the setting for each drama is suggested: the Lesbian's room with its gas stove, the newspaper office with the editors in shirt sleeves, the elegant room in Switzerland with its windows giving on to the lake. Sartre deliberately chose three rather typical news items and kept certain "true" details—that is, their naturalist color.

. . . Yet Sartre had reasons for what he did. He wanted first to get the spectator on familiar ground and then gradually bring him into existentialist drama, far from his familiar ground. In *Huis-clos,* for instance, the naturalism of each character's "case" and the realism of language and décor create an image of the beyond that is acceptable to audiences accustomed by films and theater to seeing death represented in very earthly forms. But the true subject of the play is revealed on a third level. It is neither in the anecdotal interest of a few adventures or perversions, nor in the modernist pathos of the allegory of Hell, but in the relation of one consciousness to another, in the search for a definition of the self with the help of others, in the realization that the presence and judgment of others is necessary and yet leads to an impasse.[2] On that level the whole takes on all its meaning, and we discover that the play is not a metaphor of Hell but that the image of Hell is a metaphor of the hopeless suffering of individuals in search of their definitions in the eyes of others, yet constantly brought back to themselves.

Garcin's reticence in telling about how he deserted and especially how he physically fell apart at the time of his execution is an excellent

[1] Eric Bentley, *The Playwright as Thinker.*

[2] *Huis-clos* was first published in *L'Arbalète,* No. 8 (Lyon, 1943) as *Les Autres* or *The Others.*

subject for a naturalistic psychological drama: the pacifist has a shameful secret; he acted out of cowardice. And part of the dialogue is directed toward that drama, but at one point it turns away from it and moves toward an existentialist perspective. Once it has been established that an inquiry into the motives for an act does not reveal the act's meaning, Garcin's hopeless tragedy lies in the fact that he is unable to determine the meaning of his life by himself and is condemned to live between two women—one totally indifferent to the question and the other who, needing "the suffering of others in order to exist," decides that he has been cowardly and is thus satisfied with the spectacle of his shame.

Sartre's plays lead the spectator from the universe of perception, common sense, and psychological or aesthetic habits to an existentialist conclusion, often difficult in its newness. What Sartre shows essentially is that his vision of the world is inherent in the normal universe. His method consists in bringing it out progressively. And often the progression itself makes up the greater part of the play.

Les Mains sales is presented as a politico-detective drama, based on a simple question comparable to the suspense-provoking questions in melodrama: Why did Hugo kill Hoederer? The suspense is all the more acute in that the spectator knows that Hugo's life depends on the answer. We take part in an investigation and a trial. The actual investigation, which takes up six of the seven tableaux, is in the form of a flashback concerned only with the simple fact of Hoederer's death and leaving the murder committed by Hugo in all its ambiguity. Sartre played the game of the detective-story melodrama according to the rules but he stopped short of melodramatic satisfaction. The "secret" we are supposed to uncover is not uncovered and we understand that it is impossible to uncover it. In a sense the naturalistic melodrama destroys itself under our very eyes, leaving hero and spectator open to whatever lies ahead. Having finished his long demonstration and created the necessary vacuum, Sartre can then go on to lead both spectator and hero into the true subject of his play. In the last fifteen minutes we discover that the meaning of Hoederer's murder does not lie in Hugo's reasons for it, which in any case remain ambiguous. Hugo's true motive is the one he chooses *afterward* when, fully aware of the situation, he determines—through his own death—the meaning of the situation and the value of Hoederer's life and his own. Somewhat the same gradual transition takes place within Goetz and the spectator in *Le Diable et le bon Dieu*, although its dialectic is not so clear because of the play's enormity.

. . . Camus' and Sartre's aesthetics are as different as their general ideologies are similar. In Sartre, innovations in form are secondary to content. In Camus, aesthetic consciousness is inseparable from the substance. Yet their intentions are much alike in that both have tried to give French audiences theater that is neither an agreeable repetition of past masterpieces, even recent ones, nor a purely modernist aesthetic thrill.

They have also agreed on the idea of an art that is completely concerned with and in terms of our times. Their common purpose has been both to describe the man of today and to write for the man of today. Such is doubtless the intention of all writers, but in Sartre and Camus it takes the form of a conscious rule, affirmed and reaffirmed as a writer's first duty. An acute consciousness of the modern world and a true identification with its problems and demands have determined the themes and aesthetics of both. And although Camus had time and again refused to be labeled "existentialist," he *can* be considered committed or *engagé,* if literary *engagement* is taken in its broadest sense as writing for one's time, directly or indirectly about one's time, with man's freedom as an ultimate goal.

In the light of such an attitude many literary positions must be rejected as survivals of a dead past. Psychological analyses in classical terms, reducing man to a determinism which is now thought to be precisely not man; historical and picturesque reconstruction for itself; freezing man in the ice of dead essences; the exclusive cult of beauty; placing the meaning of the world outside man—all are eliminated, not absolutely, but relatively: the present and man's tragedy at this moment of history are considered more important and rich enough to take precedence over any other concern.

Thus the central problem of Malraux's novels has been brought to the theater by Sartre and Camus. They chose their subjects among the most burning issues of our times: wars, oppression, rebellions, revolutions, and through them reached the so-called universal themes—but stated in new terms. Instead of traditional psychologism, the entire human being is called into question.[3]

. . . In trying to make this clear in their plays and also in order to reach the largest public possible, Sartre in his works as a whole and Camus in *L'État de siège* were often forced, given the difficulty of their philosophies, into simplifications and sometimes even concessions. Sartre gave in and used boulevard-type details and facile naturalist techniques, especially flagrant in *Les Séquestrés d'Altona.* He also spelled out certain of his arguments in easily assimilated formulas, and by seeming intellectually clearer, sacrificed many nuances necessary to a complete understanding of his philosophy, while losing in dramatic reality as well. As for Camus, his often abstract maxims, used as articulations, are often more intellectual than dramatic.

For theirs is a theater of ideas—exactly the kind Gide had hoped to see created by Giraudoux. Neither Sartre nor Camus are primarily

---

[3] As if by chance, a whole group of "engaged" plays appeared on Paris stages during the Forties and Fifties, presenting the point of view of the right as well as the left. Aside from the Anouilh plays that skirt existentialism, the most interesting works, in reaction or in imitation, are Thierry-Maulnier's *La Maison de la nuit* (1953) and Colette Audry's *Soledad* (1956).

playwrights. Sartre is above all a professional philosopher. Camus is obviously more of an artist and was always active in the world of theater,[4] but all his works are dominated by intellectual searching and the examination of ideas. Yet what distinguishes their plays from other "philosophical" theater is the absolutely dramatic and concrete nature of their philosophy itself. The fundamental problem of the definition of man and the world is truly embodied in living acts.

[4] For example, his collaboration with "Le Théâtre du Travail," founded in Algiers in 1935, and his many adaptations.

Sartre's Struggle for Existenz

by Eric Bentley

I

The new French theater, the theater of the Resistance, the theater of Sartre, Anouilh, Camus, and Simone de Beauvoir, has had a queer, uneven, stormy history in France. It is now beginning to have one over here. Sartre's first play, *Les Mouches,* has been ignored by the commercial theater but was produced almost simultaneously last year by the theater workshop of the New School, Vassar College, Western Reserve University, apparently in fact by every academy that knows what's what. *No Exit* was played on Broadway and had to be discontinued, not because nobody was paying to see it, but because the owners of the theater were up to their usual mischief.

Somebody else must also have been up to some mischief, for the following news item appeared in France:

Jean-Paul Sartre se mit dans une colère terrible lorsqu'il apprit la façon dont on avait monté sa pièce *Huis-clos* à New York. . . . Les Américains en ont fait une farce énorme qui déchaine l'hilarité des spectateurs, comme s'il s'agissait d'un fabliau grivois du moyen âge. Fataliste, en dépit de ses enseignements, Sartre a pris la partie de rire. "Les Américains ne comprendront jamais rien à l'existentialisme," grogne-t-il plaisamment. Le public new yorkais, que Sartre rejette ainsi dans la foule des bourgeois obtus, rassemblait tous les snobs élégants qui ne voudraient pour rien au monde manquer les grands "events" théatraux et quelques intellectuels "sophistiqués" vivement désireux de prendre contact avec la pensée française. . . .

[Jean-Paul Sartre was terribly angry when he learned how his play *No Exit* had been staged in New York. . . . The Americans had turned it into a gross farce that had the spectators laughing hilariously as though it were a suggestive medieval tale. A fatalist in spite of his teachings, Sartre decided to laugh it off. "Americans will never understand anything about existential-

"Sartre's Struggle for Existenz," by Eric Bentley. From the *Kenyon Review,* X (1948), 328-334. Reprinted by permission of the author and the *Kenyon Review.* Eric Bentley wishes to call special attention to the date of his piece—1948. Writing in 1962, he would think differently about certain matters, and he would also wish to take in what M. Sartre has written in the period 1948-1962.

ism," he grumbled goodhumoredly. The New York audience, which Sartre
thus equated with the bourgeois numbskulls, contained all the elegant snobs
who would not miss the main theatrical "events" for anything in the world,
and also a few "sophisticated" intellectuals eager to keep up with French
culture. . . .]

This report of the most considerable Sartre production in America is
matched in unfairness by a report I happened to see which was sent to a
leading New York producer after the production of Sartre's two latest
plays in Paris. The Paris agent wrote that *Les Morts sans sépulture* was
merely sensational and had no merit and that *La Putain respectueuse,*
though obviously the work of a brilliant and even great writer, was
scandalously anti-American and thus impossible as a Broadway project.
More recently, I have seen another shocked account of Sartre's un-Amer-
ican activities in *Theater Arts* and a plot summary of *La Putain* in the
front pages of *Time.*

Reverse the assertions of our theatrical shysters and you get something
closer to the truth. *La Putain* is not an offence against the American community, nor, unfortunately, is it a great play. *Les Morts,* on the other
hand, is not merely sensational and it has a great deal of merit.

The trouble with *La Putain* is that the characters and situations are
simplified to the point where we begin to laugh contrary to the author's
intention. I should think that in any American production the actors will
have to fight to keep the play from being ridiculous. For, if there is a
joke in the idea of a Yankee at the court of King Arthur, there is one
also in Sartre conducting the Struggle for Existenz at a Louisiana hot
spot, a Frenchman at the court of the late Kingfish. Like Simone de
Beauvoir's *Les Bouches inutiles,* Sartre's *La Putain* is as crudely abstract
as the proletarian literature of ten years ago. (To avoid misunderstanding,
I should interject that the politics of *Les Bouches inutiles* is *New Leader*
rather than *New Masses. La Putain,* I imagine, would be equally con-
genial to both periodicals.)

All the same, *La Putain* would be worth producing if only to show
a New York audience that a play by an intelligent, philosophical author
may be more stirring in the theater than a play by a mere entertainment-
monger.[1] In Sartre's novels and speeches, theatricality is a notable fault.
It seems to stand in the way of sincerity. But in the theater theatricality
can hardly be considered out of place. In the theater Sartre may even get
away with such old gags as he uses in *La Putain*: the stagey exploitation
of a bracelet which brings bad luck, the ironic repetition at the end of
a line used at the beginning, etc. And the play is something more than
anti-anti-Negro propaganda because Sartre contrives to give a certain
meaning and intensity to the relationship between the whore and the

---

[1] It has been produced, since this was written, by New Stages Inc. in Greenwich
Village.

senator's son (the two main characters). The histrionically pointed irony of this relationship is that it begins with the young man's blushing "respectfully" at the whore's nakedness and ends with the whore's being so "respectful" in her turn that she sells her soul as well as her body to the young man: she now drops her plan to kill him, though he has tricked and pushed her into giving false evidence against a Negro, and instead, agrees to be his mistress.

II

In *La Putain,* Sartre is engaged—one might perhaps say, *chiefly* engaged—in the old French sport of bewildering the bourgeoisie; but, fond as he may be of our southern novelists, he has no imaginative grasp, and perhaps little factual knowledge, of the American South. It is the desperate externality of the whole thing that makes the play slightly ludicrous. *Les Morts sans sépulture* presents a situation which Sartre knows and feels from the inside. Decidedly it is a better play.

It is interesting that *Time* did not tell the story of it. It is interesting too that Gabriel Marcel in *Theater Arts* and the Paris agent whom I have already quoted begin to tell the story and then break off in the middle, protesting that the play is sheer Grand Guignol. M. Marcel reiterates the neoclassic doctrine that scenes of torture should take place offstage. And there is sense in this: it *is* impossible to take in a drama if one's sense of physical suffering becomes too acute. But how did this discussion arise from *Les Morts?* The worst tortures of Sartre's story do take place offstage and, so far as I can judge from the script, we do not see as much physical horror in this play as in many movies (e.g., *Open City*). Could it be for other reasons that our accredited judges of the drama fail to speak of a play as a whole? Could we say of the present run of drama "critics" that they all go home before the end—some literally, others figuratively? And that this, when the play is a good one, might be unfortunate?

Since very few of my readers can have seen or read *Les Morts,* it will be well to explain what happens in the play. M. Marcel's summary is accurate as far as it goes:

> The scene is laid somewhere in the Alps, at the beginning of July 1944. A small group of resistants have been captured by the *milice* . . . in a pro-Maquis village, the population of which has been massacred. The resistants have been temporarily reprieved in order that they may be questioned. . . .
>
> Actually they have nothing to tell; they do not know anything. They are even ignorant of the whereabouts of Jean, their chief, who was not with them when they were seized. They will be tortured for nothing; there will be no point to their agony. François, only fifteen, the youngest among them, rebels violently against the idea of martyrdom; nothing had prepared him for this outcome.
>
> A dramatic scene ensues: Jean, arrested separately, is brought in by the

milice, who are unaware of his true identity. Jean explains to his comrades that he is sure to be released, as he was able to assume a false identity. He is not a coward: it is horrible to him not to share the fate of his comrades but he has *no right* to share it; in fact he must be liberated in order to warn others who will otherwise inevitably fall into a trap. Jean's conduct is irreproachable, but a chasm widens relentlessly between him and the others, for the simple reason that he will live on and they will die after torture.

The greatness of the play for me lies in this anomaly for which no one is to blame yet which has the effect of actual wrongdoing. On top of this, young François, who is determined to extricate himself from this hell at any price, declares that when they question him he will tell the truth, he will denounce Jean. The others then, without anger but simply because they are compelled to do so, strangle him on the stage. They do it with the consent of the older sister, Jean's mistress, who had been the one originally to involve the youthful François in this dangerous and fatal business. . . .

At this point, rather than tell us what happens next, M. Marcel indulges in some avuncular moralizing. His summary has not brought us even to the end of the second act.

After the death of François, Jean is set free, but not before suggesting to the others a stratagem by which they too will probably be able to obtain their release. They are to pretend to give way and tell where Jean is; the *milice* will go to the designated spot and find a corpse which they will take for Jean's. The *maquisards* do not at first intend to use this stratagem. They have prepared themselves for death and do not want to give the Vichyites the pleasure of a seeming victory. The culminating scene of the play is that (in the third and last act) in which they are given a few minutes to decide between intransigence and what their opponents will take for surrender. It is a truly and traditionally dramatic situation. A decisive and morally significant choice confronts the *maquisards,* and the conflict is recorded and resolved in fighting words. It is the sort of situation that Sartre can handle very well. Indeed, a generation that has forgotten Strindberg probably knows no dramatist who can handle such things better.

The morality of heroism is complex. A hero is prepared to die for the cause if necessary. But if he wishes to die when it is not necessary, when indeed his life might well be of more use than his death, he is not rising to heroism but descending to heroics. As a theoretical point, this is simple, and one can imagine, say, Maxwell Anderson making a play out of the theoretical simplicity. Practically, the point is complex, since one is never sure of one's motives, nor can one be sure of the consequences of either of two alternatives. It is out of such moral ambiguities that Sartre creates his most impressive scenes.

On the other hand, M. Marcel's observations are not false. The widening gulf between Jean and his comrades, the calamity "for which no one is to blame yet which has the effect of actual wrongdoing": these are subjects which call forth Sartre's best dramatic talent. The mistake is to see such scenes in isolation from the whole. Sartre's plays have form. After their own fashion, they are "well made." The end of *Les Morts* cannot be ignored, because it is an integral part of the whole, because it is the culmination of the action, because we are swept along to it on a wave of very powerful feeling. It is also an interesting ending in itself, being a resolution of a problem and an affirmation of life without being encouragingly sentimental in the manner of Socialist Realism. The three surviving *maquisards* decide to live; but history does not endorse their decision. The shrewdest and cruellest of the Vichyites cancels the orders of his forgiving colleague and has the *maquisards* shot, Jean or no Jean.

III

What does Sartre have to offer the theater? This would be a crass question to ask of your average playwright or even of most great ones. A playwright offers plays—which have merit in the degree of his talent and integrity. But Sartre is not merely a playwright, nor merely a novelist, an essayist, a lecturer, a philosopher. He is a literary politician in the best sense, a leader of a movement, an oriflamme. The plays of such a man may make dramatic history like those of Diderot and Hugo even if they are not masterpieces like those of Musset and Becque.

Undoubtedly a public figure, a brilliant figure, Sartre has in abundance the defects of his qualities: he can be superficial, perverse, clever, naughty. The lecture which he gave two years ago under the auspices of *View,* and which was printed in *Theater Arts* (June 1946), was the typical Sartre compound: bold to the point of temerity, confident to the point of cocksureness, magnificent to the point of pretentiousness. Consider the tactics of this defense of the new French drama. First Sartre picks his enemies, and apparently finds it necessary to attack not only psychological realism but also Maeterlinck and not only Maeterlinck but also (!) Racine. As allies he chooses Corneille and Sophocles.

Now are not both the offensive and defensive sides of this strategy ill-advised? Suddenly to attack a great writer because his purposes are not in harmony with yours, suddenly to claim the support of another great writer in order to establish your respectability—these are not new gambits. If the author of *Huis-clos* likes to prate about classic austerity so does the composer of *Sacre du Printemps;* and Sartre resembles Corneille even less than Stravinsky resembles Bach. What Sartre the dramatist actually learns from the Greeks is something as external as what Sartre the novelist learns from the Americans. Indeed when we know that he speaks in the same breath of Faulkner and Steinbeck (*Atlantic Monthly,* August 1946), we can hardly be surprised to find him equating Anouilh's *Antigone* with Sophocles'.

In his lecture on the theater, Sartre passionately denounces other schools of drama and easily establishes that they give only a partial picture of life. He proposes to replace this picture with nothing less than the whole truth! Racine was one-sided and wrong, Corneille "gives us back man in all his complexity, in his complete reality." Psychological realism is one-sided and wrong, the new French school throws "light on the main aspects of the condition of man." "We do not reject psychology, that would be absurd: we integrate life." "All," Sartre tells us, that the new French drama "seeks to do is to explore the state of man in its entirety and to present to the modern man a portrait of himself, his problems, his hopes, and his struggles." Yes, that is really "all."

Sartre's magniloquence is no doubt very useful in allowing him to have everything both ways. Take one example: the crucial matter of the relation of the audience to the actor. In several sentences of the lecture, Sartre speaks in favor of a stronger identification of spectator and performer, of greater *Einfühlung:* he wants the spectator to participate more fully because "the theater ought to be . . . a great, collective, religious phenomenon." In other places, though, he speaks of the need for distance and approaches Bertolt Brecht's conception of *Verfremdung.* "To us," Sartre says, "a play should not be too *familiar* . . . even as it speaks to the spectators of themselves it must do it in a tone and with a constant reserve of manner which, far from breeding familiarity, will increase the distance between play and audience."

Luckily, when the mountain has finished rumbling, something more than a mouse emerges. Sartre has a very nice little theory of the drama. He demands a theater of situation rather than character, of theme rather than psychology. Of course these statements are characteristically ambiguous. Sartre cannot dispense with character ("we do not reject psychology"!); he can only show it in a different light and in contact with other things. On some future occasion I should like to analyze the existentialists' treatment of character. For the present I must be content to remark that Sartre is concerned—in his lecture—with the rejection of Zolaist determinism. Far from being a creature of environment, says Sartre, man has a will. In fact that is perhaps his most important possession. Within the ring of circumstance he chooses and determines his fate. In this sense character is *more* important for Sartre than it was for the naturalists.

There is nothing new in making will and the conflict of wills central to the drama. Nor is there anything new in the dramatic technique which Sartre proposes: concise dialogue with "ellipses, brusque interruptions," "dramas which are short and violent, sometimes reduced to the dimensions of a single long act." Although one will not find such ideas in the prefaces of Corneille, one will find them in many other places, such as in the pronouncements of those realists and naturalists whom Sartre abhors.

If Sartre would stick to the theater, in which he is so richly talented, he could afford to let dramatic theory alone. In his programmatic utterances, as in those of Brecht, there is a lot of blarney. The theories are an attempt not only—which is legitimate—to explain the practice of a new type of theater but also—which is gratuitous—to give that practice an artificially high status. Perhaps some artists need to keep their spirits up in this way. If so, I hope Jean-Paul Sartre is not one of them. I hope he will choose to develop his very considerable dramatic gifts even at the expense of that other very considerable gift of his: the gift of the gab.

Comedian and Martyr

by Robert Champigny

There is . . . a category of alienation which cannot be avoided by
man as man: it is the alienation imposed on man by the presence of
other men. Insofar as we *are,* it is other people as well as ourselves who
decide on what we are. . . . In *L'Être et le néant* and in the short essay,
Visages, the appearance of "the Other" is given a magic quality. In
Esquisse d'une théorie des émotions, one could already read: "Man is always a sorcerer for man and the social world is first of all magic." The self
of the Sartrean man is intimately haunted by the Other. It is this
eminently theatrical atmosphere which is the subject of *Huis-clos,* the
basis of the often misinterpreted aphorism: "Hell is the others." This
fundamental experience indicates one of the limits within which morals
have to be thought and lived. It contributes to making morals a perpetually renewed question instead of a set of wise formulas.

Goetz is not prepared to cope with this kind of alienation. When the
peasants to whom he gives his lands prove unable or unwilling to interpret this action in the light in which Goetz likes to see it, the latter
exclaims: "The good will be done against all" (p. 136).

Goetz wants to be "the one who does the good at once" (p. 141). But
his charitable gesture, his "good" *gesture* can become a good *action*
only if the peasants take advantage of it. Man cannot coincide with
being, he can but play at "being." Goetz is still an actor who needs
spectators to assure him of the reality, meaning, and value of his role.
His spectator had been God, but now that he wants to be the hero of the
good, he is obliged to commit himself with reference to other men. His
good has somehow to be recognized as good by the peasants: "No one
can choose the good of others for them" (p. 159).

Thus, to his dismay, Goetz discovers ethical reciprocity. He is rejected
by the peasants as he was rejected by the ruling classes. He is not one of
the poor, but a former rich man (p. 137). He tries to do good through
charity, but fraternal love is the sanction of a good action, and as a

[1] Sartre, *Esquisse d'une théorie des émotions,* p. 46.

giver, Goetz cannot be fraternally loved. The class-consciousness which frustrates Goetz's intention is an obvious allusion to the contemporary French situation. The answer to the social problem, in Sartre's opinion, is not charitable gestures, but revolutionary action.[2]

Goetz's difficulty is reminiscent of that of Orestes at the beginning of *Les Mouches*. They are both emerging from the morals of non-being: aesthetic wisdom in the case of Orestes, evil in the case of Goetz. But the situation is far more intricate this time, and Sartre will not let Goetz off as easily as Orestes. He will make his character enter two blind alleys before he is allowed to "find his way." The difference between the difficulties of Goetz and the difficulties of Orestes reflects to a certain extent the difference between the France of 1942 and the France of 1950.

The act of giving has not established satisfactory relations between Goetz and the peasants. Goetz might perhaps become a peasant himself, but then he would not be the-one-who-does-good. He is not thinking of a solidarity through work, of a solidarity based on reality; he is longing for a fraternity through love, for a fraternity based on magic. Tetzel, the seller of indulgences, is loved by the peasants through religious magic. And the only person who has ever loved Goetz, who still loves him, is the dying Catherine (p. 63). Goetz has been loved through fleshly magic, not as a brother but as a master.

He takes advantage of these two lessons: he pierces his hands and presents his wounds to the peasants as divine stigmata. The directly narcissistic aspect of this gesture has been commented upon.[3] By inflicting a wound on his own flesh, Goetz tries to appropriate symbolically his existence and cancel its contingency. But Goetz's intention is first of all to incarnate himself in the eyes of others, though the ultimate goal remains to possess himself and the others through his sacred incarnation.

Incarnation, not embodiment. It seems relevant at this point to recall the distinction which has been made between flesh and body. Embodiment implies realization. It is the necessary instrument of the morals of doing. Incarnation permits exhibition, a certain category of gestures: those of the priest, of the actor.

It is therefore not surprising that Goetz chooses incarnation. By wounding himself, Goetz not only chooses his incarnation, but through his theatrical gesture, he fascinates the peasants: "At last! they are mine!" (p. 194). Goetz can now play the role of the prophet.

He has apparently reached his goal: he is loved. Doing was but the means; to be was the end. He may even think that he has "recuperated" his being. He has become an idol, he has given away his lands—but in order to possess the souls and hearts of the peasants.

---

[2] The criticism of Christian morals, implicit here as in other parts of the play, is mainly directed against those who consider that it is enough to utter the magic words "love" and "charity" for all problems to be solved.

[3] See Douglas, "The Self-Inflicted Wound," above.

Let us compare the situation which has been reached in *Le Diable et le bon Dieu* with the situation at the end of *Les Mouches*. The denouement of the latter is a question: How will the Argives react to Orestes' speech? Orestes' project has been conceived in the light of freedom: he has assumed his responsibility, he has chosen his good, and his action has been meant to help the Argives assume their moral freedom. But a more probable result is that the Argives will turn Orestes into a scapegoat, reduce his action to a gesture. And in his speech Orestes himself encourages this interpretation.

But he leaves, the play ends, and we are left with a question. In *Le Diable et le bon Dieu*, Goetz's desire "to do the good" does not take moral freedom either as a basis or as an end. Unlike Orestes, Goetz is caught in the web of theological morals. With him, we have no hesitation: he deliberately assumes the role of scapegoat and prophet.

Yet *Le Diable et le bon Dieu* will take us farther than *Les Mouches*. For Goetz will not be permitted to leave. He will remain to the end caught in a social context. *Les Mouches* tells us what the reaction of the Argives will probably be after the speech and departure of Orestes; it tells us what the reaction of most French people *was* to the myth of the Resistance, once the occupation was over. Goetz's conversion to the morals of doing for the sake of freedom is not so quick as Orestes' conversion. But it involves a more realistic commitment.

Goetz's triumph brings about his downfall. The play illustrates the tragic irony which is already present in the description of the magic dialectics of love in *L'Être et le néant*.

First of all, Goetz has sacrificed the means to the end. In order to make the peasants recognize his good as their good, he has assumed the role of the prophet. As far as he is concerned, he has abandoned the morals of purity, since his gesture is designed to deceive, to fascinate, to subjugate.

Moreover, the end attained by Goetz does not justify the means. At the beginning of Act III, the spectator witnesses an example of mass-education which might more aptly be called catechism, propaganda, or "brain-washing." In Goetz's village, the peasants are taught to love all men and practice nonviolence. A certain abstract concept of the good has been set up as an absolute, without consideration for the actual situation, and all that man has to do is to learn the recipes by heart and apply them mechanically.

Goetz's reign of sweet tyranny could perhaps be defended from the point of view of sedate wisdom: at least, the peasants enjoy a life of material and psychological peace, or slumber. But Sartre soon denies even this matter-of-fact success. A group of armed peasants, angered by the refusal of Goetz's people to join them in their struggle, destroy the village and slaughter its peaceful inhabitants.

Here again the allusion to the modern situation is obvious: no group of men can now achieve material happiness and spiritual peace, or sleep, in complete isolation from the rest of mankind. However intended it may be, the policy of the ostrich becomes every day less effective and less innocent. Humanity is no longer an abstract or sentimental, literary or scientific, myth; humanity has become, so to speak, a human concern. Sartre, always anxious to think in relation to his time, rather than *sub specie aeternitatis*, has pointed out this advent of the human age.[4] It bolsters, on the objective side, the subjective statement that "in choosing myself, I choose man." In *L'Être et le néant*, the stress was laid on the "I" and on the "you." [5] Now the "we" receives an equal emphasis. Unlike Gabriel Marcel, whose point of view on morals is somewhat obsolete, Sartre focuses his attention on the collectivity rather than on private relations (*e.g.*, the couple, the family, the local community).

The destruction of Goetz's paradise on earth, the refusal of Nasty's army to listen to Goetz when he urges them not to fight, make the hero abandon the role of prophet and paternalistic tyrant. By now, the actor has acquired enough suppleness and resiliency to snap into the new role which the relentless dramatist has kept in store for him: that of the masochistic hermit.

Goetz's dialogue with men has proved a failure, either through the perversity of circumstances, or through the actor's unwillingness to let anyone steal the show from him. Goetz returns to his old ways: a dialogue with God. God is a much more agreeable interlocutor. He remains absent from the stage, and one can make Him say whatever one wishes Him to:

> There we are, Lord: We are face to face again, as in the good old days when I was doing evil. Ah! I should never have meddled with them: They are a nuisance. They are the brushwood one must push aside in order to come to you. I am coming to you, Lord, I am coming; I am walking in your night; lend me your hand. Tell me: the night, it is you, isn't it? Night, the harrowing absence of everything! For you are the one who is present in universal absence, the one who is heard when all is silence. . . . (p. 235)

Goetz explicitly returns to the sterile dialectics of being and non-being, of being and having, which in fact, as has been pointed out, he has never been able to outgrow: "Until I possess everything, I shall possess nothing. Until I am everything, I shall be nothing." (p. 236)[6]

---

[4] See Sartre's comment on the advent of the atomic age: "Mankind had, one day, to dispose of its death. . . . We can no longer talk of a *human species*. The community which has made itself the guardian of the atomic bomb is above nature for it is responsible for its life and for its death. . . . That is what we feel today in anxiety" (*Situations*, III, 68-69).

[5] See *L'Être et le néant*, p. 484 *et seq.*

[6] Parodies of Christian terminology are numerous in the play. In this case, the mystics' verbal games with nothingness and totality are the target. The passage reads like quotations from John of the Cross or Meister Eckhart. See *Saint-Genêt*, p. 191.

In *Saint-Genêt,* Sartre comments on what Genet calls "the eternal couple of the criminal and the saint." In *Le Diable et le bon Dieu* the author stresses the theoretical similarity between Goetz's first role and his new role, that of the masochistic hermit. In both cases, the apparent goal is *not* to *be* through *not* having. But this time, God is supposed not to condemn, but to reward. Goetz had been against God and man. Now he sides with God against man.

Since he is a man, he must punish himself:

> I asked you, Lord, and you answered me. Blessed be Thou for Thou hast revealed to me the wickedness of men. I shall punish their sins through my own flesh. I shall torment this body. . . .(p. 239)

After playing the Pharisee (of evil, then of the good), Goetz has turned his talent to the role of the Publican. The Publican cuts himself in two: he is the breast which is beaten, but he is also the hand which beats the breast. Goetz still plays the scapegoat and the prophet. But he now tries to play these roles to himself. He thus avoids the alienation imposed by other men. Goetz tries to recuperate his being by tormenting his flesh, and at the same time to possess the whole of mankind symbolically through his flesh.

The Publican presents himself as a sinner: he *has* a body, he *is* a sinner. But in so far as it is he who presents himself as a sinner, he is not a sinner. His passive flesh is but a symbol of man and of his wickedness. Thus, though this thought remains lost in a smoke-screen of bad faith, the Publican ceases to be a sinner and becomes a judge. Yet, since God, and no man, can be the judge, the Publican can but *play* the role of the judge.

The Publican and the masochist try to transform the ambiguity of human condition into a duality: sinner and judge, breast and hand. But it is the Others who hold the key to our objectivity:

> I need someone to judge me. Every day, every hour, I condemn myself, but I cannot manage to convince myself because I know myself too well to trust myself. I do not see my soul because it is right under my nose. I need someone who would lend me his eyes. (p. 259)

By means of this projection, Goetz could perhaps manage to play both roles with a good conscience. But Hilda refuses to enter this theatrical scheme, she refuses "to play the game" (p. 251). Then comes Heinrich, who has wagered against Goetz that the good can not be done. His hatred for Goetz seems to guarantee a satisfactory duo between judge and sinner.

Unfortunately, Heinrich is still Goetz's alter ego. Hilda has refused to play the role of judge as Goetz would have liked, and Heinrich, as a judge, resembles Goetz too closely for the comfort of bad faith.

Goetz pretends to be conversing with God (a God who reveals himself only through silence); as for Heinrich, he has managed to pretend to himself that a devil is his constant companion, without, however, being quite able to believe in the existence of this devil (p. 243).

Under these conditions, the judgment scene achieves a result contrary to Goetz's apparent purpose. Heinrich, embarrassed by Goetz's exhibitionism, which so closely resembles his own, forgets his lines, so that Goetz is obliged to prompt him and himself assume the role of the judge. The dialogue becomes a monologue. This brings about the "conversion" of Goetz, in terms which remind us of Orestes' conversion:

> I wondered at every moment what I could *be* in the eyes of God. Now I know the answer: nothing. God does not hear me, God does not know me. . . . God is the solitude of men. There was only myself: I alone decided on evil; I alone invented the good. . . . (p. 267)

The spectator is meant to understand that Goetz has ceased to play hide and seek with himself, has ceased to set up screens—God, the devil, evil, the good, being, nothingness.

The judgment scene has the effect of an exorcism. The travestied monsters disappear from the ballet. The presence of Heinrich does not act as a screen, but as a mirror, with a cathartic result: Goetz kills Heinrich, the symbol of his theatrical possession, and proclaims the death of God (p. 268).

The naïve enthusiasm of Goetz as he awakes from self-hypnosis and announces to Hilda that "God is dead" should not be construed as indicative of the author's mood. A more adequate echo of this mood may be found in Hilda's answer: "Dead or alive, what do I care? I have not bothered about Him for a long time" (p. 270). In other words, the metaphysical question of the existence of a divinity is irrelevant to the moral problem: "Even if God existed, it would not change anything." [7] The believer is responsible for his god. It is not the metaphysical problem of the existence of a divinity that concerns Sartre; it is the psychological and ethical implications of a hieratic way of thinking.

Besides a subjective denouement, the play provides an objective denouement which gives to Goetz a place in a collective enterprise. From this point of view, *Le Diable et le bon Dieu* takes us farther than *Les Mouches* and, unlike the latter but like the *Oresteia* of Aeschylus, includes the theme of reconciliation.

This reconciliation, however, must be carefully distinguished from a

[7] Sartre, *L'Existentialisme est un humanisme*, p. 95.

religious communion or a sentimental unanimism, from the kind of "human myth" which brought tears to the eyes of the "self-taught man" in *La Nausée,* from the kind of human myth which made Shelley exclaim at the end of *Prometheus Unbound:* "Man, oh! not men."

The denouement of *Le Diable et le bon Dieu* includes a criticism of this concept of reconciliation. The criticism is both realistic and idealistic. It is realistic in so far as the actual situation is concerned; it is both realistic and idealistic from a broader philosophical point of view.

On awakening from his self-hypnotic game, Goetz tries to forsake solitude and participate in a common human enterprise. In a speech which can be taken as expressing the author's views,[8] Goetz shows the results of his Sartrean conversion:

> The men of today are born criminals. I have to claim my share of their crimes if I want to share their love and their virtues. I used to long for pure love: This was absurd; to love is to hate the same enemy: I shall share your hatred. I wanted the good; this was absurd. On this earth and at this time, good and evil are inseparable. . . ." (pp. 275-76)

This realistic criticism is directed against the myth of universal love. To love all men is to love none. It is easy to be a unanimist in words, but any ethical enterprise draws its unanimistic atmosphere and its efficacy from its hostility to other men. It is against men that man can be practically reconciled with men.[9]

Though, in theory, Sartre accepts the Kantian imperative which advises us to treat men as ends, not as means, he points out that, in practice, ethical action entails the treatment of men as means.

Even inside the group which is united by a common enterprise, reconciliation is partial. "Leaders are alone" (p. 277). The leader has to treat his men as means. Goetz has to kill an officer who has challenged his authority. He will have to sacrifice certain men: in war, quantitative considerations, which are immoral, must intervene. The atmosphere is not that of a class in philosophy. The situation does not permit a leisurely education of the masses.[10] The leader cannot achieve with his men the kind of spiritual comradeship which is supposed to have graced the relations between Socrates and his disciples. Nasty and Goetz have even to pretend to share the belief of their men in magic: a witch is supposed to make them invulnerable. The leader is reconciled with his men through lies.

Thus, in the eyes of Sartre, the morals of liberation are not an idyllic

---

[8] See *Saint-Genêt,* p. 203: "We are not angels and we have not the right to 'understand' our enemies, we have not yet the right to love *all* men."

[9] Compare Beauvoir: "Any action for the sake of man has to be directed against men" (*Pour une morale de l'ambiguïté,* p. 139).

[10] Compare *Ibid.,* p. 137.

solution, but they do make possible a proper formulation of the ethical problem. In any case, violence is inescapable. When Goetz, as a self-styled prophet, tried to appropriate the minds of the peasants, he was already using violence. But in this case, the means was mistaken for the end, or the end was unauthentic. The advantage of the morals of liberation is that the end is authentic. But it cannot claim purity of means. It is in this sense that, with reference to the present situation, Sartre has recognized that authentic morals are "impossible":

> Any morality which does not present itself explicitly as *impossible today* contributes to the mystification and alienation of man. The moral "problem" arises from the fact that morals are *for us* both unavoidable and impossible. Action must give itself its ethical norms in this climate of unsurmountable impossibility. It is in this light, for example, that one should consider the problem of violence or that of the relation between the means and the end.[11]

And he reiterates this statement as a corrective to his criticism of Christian morals: "I do not present these contradictions to condemn Christian morals: I am too deeply convinced that *any* morals are both impossible and necessary." [12] Sartre's main objection to the more authentic brands of Christian morality is that today they provide an inadequate statement of the ethical problem and can serve only as a mask for irresponsibility.

The reconciliation of Goetz with some of his fellow-men bears some analogy to the reconciliation which occurs at the end of the *Oresteia*. There is nothing idyllic about the Aeschylean reconciliation. And it is far from being universal, since the reconciliation between Athenians and the alliance with Argos are urged for a practical enterprise which is war. The difference, of course, is that in the *Oresteia* we are dealing with a war between states, whereas in Sartre's play we are dealing with a war between classes.[13]

It is tempting to consider the situations depicted in *Le Diable et le bon Dieu*—particularly the denouement—in the light of the present situation in France. From this point of view, however, an important difference must be noted between the fiction and the reality. The denouement—Goetz's choice—has no application to the present situation in France. The situation is revolutionary, but a revolution is impossible This is one of the reasons why Sartre considers that morals *today* are both necessary and impossible. Even though the denouement is far from idyllic, it appears to be wishful thinking when viewed against the background of contemporary France.

---

[11] Sartre, *Saint-Genêt*, p. 177.   [12] *Ibid.*, p. 211.
[13] The objective denouement of the play corresponds to some extent to the views on French politics which Sartre entertained at the time: he was favorable to the formation of a new Popular Front.

More broadly examined, the question of reconciliation does seem to be resolved on one level of action in *Le Diable et le bon Dieu.* If the actual situation at the end of the play does not permit a communion between oppressor and oppressed, or even between leader and men, there is at least communion among the soldiers. It is as an ordinary soldier that Goetz wants to enlist: "I want men everywhere—around me, above me, so that they may hide the sky from me. Nasty, allow me to be a nobody" (p. 277).

This time, the criticism of the myth of communion is both realistic and idealistic. What tempts Goetz now is no longer the desire to be a hero (of evil or good), but to become a nobody, a thing, an innocent, irresponsible instrument. But one does not return to innocence. In so far as soldiers are men, even a soldier cannot become a pure thing, cannot completely dissolve his subjectivity into the collective myth.

Moreover, if perfect communion is practically impossible, it should not be set up as an ideal, either. Sartre does not stress communion, but solidarity. Goetz says to Hilda: "We shall be alone together" (p. 277). This formula can be taken not only as a statement of fact but as a judgment of value. Sartre stresses both solidarity and aloneness, for they imply each other. It is through the subjectivity of others that our autonomous subjectivity, our aloneness, is revealed to us.[14] It is because Sartre wants his philosophy to be a humanism, it is because he wants his "myth" to be human—not animal, not divine—that he stresses aloneness and solidarity, not communion. A reconciliation between men will be ethically valid if they are reconciled within themselves and with each other to the principle of aloneness and reciprocity, to the principle that there can be no valid ethics for the man who has not assumed his aloneness. The rest belongs to sentimental and mystical literature, to totalitarianism or pseudo-science.

For Blake, too, the chief enemy was alienation: he had to fight it in his own religious mind. *The Marriage of Heaven and Hell* might be a better introduction to *Le Diable et le bon Dieu* than Nietzsche's *Beyond Good and Evil.* Like Shelley, Blake strives toward an integration of the divine, but, unlike Shelley, he does not intend to set up a sentimental concept of mankind as a substitute idol. Blake stresses subjectivity. His ideal city is not a city of stultifying peace and drugged communion, it is the place of endless "spiritual strife." In the same way, Sartre does not imagine any order as the ideal. An order can be only a relative end; it must be conceived as a means for further negations and projects, as opening more opportunities for freedom. But Blake is a poet; he realizes his city symbolically for himself. Sartre stresses solidarity and thinks in relation to the social situation. Goetz's last words are: "There is a war to make and I will make it." But one does not make a war as one *makes* an epic poem.

[14] See *Saint-Genêt,* p. 543.

And a play is not an epic poem. The theater is the best medium for a philosophy of ambiguity, of clashes between freedoms (between freedom and itself), of aloneness and reciprocity.

In the really creative and poetic aspect of the morals of doing man is not placed face to face with man, but with things. There is no alienation there, for things have no subjectivity. There is no clash between freedoms, but a clash between freedom and nature.

The theater cannot deal with the really positive aspect of the morals of doing, it cannot deal with making. For things are absent. The character exists only in relation to the other characters. His subjectivity is revealed negatively rather than creatively. He has only the other characters to work on, and he cannot create them: their freedom means his failure. Failure is experienced when he tries to possess the others and conversely when the others try to possess him. His subjectivity is revealed through these failures.

In so far as we *are* (this or that), it is the others as well as ourselves who decide on what we are. This point of view is pure theater. And it is pure theater that is implied in this formula: "As a successor to the theater of *caractère*, we want to have a theater of situations." [15]

The word *caractère* refers to a certain tradition of French literary psychology. The English word "character" does not quite translate it. The play of *caractère* uses events and situations to bring out certain characteristics, in the same way that, by clever lighting, one brings out the interesting qualities of a statue. The play of *caractère* could also be compared to a lesson in anatomy.

The play of situations as it were throws the character outside himself. The character does not come into the play as a certain object to be gradually revealed. The character will have to interpret what he "is" from what the other characters tell him he is. His being is perpetually in question. He has to choose himself, he will be what the other characters make him and what his reactions to this attempt at possession will be.

Of course, there is nothing particularly new about this conception of the theater. What Sartre brings to this conception is greater awareness. It must also be noted that there can be no pure play either of *caractère* or of situations. In *Le Diable et le bon Dieu,* the character is not a pure ghost when he enters the stage. The character has a certain past. But Sartre tries not to present this past as an "eternal nature."

First of all, we are meant to understand that this past is a choice, an "original choice." This choice, implicitly made by the child, is not authentically ethical, since the child is unaware of responsibility and reciprocity. It is a choice to be (or not to be). Thus Goetz enters the stage as a project not to be, through not having, or as a plan to be the evildoer.

[15] Sartre, "Forgers of Myths," p. 326.

This original choice, since it is conceived as a choice, must be distinguished from a nature established once and for all. *Le Diable et le bon Dieu* shows us that two things may happen: metamorphoses and an ethical conversion. Metamorphoses, as we have noted in the case of Goetz, bring about changes which the psychology of *caractère* might not allow: Molière and Balzac did not permit Harpagon and Grandet to become spendthrifts. Sartre tries to make these metamorphoses credible by the use of situations which rock the character to his foundations. Yet, as we have also noted, these metamorphoses do not effect a radical change in the original choice. Throughout his metamorphoses, Goetz's morals remain the morals of being. He rings the changes, so to speak, on the ontological failure, on the failure to *be*.

The radical change is supposed to come with his conversion. The character breaks with his original choice and abandons the sterile pursuit of being. It is this possibility of conversion which makes Sartre's moral philosophy more optimistic than the psychology of *caractère,* or traditional psychoanalysis. It indicates Sartre's faith in man. Faith, not belief; for the endless variety of metamorphoses shows how difficult it may be to break the vicious circle of the original choice, the circle of the comedian and martyr.

In any case, either through metamorphoses or conversion, Sartre's play of situations tries to make us feel that anything may happen to the character. His being is at the mercy of the other characters and of himself; it depends on situation and action. *Le Diable et le bon Dieu* is made up of perpetual clashes between freedoms: Goetz and Heinrich, Heinrich and Nasty, Goetz and Nasty, Goetz and Hilda, Goetz and the peasants, etc. In Racine's tragedies the character was permitted to compose his soul leisurely through the use of a confidant. Sartre eliminates the confidants, or rather he turns the confidants into enemies.

These clashes between freedoms reflect the characters' attempts to possess each other. One character hopes to recuperate his precious being from another. But as this attempt fails again and again, illumination may come at last. The character may abandon the sterile pursuit of his being and turn to the morals of freedom.

A theater can be "moral" in two opposite ways: the hero may be presented as a model, as an idol, or he may be presented as a telltale mirror.

In the first case, the theater is the servant of the morals of being, and we are dealing with a moralizing, rather than a moral, theater. The hero glorifies the natural attitude, the desire to *be,* and our own "original choice" may be flattered and countenanced through a metamorphosis: the desire to be like the hero.

Sartre tries to use the theater not as a drug but as a purgation. *Le Diable et le bon Dieu* provides an even better illustration of this practice than *Les Mouches*. The moralizing theater glorifies the original choice, the morals of being. This is what Sartre's play tries to undermine. In "real" life, the thickness of things, temporal screens, the routine of daily occupations permit us sluggishly or drunkenly to lull our desire to be. But the theater makes freedom clash against freedom, it presents a perpetual attempt at reciprocal possession. On stage the reverberation of the symbolic gesture, or word, is immediate. And in Sartre's theater the use of "extreme" situations produces a brutal ilumination. The original choice with which the character coincided when he entered the stage suddenly appears as a theatrical mask. The current of bad faith does not find any resistance in which to spend itself; bad faith is, as it were, short-circuited.

What Sartre says of Genet's theater is, in this respect, applicable to his own plays, more especially to *Les Mouches, Huis-clos,* and *Le Diable et le bon Dieu:* "Genet betrays his characters, he unmasks them, and the comedian whose imposture is exposed finds himself in the situation of the wicked man dispossessed of his weapons." [16]

Through a hero, the moralizing theater glorifies our desire to be. *Le Diable et le bon Dieu* exposes the spectator's spirit of seriousness and bad faith by turning the hero into a comedian and martyr (*i.e.,* a witness). The play is not supposed to act as a drug on the spectator, but as a homeopathic treatment.

[16] Sartre, *Saint-Genêt*, pp. 561-62.

Les Séquestrés d'Altona

by Oreste F. Pucciani

Les Séquestrés d'Altona is the dramatic story of Frantz von Gerlach, a Nazi war hero, who has been living in voluntary confinement in his father's house since 1947. He returned from the Polish front in 1946. His battalion had been wiped out. He alone escaped. Mentally disturbed because of his country's defeat and because of what appeared to him to be the injustice of the Nuremberg trials, he shut himself away in his room six months after his return and has lived there for the last thirteen years without any communication with the rest of his family except for his sister Léni. Supposedly, he cannot bear to witness the systematic destruction of the German nation by the Allies. Protected by Léni, who is incestuously in love with her brother, Frantz is unaware that Germany is thriving under the reconstruction and is again on its way to becoming a great power. Officially, Frantz is dead.

In reality, the reason for Frantz's "sequestration" is of a very different nature. Frantz is himself a war criminal, as guilty as any sentenced at Nuremberg. His crime is the crime of torture. It is thus, actually, to escape his own conscience that he has become a *séquestré*. Renascent Germany is an offense to his conscience because he knows that he has forever forfeited his right to take active part in his country's rebirth. The dramatic interest of the play consequently revolves about Frantz's confinement and the forces that will bring it to an end.

The device by which Frantz is "liberated" is the introduction of Johanna, his sister-in-law and wife of his brother, Werner, into the closed circle of his universe. Johanna is brought into his world by Frantz's father, old von Gerlach, the prototype of the great German industrialist who all his life has believed only in his own power and who has ruled his family through fear. For the last thirteen years old Gerlach has been vainly trying, via Léni, to establish some contact with his elder, favorite son. Léni, however, as the old man suspects, has not been carrying his messages to Frantz. She does not want her brother's confinement to be

"*Les Séquestrés d'Altona*." (Original title: "*Les Séquestrés d'Altona* of Jean Paul Sartre.") From *The Tulane Drama Review*, V, No. 3 (March 1961). Copyright © 1961 by *The Tulane Drama Review*. Reprinted by permission of the author and *The Tulane Drama Review*. The pages reprinted here are excerpts from the original article.

violated. It is the ideal climate in which her incestuous love can thrive. But now old Gerlach has a reason for haste. He has contracted cancer of the throat and has only six months more to live. Since he plans to commit suicide before the six months are up, he is anxious to communicate with his favorite son and in some manner discover the meaning of his own being in Frantz before his death. To circumvent Léni, the old man resorts to a trick. He persuades Johanna, his daughter-in-law, to use the secret signal by which Léni gains admission to her brother's room and pay Frantz a visit. Her purpose will be to tell Frantz that his father is doomed. Johanna accepts because old von Gerlach has offered in exchange to free her husband, Werner, from an oath which he had extracted from the latter: namely, that Werner would succeed him as head of the family business and live the rest of his life in Altona with the mission of caring for Frantz. The liberation of Frantz thus comes to involve the liberation of both Johanna and Werner as well.

Johanna becomes the catalyst which causes Frantz's mental world to collapse. Through her occurs the *prise de conscience* which is so pregnant with tragic possibilities for an existentialist. Frantz is suffering from a guilty conscience and has erected a bulwark of fiction to protect himself. But conscience for Sartre is no more than human consciousness at work in the world. When Johanna learns that Frantz has tortured and consequently rejects him, there is no longer any reason for him to remain in his room. His "sequestration" has come to its normal end. Frantz returns to reality; the reality of the Gerlach family and reconstructed Germany. His father is waiting for him. In a final act of mutual awareness the two men commit suicide together. Léni locks herself up in her brother's room. Johanna and Werner alone remain relatively free. Whether their freedom will become liberation or "sequestration" is the suspended note on which the action of the play comes to an end.

Such a condensed statement reveals little or nothing of the essential complexity of the play. Yet it is within this basic structure that the theme of "sequestration" is pursued on many levels, becoming finally a universal statement about the world in which we live. It is a tragic statement to the extent that it implies that human problems cannot be solved either by optimism or by will, but only through an awareness and finally through a course of action which reduce the problem of evil to the dimensions of a vicious circle and which permit the individual to break out of this circle once it has been perceived. Thus ethically in Sartrean freedom there comes to be an element of knowledge, but this knowledge is in itself tragic. It presupposes an element of consciousness which is prior to any act of knowing and which precludes the efficacy of any external grace. In a sense, consciousness is grace itself; it is what has been known traditionally as the "soul." In philosophical terms, it has reality, but it does not have existence. *Les Séquestrés* is a play about things which do not have existence, but which are nonetheless real: good, evil, conscience, consciousness, freedom, ambition, greatness, beauty. The fictional structure of the play manages to give concrete form to these entities. For some two hours we are present at the drama of five people who have been caught in a kind of trap. Two of them manage to get out of it: Frantz and his father. Léni refuses to the end. The fate of Johanna and Werner remains undecided. But the question remains: by what process does one free one's self from the trap of one's ideas? Again the fictional structure of *Les Séquestrés* embodies Sartre's answer: the "downstairs" room of the Gerlach family and the "upstairs" room where Frantz is "sequestered" are the two poles of a dialectic which lead us to the conclusion that we liberate ourselves by an exercise of consciousness which permits us finally to become aware of our true situation in the world. By passing from one realm to the other, back and forth in the course of the play, we become aware of a progressive enlightenment in the characters. But this enlightenment remains strictly tragic. It leads nowhere unless it is coupled with individual action. The "downstairs world" of the Gerlach family is a world of implicit violence which condemned Frantz to "sequestration" long before he bolted his own door. "There are many ways to lock up a man," says Johanna. "The best is to make him do it himself." This is the truth which Frantz slowly comes to understand. But he comes to understand also that his act of torture, willed by his father's world in which freedom was merely an abstraction, required his assent. What Frantz lacked was imagination. By the time he had acquired it, it was too late. But it was not too late for him to understand that his father's world had implied "sequestration" from the beginning and that the deeper meaning of "sequestration" was violence and torture. By following the theme of "sequestration" through the play, we shall perhaps come to some understanding of the grounds on which Sartre rests his case and unravel a few of the many meanings of *Les Séquestrés*.

"Sequestration" in its most obviously vicious form is represented by Léni and her incestuous love for her brother. One might be inclined to think that Sartre has used incest because it is a powerful dramatic device and because of the universal condemnation which it elicits. It is rather, I think, because the question of incest forces us to ask: why should incest be universally condemned? If we feel, however obscurely, that incestuous love is autistic and solipsistic, that it fails to create a bond with the world, that it destroys the family in which it has its roots and is a refusal to live according to the conditions of human life, is it not because we also feel the limitations and contradictions of family life? Society somehow understands that one of its most sacred institutions can exist only if it is renewed by elements which may well imply its destruction. Significantly, Léni's love for her brother, which has been consummated by a physical act, thrives in the close atmosphere of her brother's more literal "sequestration." It is to protect this intimacy that she has refused to be her father's messenger throughout the years. Léni is, moreover, aware that her love for her brother is part of her fanatical espousal of a certain code of tribal, family life: "Incest is my way of making family bonds tighter," she says. Her words draw an authentic shudder from the audience. We feel ourselves in the presence of evil. But what precisely is the evil of incest?

Léni's love for her brother is made up of many contradictions for which "incest" is a convenient unifying term. Léni is both victim and accomplice in her father's world. She is also the only character in the play who can move freely from the "downstairs world" of the Gerlachs to the "upstairs world" of Frantz. But her freedom exists within the limits of a kind of assimilated revolt. As the younger sister in the Gerlach family, her possibilities of action have been objectively very few. The society into which she was born required above all that she love and admire. But it offered her little opportunity to go beyond the walls of her own home. "A woman's place is in the home." In the case of Léni, born into a great German family of industrialists still committed to nineteenth century ideologies, Léni was "sequestered" from birth because she was a woman. Her mistake has been to accept this role and to follow it to its logical conclusion. Revolt and defiance have not carried her any farther than the Gerlach world where she has lucidly assumed the role which in reality has been imposed on her. In Léni the implicit incest of the Gerlach family becomes explicit. It is latent even in the other members. Old Gerlach exhibits an exaggerated sort of physical repulsion for his younger son, Werner. Johanna, who as an outsider has more perspective than any of the Gerlachs themselves, notices in her relationship with Frantz a strange sort of communion between the two brothers: "Each of you tries to find the caresses of the other on my body," she says.

But if "sequestration" can be incest, incest is "sequestration." Léni understands this when she says at the end of the play: "A *séquestré* is needed up there." And yet for all her lucidity, Léni is not really aware of what her own "sequestration" means. Like Frantz, she lacks imagination. She does not see that her love for Frantz, which requires his "sequestration," also requires his destruction. Léni's world is upside down and remains so to the end. She believes it is enough to say: "I have done as I wanted and I want what I have done." In revolt against her family, she has created a sub-world in which wrongs are put to right by the simple process of turning them around. In this sub-world she has put herself in her father's place and, as her father did when Frantz was a child, she now wants to create happiness for Frantz on the only terms which he cannot accept. Born to venerate property and power above all else, Léni believes in her power as she believes that Frantz is her property. She thinks she is free; she is in reality the most irrevocably "sequestered" of all. She cannot even understand that she herself is a victim. When she locks herself into her brother's room at the end of the play, we know that in one of its members at least the Gerlach code has achieved perfect success.

The Gerlach code has been almost as successful in the case of Werner as in the case of Léni. Born to the role of younger son, as Léni was born to the role of younger daughter, Werner has grown up among the myths of the Gerlach family which have proclaimed him "weak" whereas Frantz was "strong." We sense that his "sequestration" began in childhood and that the meaning of his "sequestration" was from the beginning *neglect*. As Léni was born to incest, Werner was born to jealousy. Rejected in favor of Frantz, Werner cannot give himself to any relationship unless it be an attitude of permanent courtship which he has adopted towards his father. He is, for example, eager to swear the impossible oath which his father requires of him regardless of what Johanna feels. At bottom, he is delighed to replace his brother as head of the family business in spite of the cost to himself and others. Jealousy of Frantz is the real meaning of Werner's love for Johanna as well as of his material ambitions in the world. Throughout the play, he progresses increasingly towards isolation. There are suggestions that alcoholism will ultimately be his refuge. Meanwhile, his relationship with Johanna deteriorates into a purely sexual obsession which excludes all tenderness and leaves little hope for the future. Yet, there is an indication that things were not always so. As a young lawyer in Hamburg, in love with the former movie star, Johanna Thiess, Werner seems to have achieved a degree of independence and freedom which vanish as soon as he is back in the ancestral home. In Hamburg he was a different man. He was successful in his profession and had a life of his own. But in Altona he becomes again the "younger brother" without autonomy and without any personal meaning except in terms of a secondary relationship to Frantz. But the question is: why did he return to Altona? And why does he refuse to leave when Johanna pleads with him to do so? Here is the secret of Werner. Like Léni, like Frantz, he agrees with his father's world. His "inferiority complex" is rooted in his own conviction of inferiority. The Gerlach family required a second son and it created Werner. Momentarily he had escaped to Hamburg, but now he is once again one of the *séquestrés* of Altona. We wonder if Johanna will not be able to help him, but the curious fact is that even Johanna is a *séquestrée* in this strange play.

Frantz is immediately aware of Johanna's "sequestration" as she enters his room. She says: "I am a *séquestrée*? I wouldn't have thought so." He answers: "*Séquestrés* have special faculties for recognizing each other."

As we come to learn Johanna's story, we understand just what her "sequestration" is. Before her marriage Johanna was a film star who had begun to enjoy a certain degree of fame. As "Johanna Thiess," celebrated for her beauty, she used to go into neighborhood theaters in order to watch the effect she made on the screen. Then suddenly she was rejected by the public. It was at this point that Johanna married Werner. To a large degree, her marriage represented an attempt to compensate for something she had lost. It is for this reason that Werner eventually has cause to accuse her. "How can I have lost you?" he says. "I never had you. . . . You deceived me as to the nature of the goods! I wanted a woman and I got a corpse."

At first glance Johanna seems to be an energetic, well-balanced young woman, ready to fight for her husband and herself. Yet as the play progresses, we see that her real kinship is with Léni and old Gerlach. Old Gerlach himself realizes this. "She was the wife for Frantz," he says. And Léni, according to the sacred tenets of the Gerlach family, classes Johanna among the "strong" rather than the "weak." When Johanna shows surprise at this, Léni says: "You do nothing and you think about death." This is what characterizes the "strong"; they do not *act*; they *are*. She is in fact an essentialist. Her form of power is her beauty. Like Frantz, she is an abstractionist in love with realities which do not have concrete existence. She understands his devotion to absolute greatness and is consequently able to enter into the extravagance and folly of his "sequestration." But there is a difference too, a difference which creates one of the dramatic springs of the play. Johanna has actually rejected her former world of the absolute in favor of a more human world in which she loves Werner. Whether she is in good faith or in bad faith is impossible to say. But the fact remains that her contact with Frantz causes a regression in her which divides her, in a sort of temporary schizophrenia, between the "upstairs" and the "downstairs" worlds. She is not, as Léni is, a free agent moving from one to the other. She is torn. And to this extent she is more conscious. The realities of Frantz's world are to an extent true for her as are the realities of her former life with Werner and her present life in the Gerlach household. She is less an accomplice than the others and more of a victim. She is at the same time more authentically free. She is originally "sequestered" only to the extent that we are all "sequestered" by the worlds into which we are born. But she has already progressed towards her own individual liberation by the time the action of the play begins. It is this that Werner does not understand in her and by his lack of understanding, he condemns her to the fictions which she has already abandoned. By the same token, she is able to reject Frantz unwaveringly when she learns that he has committed torture. But it is not possible to discuss Johanna more fully without discussing Frantz.

Both literally and symbolically, Frantz von Gerlach is the supreme example of "sequestration" in the play. He has been a true *"séquestré"* for the past thirteen years. He has been a *séquestré* mentally and spiritually all his life. Frantz's madness is the *folie des grandeurs*. When

Johanna asks him: "What is your obsession?" he answers: "I wonder if it has a name. Emptiness . . . Or why not call it 'greatness'? . . . It possessed me, but I didn't possess it."

Frantz had been born to greatness as the elder son of the Gerlach family and as the heir to his father's industrial empire. He was raised in the belief of his future power as he was raised in the myth of his father's omnipotence. But power for Frantz had many corollaries. "Human dignity," "heroism," and "humanitarianism" were among them. There was also Hitler; and there was torture. It may seem far-fetched to think that torture can be linked to humanitarianism, but in the portrait of Frantz, Sartre is criticizing the entire liberal and humanistic tradition. He is attempting to show through Frantz how a network of logic binds together in a vast pattern of "sequestration" all the concepts, myths, and even moral imperatives of the Gerlach world. It is as if he were saying: one cannot believe in power for its own sake without arriving, even in questions of beauty, at the final truth of such power: violence and the violation of human freedom. The absolute of such violation is torture. This network of logic is shown vividly and dramatically in the life which Frantz leads in his "sequestered" room.

In his room Frantz continued to dress as a Nazi officer. There was a picture of Hitler on his wall which he constantly abused impotently by throwing empty oyster shells at it. He had established, moreover, an elaborate ritual which Léni helped him to fulfill. He did not allow time to be mentioned and there was no clock in the room. Human time had merged for Frantz into the abstraction of Eternity. He drugged himself constantly on benzedrine because life required for him an abnormal measure of power. A light was always kept burning. Frantz was an optimist and a child of the Enlightenment. A window that looked out onto a garden of the Gerlach estate had been walled up. Reality could not be allowed to intrude into the dedicated world of "sequestration." Here in this perfectly artificial world Frantz dedicated himself to an essential task which Johanna described to old Gerlach as "keeping busy." He dictated into a tape-recorder a kind of poem, a long lyrical protest of innocence which was addressed to a people of "Crabs," posterity, who sat in judgment on Frantz and his times. In other words Frantz was also a writer and artist. But his work as artist and writer somehow never quite succeeded. He never managed to find exactly the words which would convince the "Crabs" of his innocence. Yet he did not abandon hope. As he said to Léni: "One day the words will come to me by themselves and I shall say what I want to say. Then I can rest." It is not difficult to see that Frantz, as a writer, belonged to a certain tradition. He believed in inspiration. He believed that a writer writes because he must and not because he has something to say. Yet he was in fact trying to say something. It was his purpose to bear witness that neither he nor Hitler-Germany had been morally guilty. The fault, if there was one, was neither Frantz's nor man's; it was the fault of history. And a perfect reading of history would contain the acquittal which he hoped to receive at the hands of the "Crabs." Frantz had even invented a fantasy that was foolproof and which would deliver the absolute truth: the glass. He imagined that this "glass," a sort of sensitive photographic plate, recorded every event, every detail of the phenomenal world. By means of it history was perfectly preserved. "All of history is engraved on it," he says to Léni, "from the beginning of time to this snap of my fingers." We can detect the liberal assumption of the scientific writing of history: the whole is equal to the sum of its parts. As we shall see, Frantz managed to say something in his "sequestration," though it was not at all what he intended. This was the fantastic life which Frantz lived in his "upstairs room." When he could bear it no longer, he made love to Léni.

"Sequestration" remains, however, a poor substitute for reality. Its main disadvantage is that it is fragile. Occasionally in sleep or in moments of exhaustion the fragility of Frantz's life would become apparent to him. Memories of the war—real memories—would burst upon him and he would wake up screaming. Truth and reality for Frantz were torture. The rest was unstable camouflage. When Johanna enters Frantz's world, his entire structure collapses.

Johanna, it is true, is the catalyst which precipitates the change in Frantz's world, but it is also true that Frantz acts as a catalyst for her. What occurs when these two *séquestrés* meet is that a third term is added to their juxtaposed isolation: their *relationship*. Something similar to "falling in love" happens to each: *recognition*. Because of this recognition they are both seen and "sequestration" becomes an impossibility. The *prise de conscience* takes place. Because Johanna is young and beautiful, she elicits a reaction from Frantz which Léni had never elicited: authentic desire. Meanwhile, for Johanna, Frantz represents the shock of being understandable. The world of each is suddenly reversed. Frantz is torn from his dreams while Johanna is plunged back into hers. This reversal is one of the great dramatic and psychological discoveries of the play. It permits the action to enter a phase of anti-action which is the perfect justification for the *folie à deux* which now envelops Johanna and Frantz and is an occasion for Sartre to demonstrate with virtuosity the intricate play between human consciousness and concrete reality. Fate no longer lurks as it does in a classic or bourgeois drama, waiting to spring. Fate is woven before our eyes from a series of human choices which have their conditions and logical consequences in previous choices within a fundamental condition of freedom. Frantz's world is returned to "reality." He desires Johanna. Human time again enters his world. He misses Johanna when she is gone and waits anxiously for her to return. He even admits that Germany is perhaps not in her death-agony. He forgets the "Crabs" and turns to Johanna in his need for justification.

Slowly there is born in him the faint hope that justification is even possible, that there might even be a possibility of a return to life provided Johanna's faith in him were strong enough. Johanna, meanwhile, is plunged backwards into an absolute, mythical world which she had nearly forgotten. She begins to believe that Germany is after all in its death throes. The world is guilty of genocide towards the German race, as Frantz says. In the city of Düsseldorf there are poor children dying by the hundreds, all victims of a senseless evil. Johanna begins to be torn by opposing "truths": a truth "downstairs" which is the realm of her liberation prior to Frantz; and a truth "upstairs" which is the familiar logic of fantasy, escapism, and "sequestration." In itself there is no logical end to this *folie à deux*. But in reality there is an end. For Frantz there is Léni and for Johanna there is Werner.

The condition of choice which is now set up for Johanna and Frantz is a choice of fact over fiction. Frantz and Johanna can have their relationship together to the extent that they recognize each other, but in order to do so they must either admit that their relationship is objectively impossible or make it possible by denying objective fact. There is no escape from this dilemma. Slowly we see that Sartre is coming to his ultimate point, that there is a *prise de conscience* intended for the audience as well as for the protagonists of the play: "Sequestration" is in fact impossible; a *séquestré* cannot engage in a human relationship and remain a *séquestré*. "Sequestration" implies by its very nature conditions so contradictory that they cannot be fulfilled by normal human consciousness. "Sequestration" is the logic of madness and crime. Its vice is that of the vicious circle. Because Frantz had chosen fourteen years before to commit torture, because Johanna had chosen to leave a world of illusion for another human being regardless of her motives, they are separated today. The facts of their lives are such that the only relationship which they could have together would have to be based on illusion. Meanwhile illusion has become impossible for both. The process of enlightenment is complete when, at the end of the fourth act, Léni tells Johanna that Frantz has tortured. Johanna's total rejection of Frantz leaves him nothing to do but abandon his "sequestration," see his father, and commit suicide. The *prise de conscience* has occurred and it has been tragic. For thirteen years Frantz has prevented it; now he can prevent it no longer. To do so he would have had to become truly mad. And this he cannot choose to do, because a free consciousness cannot choose not to be free.

We have come at last to Frantz's father. We might have begun with him since he is in reality the author of his children's "sequestration."

Old Gerlach had "sequestered" all his children from birth. But if he did so, it was because he himself was the greatest *séquestré* of all. In old Gerlach, Sartre makes his greatest indictment of the bourgeois world

which is the point of departure of the play. The thinking of this world
is circular and, as such, it is vicious and "sequestered." Its permanent
latent possibilities are the incest of Léni, the jealousy of Werner and
the torture which Frantz has committed. As an industrialist of the old
school, Gerlach had the mentality of a *condottiere*. He possessed one
truth: power for its own sake. His single ethical code was that the
end justifies the means. He taught his children to believe in his own
omnipotence as he taught them to believe in the omnipotence of God.
For Gerlach humanity divided itself into two species: the "weak" and the
"strong." There was nothing to do about it. The "strong" were born to
rule the "weak"; the "weak" to be ruled by the "strong." He met the
problem of Nazism in Germany as he met all problems: with lucid
cynicism and a philosophy of expediency. He considered himself to be
anti-Nazi because he hated Hitler. He did not understand that his hatred
of Hitler was merely an aspect of his universal disregard for all men.
To the real historical Hitler he was indifferent. He said of the Nazis:

> [I serve them] because they serve me. These people are rabble on a throne.
> But they are fighting a war to find markets for us and I'm not going to have
> trouble with them over a piece of land.

The occasion for this remark, which occurs in a flashback scene, contains, from a clinical point of view, the source of Frantz's "sequestration
complex." Gerlach had sold a piece of unused family land to Himmler
for the construction of a concentration camp. It was here, on his own
property, that young Frantz had seen the first Jewish prisoners and had
been revolted by their sordidness more than by their misery. It was here
also that he had seen a Jewish prisoner whom he had tried to help escape
brutally murdered. His father had promised that the man would not
be harmed, but he had nonetheless, because of indifference and care-
lessness, allowed the murder to occur. SS troops held Frantz while the
prisoner's throat was cut. It was at that moment that Frantz learned
that the corollary of power for its own sake is impotence. He might have
rejected his father's world at that point, but he was to make an even
more sinister discovery. "As the Rabbi lay there bleeding," he says to his
father at the end of the play, "I discovered in the heart of my impotence
that I was somehow giving my consent." Frantz's "sequestration" begins
from this moment of essential choice. As he accepted his father's world,
he also accepted its complicity with the Nazi cause. He gave his consent
to the concentration camps, the crematoria, the torture which the Nazi
world required as means to a justifiable end. His own acts of torture
merely represented an attempt to give universal validity to a world of
violence. He failed, however, because the end does not necessarily justify
the means. Scientific relativism, utilitarianism, Christian pessimism were
the great moral heritage of the Gerlach family. But in times of trial

they fail as criteria of good and evil because each, in its own way, requires a justification of evil.

> Evil, *Messieurs les Magistrats,* evil [says Frantz] was our only material. We worked it over in our refineries. Good was the final product. Result: The good turned bad. And don't think for a moment that the bad turned good.

But Frantz was not the only one to give assent to his father's world. In reality, his father's world created Hitler. . . .

Old Gerlach had been persuaded that it was enough to build a German army and navy, trade with the world, make Germany a great nation. But *for what* was Germany to become a great nation? Greatness for its own sake is the *folie des grandeurs* and Hitler-Germany was a victim of this madness. It was a world inherited from the nineteenth century. Its roots went even farther back into the Reformation and the Renaissance. "Luther drove us mad with pride," says old Gerlach. But now even pride is gone in the tragic *prise de conscience* which has come to old Gerlach and his son.

> My poor boy! [he says] I wanted you to direct the business after my death, but now it's the business that does the directing. It chooses its own men. And it has eliminated me. I own it, but I am no longer in command. . . . I made a prince of you. Today that means a "good-for-nothing."

By the close of the play, there is only one authentic act which Frantz or his father can perform: suicide. This must be their strange liberation since the committing of torture, once one understands what it is, allows no mitigation. It might have been different if old Gerlach had refused to sell his land to Himmler, but he did not. He thought the end justified the means, but he was mistaken. It seems logical to think that *Les Séquestrés* is Sartre's way of avoiding the same mistake.

. . . In his room in Altona, Frantz wrote as Sartre writes from a room in Saint-Germain-des-Prés. After his death, he is survived by a series of tapes as Sartre will one day be survived by a series of volumes. It is one of these tapes, a very special one, recorded on the 17th of December 1953, a day of "inspiration and insight," which he leaves as a gift to Johanna. At the end of the play Johanna turns it on. She and Werner listen for a while. Then they leave the stage while Frantz's disembodied voice continues to address the audience:

> . . . The thirtieth century doesn't answer. Perhaps there won't be any more centuries after our own. Perhaps a bomb will snuff out all the lights. Everything will be dead. Eyes, judges, time. Night. Oh, Tribunal of the Night, you who are, have been and always will be, I have been, I have been!

I, Frantz von Gerlach, here in this room, took my century on my shoulders and said: I am responsible for it. On this day and forever. So what do you say?

Who knows what a "Crab" would say? But this at least can be said: Frantz had intended a self-defense. He wrote a self-indictment instead. He believed that one day the words would come by themselves and then he would be able to say what he really meant. They finally did and they proclaimed him guilty. We must conclude that this is what Frantz was trying to say from the beginning. It is also Sartre's way of speaking about torture in France.

III

Fiction: Style

The Rhythm of Time

by Fredric Jameson

The writers with the most striking, most nakedly accessible sense of time are those who use long sentences: the exaggeration of the rhythms of normal breathing yields a kind of time whose texture is gross and easily perceived. And among these sentences long enough to let us listen to the beat of time, short sentences, expletives, recover some of their original shock, enjoy new and jarring force. But sentences of more ordinary length can function within some larger unity that controls their cumulative effect: the rhythms Flaubert made his paragraph divisions yield are well-known. Such forms, in which the individual sentences, beaten into solidity, are set together piece by piece into a whole that gives them their meaning, suggest an idea of the work of art as a craft, like handiwork in silver, an idea which hardly survives at all in the universe of mass merchandise contemporary artists inhabit.

The time of Sartre's world is regulated by an instrument in appearance more extrinsic to literature than any of these schemes. Once more, it is a question of the ways sentences are connected together, but it is as if the sentences themselves counted for little in the process, possessed little intrinsic weight or effect upon it, like the bits of valueless material which modern sculptors join together into a form that rises above the cheap or ephemeral nature of its contents. The pace at which this world unfolds is supervised by punctuation.

Of course punctuation has always performed this function. But it has become so standardized that writers who use it as the schools or newspapers direct have no alternatives to choose from at the moments when they are obliged to punctuate. And where there is no possibility of doing something in different ways, there is no possibility of a style. We know this so well as readers that ordinarily we hardly even notice the punctuation at all: we do not have to, the convention is fixed, in a given case a given symbol will make its appearance. Limiting the writer's freedom in this matter even further are more curious restrictions: the colon, for example, is almost never seen in narration; some misfortune, possibly in its appearance, prevents it from ever straying out of the humdrum circle of expository prose.

The freedom with which Sartre uses these inherited symbols recovers for us some of their original freshness; he disposes of at least four different ways of linking sentences together, and this chaos begins to take on some appearance of order if we keep in mind that the marks are in his hands fairly precise symbols of different possible relationships between the complete sentences they separate:

Daniel s'emplit d'une eau vaseuse et fade: lui-même; l'eau de la Seine, fade et vaseuse, emplira le panier, ils vont se déchirer avec leurs griffes. Un grand dégoût l'envahit, il pensa: "C'est un acte gratuit." Il s'était arrêté, il avait posé le panier par terre: "S'emmerder à travers le mal qu'on fait aux autres. On ne peut jamais s'atteindre directement."

[Daniel filled up with muddy and insipid water: himself; the water of the Seine, insipid and muddy, will fill the basket, they'll tear each other apart with their claws. A strong revulsion came over him, he thought: "It's a gratuitous act." He had stopped, he had set the basket on the ground: "You've got to hurt other people to make yourself feel it. You can never get at yourself directly."][1]

The mingling of thought and objectivity in this passage is characteristic of the third person narration of the later novels, and obviously has something to do with the blinking rapidity with which the punctuation varies and succeeds itself. The rhythm of this paragraph is controlled by three instruments, each one marking a pause longer and more absolute than the others: the comma, the semicolon, and the period. The period comes as a deep silence, a consequential gap; it has something of the force of the past definite tense: after each one new areas are uncovered or new things happen. It is uncertain just how distinct the opaque watery feeling Daniel experiences is from the sudden revulsion

---

[1] *L'Âge de raison*, p. 94.

which also "fills" him, but in any case the revulsion is the accession of
this feeling to a new plane; it has been named, and through the name
the vaguer feeling takes on new shape and new intensity. The separation is even more striking after the next period. The sentence which
follows it is a skip backward in time; its events, described in the
pluperfect, have already happened, but have happened on such a different
level from the feelings and thoughts that were going on simultaneously
that they have had to be cleanly divided from them, there was no room
for them in the earlier sentences. The mind, busy with its unpleasant
sensations, did not notice the pause and the setting down of the basket
until after it had already taken place.

This silence latent in the period is by no means intrinsic to it through
some kind of "nature" that it might possess: its meaning is a function
of its use, and the shock, the sudden break it causes, becomes easier to
sense when we realize that the normal connection in this special world
between straightforward sentences describing concrete actions is not the
period at all but the comma. It is because we grow, over pages and
pages, accustomed to this privilege of the comma, trained to it, that the
period comes to strike us with the force it does. And it is certain that in
a consecutive reading, attentive to the continuity of the narration, we
have no trouble passing across the distance the period leaves between two
sentences, and that the selection of small passages, their isolation and the
slower reading they profit from, all exaggerate the effect of this punctuation far beyond what it is in a normal reading. But the magnifying and
exaggeration of a phenomenon simply permits us to register more
clearly what had to be there in the first place.

When the period is frequently used in a paragraph, the past definite
is called into play and the effect is that of a jerky moving forward in
time:

> Les chats miaulèrent comme si on les avait ébouillantés et Daniel sentit
> qu'il perdait la tête. Il posa le cageot par terre et y donna deux violents
> coups de pied. Il se fit un grand remue-ménage à l'intérieur, et puis les
> chats se turent. Daniel resta un moment immobile avec un drôle de frisson
> en aigrette derrière les oreilles. Des ouvriers sortirent d'un entrepôt et
> Daniel reprit sa marche. C'était là.

> [The cats shrieked as if they had been scalded and Daniel felt himself going
> out of his mind. He sat the cage on the ground and gave it a couple of
> violent kicks. There was a tremendous rumpus within and then the cats
> were silent. Daniel remained motionless for a moment with a strange elec-
> tric sensation suddenly shooting through the back of his head. Two workers
> came out of a warehouse and Daniel began walking again. The place was
> here.][2]

[2] *Ibid.*, p. 96.

Each of these sentences is a complete event; the past definite hermetically closes off each of the verbs. We pause at each period and it takes a little effort to leap into the next sentence. And the frequency of *and*'s in this passage indicates a will to connect in some way the small units which threaten to fall apart; the *and*'s attempt to weaken the divisive period-time, and the pressure of this time is so great that at one point one connective has to be intensified to *and then* in order to hold things together.

This abnormal strength of the period accounts for the very frequent use of the semicolon: it is as if the period were so strong it had to be used with care, reserved for the most significant moments, so as not to wear it out and for fear it prove too powerful for the structure it is supposed to hold together:

C'était une place populeuse avec des bistros; un groupe d'ouvriers et de femmes s'était formé autour d'une voiture à bras. Des femmes le regardèrent avec surprise.

[It was a bustling square with bars along it; a group of workers and women had gathered around a pushcart. A few women stared at him with surprise.][3]

The group around the pushcart is part of the scene described in the first sentence; it develops the description of the square, but it is too leisurely, too contemplative, to warrant the sudden rush of motion which the comma would call up between the scenic framework and the detail. But the two sentences are static, descriptive; neither of them has enough autonomous energy to stand alone, bounded by a period, without falling flat. The semicolon offers a kind of neutral pause, and the real break is saved for the next sentence, so that when the women look at Daniel it will come with the shock of a completely new occurrence.

Let us recall for a moment some of Roquentin's ideas about narration. His criticism struck at the anecdote and only indirectly at the novel. The anecdote is a kind of primitive stage of the novel, distinguished from it above all by its length; the anecdote is short enough so that its beginning and its end can both be held together within the mind without much trouble, whereas the novel (even if it tells a story which can be converted into an anecdote) represents an enormous amount of time that passes in front of the mind and then is lost to view, never wholly existing in the present, always part memory or part anticipation. Roquentin shows how sentences like: "It was dark, the street was empty." are secretly charged with their energy from the impending climax of the story. We know that something is about to happen, and soon, and that these details are only apparently unimportant, that they must have meaning and are to be watched attentively. The end of a novel, much

[3] *Ibid.,* p. 95.

further away, does not exercise this power of gravity over the in-
numerable sentences that precede it. Only toward the last pages, and
at the very beginning, of the novel, is time obviously distorted and
stylized in the way Roquentin described; and this distortion can in the
hands of a self-conscious artist turn into a bravura piece, a kind of
exhibitionistic gesture to show his shaping power over what he narrates
before effacing himself. Here (and in the weaker reflections of these
moments which are the beginnings and endings of chapters) he can
lead us into his story with the most breath-taking details, the most
startling perspectives, and break it off at similar points, in the grand
manner. For beginnings and ends are artificial, they are not "in nature."

The sentence is not in nature either. Sentences must also begin and
end, and as long as our attention is directed to their succession, to the
continuity of their subject matter, we are not aware of any violence done
to time. But when we examine them more closely, focusing on small
areas and attending to the manner in which they are linked together,
we find that the time of the novelist, taken for granted, flowing on
smoothly before, threatens to fall apart, to leave a ruin of separate
moments and separate events, with no way of getting from one to another
except by fiat, through a solution by violence.

This possibility of a breakdown in the continuity of sentences is the
reflection on an aesthetic level of a technical philosophical problem:
that of a theory of time. The conflict between the unity of time, its
continuity, and the divisibility and multiplicity of the individual
moments, a conflict out of which such things as Zeno's paradoxes arise,
does not offer a choice between irreconcilable alternatives but a formulation of two requirements, two simple and incontrovertible facts about
time which the new description will have to take into account. Sartre
unites these opposites in conceiving time as a "unity which multiplies
itself," a relationship within being, and within a being split against
itself. Time is therefore not a *thing,* the nature of which we can describe.
It is not somewhere *inside* the world, it is the way we live the world;
we are temporal in the structure of our being and time is one of the
negations that we bring to the pure simple being of the world by
surging in its midst.[4] We *are* time, are its privileged place of existence.

This has immediate implications for the literary problem we just
described. Since we are our time, it is up to us whether it turns toward
us the face of continuity or that of divisibility. There are no real beginnings, and yet our time is full of beginnings and endings. We constantly interrupt a time continuity to do something else, our time sense
expands and contracts like an accordion: fast or slow, continuous, absorbed, or jerky. It is on this possibility of variations in the quality of
time that the variations we have discovered in Sartre's narration are

---

[4] See *L'Être et le néant,* p. 181ff.

founded, and the effect of the period, in particular, is inconceivable with-out some possibility of a kind of absolute break in time which it could echo.

This absolute break is the moment or instant: but the break must somehow take place within time, or time would cease altogether. It cannot take place within the unity of action, of a project, otherwise it would slip back into a continuity. The only moments free enough from a continuity of time already past and from the ceaseless rush into the future to qualify as moments, are those which are in themselves both the end of something and the beginning of a new thing.[5] The moment is no longer strongly attached to the dying continuity, and the new one has not yet taken on enough life to catch the moment up in its motion. Yet these instants are in their turn merely the reflection of a more basic reality and happen on the basis of a more fundamental possibility. These partial beginnings can happen only because beginnings are somehow possible, or at least a certain type of beginning is: that of the original choice of our being, the unjustifiable choice that gives meaning to our smallest attitudes and acts, that accounts for our tastes, our ambitions, our habits. All of these are themes within a unity, parallel expressions of an underlying reality. The description of this original choice takes the form of a kind of myth, as the "look" did: it is the abstract structure which all later choices carry within themselves like a meaning, and inso-far as it is the structure of an act, it cannot be reduced completely to an abstract idea but preserves the act's shape. Yet in another sense, since it precedes our time itself and is itself the basis of the quality of the time we live, it can never be localized in a moment of our personal history: we are not born grown-up, and there is never a full dress moment in which we can be said to have chosen ourselves, and yet everything happens as though we had. In certain cases, as with the childhood trauma of Genet,[6] the original choice can even crystallize into a drama which can be temporally represented, whether in fact it happened all at once or not. The "myth" of the original choice is therefore an instrument of analysis that risks perpetuating itself as a concrete image.

There are nonetheless certain specialized moments of our personal his-tory that seem to stand in a more privileged relationship to this moment of original choice than do the ordinary contents of daily living, moments that have a feeling of beginning about them stronger than most, that we think of as change, as absolute dates. Such are those rare moments, in which in our freedom, the original choice is abandoned for some new choice of being. There are no "reasons" for such conversions, as Sartre calls them; the idea of a reason for doing something, a motive behind a project, has meaning only *within* a global choice; and very often a will

---

[5] See *L'Être et le néant*, pp. 554-55.

[6] See *Saint-Genêt*, Chap. 1: "L'enfant mélodieux mort en moi." ["The melodious child dead within me."]

to change completely, the passionate desire to alter from top to bottom that choice which is ourselves, is a kind of rationalization, a struggle against ourselves which is part and parcel of our original choice and not in any sense set against it. Yet these sudden conversions show our freedom at its most absolute, freedom exercising an ultimate power over all reasons and all values, and they have for us therefore a very special fascination, an excitement which the tone of the following passage betrays:

> At every moment I am aware that this initial choice is contingent and unjustifiable. . . . Hence my anxiety, my fear of being suddenly exorcized, of suddenly becoming radically other; hence also the frequent coming into being of these conversions which wholly transform my initial project. . . . Think for example of the *instant* in which the Philoctetes of Gide suddenly abandons everything, his hatred, his fundamental project, his reason for being and even his being itself; think of the *instant* in which Raskolnikov decides to give himself up. These extraordinary, marvelous instants, in which the older project collapses into the past in the light of a new project which rises on its ruins and which has hardly even taken full shape yet, these instants in which humiliation, anxiety, joy, hope are all inextricably united, in which we let go of everything in order to seize something new, in which we seize the new in order to abandon everything, such instants have often seemed to furnish the clearest and most touching image of our freedom. But they are only one manifestation of it among others.[7]

In other words, if we are free at all, we cannot be "more" free at certain moments than at others; freedom is not a quality that we possess degrees of; so that in spite of everything, from the point of view of the idea of freedom, these conversions are not more privileged than any other moments of our lives.

Yet from the point of view of the notion of an original choice, the conversions are in a sense the *only* real moments in our lives, the only real events. This curious difference in perspectives, where an idea suggests more than it really means, suggests something radically different from what it is supposed to mean, is perhaps attributable to the "myth"-like nature of the notion of choice. We will see later on also how certain notions, above and beyond their purely thought content, because their formulations are very close to images, tend to have this double development, in which from their images consequences can be drawn, secretly, implicitly, mistakenly, which range far beyond anything the pure thought of the notion ever intended to convey. In the case of the original choice, in terms of which every detail of a life can be interpreted (an interpretation and a method which Sartre has called "existential psychoanalysis"), the unique individual force of the events of a

---

[7] *L'Être et le néant*, pp. 554-55.

life seems to fade, the events become mere expressions, simply manifestations of the ever-present single choice. So that we approach the
strange image of a world in which nothing happens, in which the same
thing repeats itself over and over in different forms, in which only one
real solid event—the choice itself—has ever taken place and in which
only one new event can take place: the conversion, the sudden reversal
of values at any time possible. That these extensions and suggestions
latent in the notion of choice do not really do justice to Sartre's practice
as a novelist is apparent from the impression of a richness of action
which his books leave with us. There is little overt effort made to show
in some manner an original choice operating behind each of his characters—such an effort would have resulted in a kind of personification, a
kind of world of "humors," of character-ideas in action rather than real
people. And yet the moment of conversion, so dependent on this whole
complex of ideas, occupies a place of great importance in this work. The
conversion can seem a waking up, as it does in the consul's office in Indo-
china, where Mercier urges Roquentin to accept a place in the new ex-
pedition:

Je fixais une petite statuette khmère, sur un tapis vert, à côté d'un appareil
téléphonique. Il me semblait que j'étais rempli de lymphe ou de lait tiède.
Mercier me disait, avec une patience angélique qui voilait un peu d'irritation: "N'est-ce pas, j'ai besoin d'être fixé officiellement. Je sais que vous
finirez par dire oui: il vaudrait mieux accepter tout de suite." Il a une
barbe d'un noir roux, très parfumée. A chaque mouvement de sa tête, je
respirais une bouffée de parfum. Et puis, tout d'un coup, je me réveillai
d'un sommeil de six ans. La statue me parut désagréable et stupide et je
sentis que je m'ennuyais profondément. Je ne parvenais pas à comprendre
pourquoi j'étais en Indochine. Qu'est-ce que je faisais là? Pourquoi parlais-je
avec ces gens? Pourquoi étais-je si drôlement habillé? Ma passion était morte.
Elle m'avait submergé et roulé pendant des années; à présent, je me sentais
vide.

[I was staring at a little Khmer statuette, on a green cover, next to the
telephone. I felt as if I were filled with lymph or with tepid milk. Mercier
was saying, with angelic patience that concealed some irritation: "As you
are well aware, I have to receive an official appointment. I know that
sooner or later you will say yes: it would be better to do so at once."
   He had a reddish black beard, highly scented. Every time he moved his
head I got a whiff of the perfume. And then, all of a sudden, I woke up out
of a sleep six years long.
   The statue looked disagreeable and stupid and I realized that I was profoundly bored. I couldn't manage to understand why I was in Indochina
at all. What was I doing there? Why was I talking with these people? What
was I dressed so oddly for? My passion was dead. I had been submerged in
it, swept along by it, for years; now I felt empty.][8]

[8] *La Nausée*, pp. 16-17.

Here is a moment in which freedom suddenly stirs convulsively, shatters the crust of habits that had seemed to be forming around it, emerges without any connections at all, without any obligations, into a world which had gradually forgotten it was there. And yet the astonishing thing is that this sudden self-assertion of freedom is presented in terms of its opposite: it is something that happens to Roquentin, he himself does nothing, seems hardly responsible for it. He seems merely the passive locus of a wholly impersonal event, like a sudden bodily reaction. He merely "wakes up," and wakes up after it is all over. His passion does not die, he realizes that it is dead. The moment, the leap in time from one world-choice to another, is so sudden and so radical that it apparently eludes the instruments which were supposed to register it. It is deduced after the fact, from its consequences. For this moment is in the beginning wholly negative: the new passions, new interests, new thoughts, which will gradually fill this void have not yet appeared; the astonished mind is alone for the time being with the trophies of its former enthusiasm. That is why the image of death is the privileged expression of this change: the image of the loss of everything familiar, everything to which we are passionately attached, of the pain of the organism acceding to a new condition—so that the emptiness, the abandonment of the consciousness is its first sensation.

The most shocking, polemic statement of this event is the death of love: such moments take on their significance when opposed to the heavy burden of works composed from the very beginnings of literature to glorify love as a divine, irresistible, irrational force—one which begins with the inevitability of a chemical process, mastering the soul and setting it under very real slavery. It is not the reality of these feelings which is denied; but the test of a literature of freedom is the presentation of just such a passion—showing it as it is, with all the passivity it involves, the feeling that it seizes us without our consent, and showing at the same time that it is freely assumed, and that we somehow put ourselves into a passional state, that we make ourselves passive to be "enslaved" by our own freely chosen passions. Yet the direct description of the passion is somehow insufficient. Love, like the passions of Roquentin, is a value, and each value tends toward self-sufficiency, toward absorbing the whole world into itself at the exclusion of everything else. It denies its existence as "a" value and insists on being Value pure and simple. The value is moreover a kind of absence: it is that which consciousness lacks, that path by which consciousness hopes eventually to arrive at its own special form of being: a lack which propels consciousness forward in time, and which all of the acts of consciousness are designed to fill. So that very often the value itself escapes detection, and people even deny they have any: only their acts, often performed under motives which their doers attempt to conceal from themselves, show secretly the ever-present influence of this absent center of gravity. Yet in the moment of the death of a value, the eye manages to register it directly; suddenly it becomes aware of what was there now that it is gone; and in the place where the value used to be it seizes it as the outline of an absence.

Thus the real meaning of love as freely chosen, a meaning obscured during its existence by the passive nature of the feeling which is lived as being submitted to, suddenly emerges when love dies. Like the other moments, the death of love happens abruptly and without transition: the person merely wakes up into a world from which his love is gone, he remembers the former gestures inspired by it without any longer understanding them. This sudden absence is not *caused,* is wholly gratuitous. Yet it can happen against the background of a world so unexpectedly and radically altered that the older value, persisting a moment in its new surroundings, becomes incomprehensible, and then vanishes altogether. This is what happens in *Dead without Burial,*[9] after Lucie has been tortured and her world sealed off by the imminence of death, when her love for Jean, a kind of peacetime love nourished by the idea of a continuing future, suddenly proves to be at cross-purposes with the passion in which she wants to live her coming extinction. Love has nothing to offer her in such a world; it is a toy she drops without regret.

Yet we should not make any mistake about the tone of these sequences. They have no trace of any sadness at the evanescence of human passions or emotions; they are painful, "humiliation, anxiety, joy, hope" all mingled together, but they have no built-in effect. The very same moment, which in *Dead without Burial* had some of the somberness of approaching death, becomes in *Kean* pure comedy, in the astonishing scene in which the passion shared by Kean and Elena suddenly gives way beneath them and drops them from Alexandre Dumas into a play of a different nature altogether.[10] If there is any dominant tone in such moments at all, it is more likely to be excitement, which does not have to be wholly free from anxiety: a kind of relief of the consciousness at finding itself once more naked and without any ties, left with absolutely nothing. There is in it some of the exhilaration of all negativity, all destruction.

It is the ever-present possibility of such moments of radical change, the constant threat that time will collapse into one of these moments and then reissue wholly altered, that lends the world of Sartre that jerkiness we have discovered behind the use of the period. It is as if time might suddenly begin to divide itself into infinitesimal separate units and as if this process, like a chain reaction, once begun could never be arrested. And against this threat a host of smaller mannerisms stand guard: verbs of unusual violence, especially in the philosophic works where milder ones might have been used, keep things moving explosively forward: such verbs as "die," "surge," "seize," "invade," and so on. But such verbs have ambiguous effects: they do keep things going but

[9] See *Morts sans sépulture,* Tableau III, scene 2.
[10] *Kean,* Act V, scene 4.

at the same time they separate the new thing bursting into being somewhat irrevocably from all that has preceded it, as if it had been separated
by the enormous gap of one of those instants. And the constant series
of *and's* and *then's* and *afterward's* push the minute separate events
forward, both linking and dividing them. On every page we find
adverbs of violence attempting to bring new events to birth: "suddenly,"
"brusquely," "all at once"—all these lend a kind of abruptness to this
world which occasionally looks like the jerky, over-rapid and sectional
movement of the early movies:

> Elle verse sans répondre; tout d'un coup il retire prestement le doigt de son
> nez et pose les deux mains à plat sur la table. Il a rejeté la tête en arrière et
> ses yeux brillent. Il dit d'une voix froide: "La pauvre fille."

> [She pours without replying; all of a sudden nimbly he withdraws his finger
> from his nose and spreads both hands out on the table. He has his head
> tossed back and his eyes are shining. Coldly he says: "Poor girl."] [11]

The new gesture is so rapid that it will not all fit into the sentence
which was supposed to circumscribe it and leaves some trailing, static
now that the gesture is over, into the next ("He has his head tossed
back"). There are long waits, unexpected things suddenly happen, time
slows again and stops and then moves.

That jerkiness does not become intolerable because it is not the only
kind of movement in this prose. In the silences of the period, time
shows its possibility of being discontinuous, fragmented; the requirements of a sentence seemed to image faithfully this starting and stopping
of time. Time's continuity is in some ways harder to fix. The basis for
it could not be in the sentences themselves unless they were highly
unusual like Faulkner's, but in the continuity of our reading, which
provides the solidity with which the impression is filled out.

Sometimes the continuity is illusory: such is the movement which the
colon provokes, a mere flash which quickly abolishes itself: "Daniel
filled up with muddy and insipid water: himself." The colon here is a
little pause, a slight catching of the breath before the last word is uttered
which permits the sentence to fall, finished. It signifies equivalence
between the two parts, an identity so great that the two sections seem
to be held apart artificially and by force only. Once the colon is bridged,
once the mirror-sentence on the other side of it has joined its predecessor,
the two seem to merge into one like a rubber band stretched and snapping back, and they glide as a single unit into the past. The separation
can be as slight as the distance between looking and seeing, between
seeing and identification:

[11] *La Nausée,* p. 87.

De petits monstres mous rampent à terre et regardent le gai troupeau de leurs yeux sans prunelles: des masques à gaz.

[Limp little monsters crawl on the ground alongside and stare at the joyous troop through the empty sockets of their eyes: gasmasks.] 12

The colon permits not an abstract description of the process of seeing something and then realizing what it is, a description that would use weak and faded words like "realize" and "it occurred to him suddenly," but a concrete presentation of the event in which we participate ourselves. We are suddenly lifted out of the realistic world of the rest of the novel, lifted higher and higher into fantasy the length of the whole sentence, until suddenly the single withheld word is released and the world immediately settles back to normal again. The sentence no longer displays a merely static meaning; it imitates with its own small drama the drama of its subject matter. And yet the drama caused by the colon is partly an artificial one: the colon assures us that there is no difference at all between the one and the other sentences it separates and yet it separates them. The colon unity throws up beyond itself the presence of the thing as it really is, the unified thing of which the two sentences are merely aspects, and then against this, the sentence which attempts to seize the solidly settled object through motion, through the illusory, snapping motion of the two temporarily separated parts rejoining. The sentence, the subjectivity, creates an illusion of separation, a mirage of dynamism and of happening, in order to convey a basically static reality. The colon here is therefore a kind of symbol of the events in which "nothing" really happened . . . ; it is also a privileged form through which certain objects in this world find their expression.

Such use of the colon permits a characteristic solution to one of the most serious problems in modern narration, that of the "thought." There is no "natural" solution to this problem. The interior monologue of Joyce is not less artificial than indirect discourse; it has merely the virtue of a conquest, of the new. The problem exists because of the relationship between thoughts and words. If thoughts were immediately equivalent to, immediately assimilable to words, there would be merely the ordinary problem of finding the exact words, there would be no question but that words were the perfect and privileged manifestation of thoughts. But the words pronounced inside the mind can be in direct contradiction to the mind's secret awareness, they can be an attempt of the mind to fool itself. Or the real thinking can be done through acts. We can sometimes think directly with the things we handle and use, so that the full dress "thought" is only a much later entity, a kind of reflection of an immediate reality. So unless a little violence is done to the traditional

12 *La Mort dans l'âme,* p. 201.

methods of presenting thoughts, the old worn-out notions of personalities
and of the nature of thinking and of action will perpetuate themselves.

Sartre's renovation of this state of affairs is along the line of least effort,
hardly perceptible: he preserves everything, the equivalence between
thought and sentence, even to the quotation marks that give us the
impression that the thought-sentence has been lifted bodily from someone's mind and set unchanged upon the paper. But this traditional
arrangement is secretly subverted: the colon in itself would not be
enough to install any real novelty into this form; its use in direct quotation before a sentence in quotation marks is in fact one of the rare ap-
plications of this symbol which is not rejected from French narrative
prose; but the colon is the locus of this subtle change: "A strong revulsion came over him, he thought: 'It's a gratuitous act.'" The effect of
this "thought" has been prepared by its context, by the kind of sentence
that precedes it. The comma separating the two narrative sentences lends
the second, carrying within itself the burden of the thought, the same
weight as the first, more linear one. This forced equation of two un-
equal lengths would of course be present even with different kinds of
separating punctuations:

Il but. Il pensa: "Elle est enceinte. C'est marrant; je n'ai pas l'impression
que c'est vrai."

[He drank. He thought: "She's pregnant. It's funny: I can't believe it."] 13

Even here, where the "thought" section is far more complicated than the
two words it is dependent on, it has nonetheless been reduced to the
status of a mere clause by the influence and the parallel of the preceding
small sentence. What the period does here however is to alter the quality
of the movement: in the first passage the length of the beginning sentence
and the rush ahead caused by the comma help to complete the "he
thought" effortlessly with the substance of the thought. In the second
group there is an abrupt stopping short that causes the thought to tumble
forward under the acquired momentum in a kind of stumbling over its
own feet; but in both cases the "thought" has been solidified, turned into
an entity, by the parallel with the preceding sentence. What stands between the quotation marks is now no longer language of the same quality
as the sentences outside them: it is unitary, and when it happens, it has
to be at least as tangible an event as the drink the man takes or the
sudden wave of revulsion that comes over him. The shortness of the "he
thought:" is essential in lending the vague subjective event the value of
a precise gesture, and after it the colon comes as relief, it points forward,
indicating an empty space which the thought quickly flows into and

13 *L'Âge de raison*, p. 24.

fills up; it holds the door open at the end of an incomplete sentence and the completion arrives almost instantaneously. Thus the thought, when it happens to the incomplete announcement preceding it, has now all the force of an act, and the quotation marks, which were supposed to indicate naïvely that we think in words, are forced to assist in conveying the impression of a gesture of consciousness just as real and as solid as a gesture of the hand. The "words" of the thought are now a kind of illusion: the thought-sentences indicate the sudden decisive seizing of consciousness on things; they are not any longer supposed to give faithfully "word for word" what the consciousness "thought." The words of these sentences no longer stand for the words of the thoughts in question; they stand directly for the thoughts themselves, just as ordinary narrative sentences "stand for" the wordless realities they describe.

The movement which the colon generated was ephemeral and immediately abolished itself, a mere illusion of movement created to be as quickly laid to rest: an instant only, since it could bind only two sentences, could represent nothing more substantial than an exchange of energy between two points alone. The comma, on the other hand, has the seeds of perpetual motion within it: it connects complete sentences, lets them pile up one after another, and suggests no superior structure which would cause a period to happen at any given point, which would of itself set an end to the fissioning development.

But although the sentences it links are grammatically complete, the comma insists on their secret incompleteness, it urges us forward, assures us that everything has not yet been said: "He had stopped, he had set the basket on the ground: 'You've got to hurt other people to make yourself feel it.'" The center of gravity in this unit is in the thought, the other sentences slide down the incline toward it although they in no way duplicate it. The comma is precisely this slant at which complete sentences are leaned and which robs them of their autonomy. But the incompleteness is not a precise one, to be filled and satisfied by a single detail, a single subsequent sentence: it spreads out on all sides and the period that finally puts an end to it is arbitrary and dependent on the angle of vision, like a window frame that shuts off the view at an accidental point. For the comma generates a movement which whirls loose wider and wider. The colon was bounded, centripetal, moving in upon itself to vanish at a given moment; the comma has no natural term; the form which it governs is open, full of loose ends. In a sense the master image of this special kind of movement is the entire novel *The Reprieve,* in some ways nothing but a vast whirl of things linked by commas and which at its most concentrated moments shrinks to precisely the form we are describing:

Des étoffes rouges et roses et mauves, des robes mauves, des robes blanches, des gorges nues, de beaux seins sous des mouchoirs, des flaques de soleil sur

les tables, des mains, des liquides poisseux et dorés, encore des mains, des
cuisses jaillissant des shorts, des voix gaies, des robes rouges et roses et
blanches, des voix gaies qui tournaient dans l'air, des cuisses, la valse de la
Veuve Joyeuse, l'odeur des pins, du sable chaud, l'odeur vanillée du grand
large, toutes les îles du monde invisibles et présentes dans le soleil, l'île sous
le Vent, l'île de Pâques, les îles Sandwiches, des boutiques de luxe le long de
la mer, l'imperméable de dame à trois mille francs, les clips, les fleurs rouges
et roses et blanches, les mains, les cuisses, "la musique vient par ici," les
voix gaies qui tournaient dans l'air, Suzanne et ton régime? Ah! tant pis,
pour une fois. Les voiles sur la mer et les skieurs sautant, bras tendus, de
vague en vague, l'odeur des pins, par bouffées, la paix. La paix à Juan-les-
Pins.

[Red and pink and mauve fabrics, mauve dresses, white dresses, uncovered
bosoms, beautiful breasts beneath handkerchiefs, pools of sunlight on tables,
hands, sticky and golden liquids, more hands, thighs bursting out of shorts,
gay voices, red and pink and white dresses, gay voices spinning in the open
air, thighs, the *Merry Widow* waltz, the smell of pinetrees, of warm sand,
the vanilla odor of the open sea, all the islands in the world invisible and
present in the sunlight, the Leeward Islands, Easter Island, the Sandwich
Islands, the luxury shops along the seashore, the lady's raincoat at three
thousand francs, the costume jewelry, red and pink and white flowers, hands,
thighs, "this is where the music is coming from," gay voices whirling in the
air, what about your diet, Suzanne? Oh, just this once. Sails on the sea and
the skiers leaping, their arms stretched forward, from wave to wave, the
smell of the pines in whiffs, peace. Peace at Juan-les-Pins.] [14]

This cascade of sensations is pure of any individual minds; the people
leave their separate identities along with their jobs and their winter
clothing and merge into a common set of feelings, into a common world.
The holiday world directs them, not the other way around: it proposes a
series of well-traveled paths which they follow through their summer.
For a time at least this collective world is the only living entity, the
only reality. Yet take this resort as the widest frame of reference, expand
its hints and fragments, let the bodies which are attached to the hands
and thighs begin to appear, and let the situations attached to the disembodied voices little by little be guessed at, and the form of *The
Reprieve* is unmistakably present before you. This form, which attempts
to convey both the minute position we occupy in a world filled with
history and the fragmentary nature of our awareness of that world, is
supposed to be full of loose ends, open, fragmentary, in order to avoid
the god's eye view of the world which some novels that do not remain
within a single point of view suggest.

Yet in spite of its difference from the colon form, the comma also
suggests a single central reality which the sentences do violence to; but
this central reality, instead of being somehow separated in two only

to be immediately reunited again, is infinitely divided, infinitely divisible. Time, in order to move forward, must change from moment to moment, but it must also, to be continuous, remain somehow the same. The most striking changes turn out to be grammatical fictions and necessities, the apparently separate events imperceptibly fade into what preceded them and into what will follow. Like the thoughts, the revulsion, the setting down of the basket, they are all distinct because they happen on different levels and have to be separated in their presentation, and yet somehow they are all simultaneous, form part of a single large reality which we sense after we have read all of them.

This movement forward which is also a kind of repetition is a form of generosity: a fear that the event, the reality, has not been sufficiently presented, a turning around it to strike it again and again from new sides and at new angles, so that no single formulation which might have caught your mind more immediately than others, will go unsaid. This sort of repetition is familiar to readers of Sartre's philosophic works; and since these are practical expository works, it is there unashamed and unconcealed. But in narration any real repetition is generally checked by the real movement forward of time, the necessity that very shortly things be in some real sense different from what has preceded them. Nonetheless sometimes this flow forward is slowed down as much as it can be, sometimes time marks time, and little pools of repetition gather:

Mais il aurait fallu parler: Boris sentait qu'il ne pouvait pas parler. Lola était à côté de lui, lasse et toute chaude et Boris ne pouvait pas s'arracher le moindre mot, sa voix était morte. Je serais comme ça si j'étais muet. C'etait voluptueux, sa voix flottait au fond de sa gorge, douce comme du coton et elle ne pouvait plus sortir, elle était morte.

[But he would have had to say something: Boris felt himself unable to speak. Lola was beside him, tired and all warm and Boris couldn't tear the slightest word loose, his voice was dead. I would be like this if I were a mute. It was voluptuous, his voice floated deep down in his throat, soft as cotton and it couldn't get out, it was dead.] [15]

This repetition, the describing in different ways of the same phenomenon, is not exactly circular: with each phrasing it rises to a new level, and the image of the "dead" voice, colorless and figurative at first, becomes real by the end of the passage. The mere abstract feeling of not being able (not wanting) to talk has become the awareness of a part of his body, an organ, actually gone lifeless. Such a sudden unfolding of development, the quick rushing into being of variations on a single motif, is the characteristic form of a kind of Sartrean poetry. The passages begin with a single central datum or conceit: in this case the voice

[15] *L'Âge de raison*, p. 28.

not working, the idea of the voice as a thing which operates like an organ of the body; and then this central "inspiration" is systematically exploited, used in as many different ways as possible, developed as exhaustively as possible, until a kind of feeling of completion is reached, the thing is there before us, and the continuous movement of narration sets in again.

In its most characteristic use, therefore, the comma ceases to be simply the rhythm at which events unfold, and turns into a kind of momentary departure from the narration, a form that develops above the line of the narration like a pause. There is a point here beyond which our analysis cannot pass: the coming into being of the "idea," the central image, the motif itself, the "inspiration"; this surges out of nothingness, the *Einfall* is a kind of irreducible. And yet there is a quality about all of this Sartrean rhetoric, or poetry, which can be formulated: we feel a kind of contortionism in it, a straining which nonetheless remains graceful, lands back on its feet. The motif surges in a kind of receptive tension in the author's mind; at points in the steady continuity he strains his imagination for a certain kind of perception and suddenly, out of nowhere, the right thing comes. But this pressure of the imagination does not exist in a void: it is not content it seeks, but a special way of treating content which is already given in the story line. It is as if the things of the narration were constantly being stared at to yield up a kind of poetry, as if the things were being constantly forced to take the shape of a subjectivity, to take on some of the grace and the autonomous movement of a kind of thought. But what it is that happens to these things, what can happen to them, what this specialized attention directed on them means, we will only find out by leaving behind us the forms into which this content organizes itself, and interrogating the content itself directly.

IV

Literary Criticism

Existentialism and Criticism

by René Girard

Literary criticism as it is practiced in *Saint-Genêt: comédien et martyr* is primarily the application of existentialist psychoanalysis to a writer. It is a search for that original choice of being, that *project* which is Sartre's pass key to a man's personality, to his *Weltanschauung* and—if he is an artist—to his works of art. Genet's literary works are not treated differently from the other aspects of his behavior: they provide clues to the original choice and they illustrate it.

Far from narrowing the range of inquiry—which would be true if the project only colored the author's writings, as we say, for instance, that Flaubert's pessimism colors his novels—this approach is the only one, in Sartre's eyes, which can exhaust the work's significance. Nothing is dismissed as accidental or incidental; there is no formal characteristic of style or composition that does not constitute a new effort to achieve the chosen goal.

In a ten-page commentary of a single image: "The gardener is the most beautiful rose in his garden," the critic shows, for example, that his author brings disparates together not in the brutal and overt surrealist manner but insidiously, so as to subvert the values of the unsuspecting reader and induce him to accept the hidden premises of an inverted

"Existentialism and Criticism." From *Yale French Studies*, No. 9 (Winter 1955-56), *Foray through Existentialism*. Reprinted by permission of *Yale French Studies* and the author.

morality: evil is good; good is evil. Which brings back Genet's homo-
sexuality, his thefts, his imprisonments and, ultimately, his original
choice of *evil*.

Perpetual projection into the future, the choice is also an event of the
past; a psychic "crystallization" has occurred around an original crisis.
Genet's biography is therefore an integral part of the structural analysis.
Caught at the age of seven in the act of "stealing" some worthless object,
branded as "evil" by his rigid foster parents, the docile child has *chosen*
to see himself as the almighty adults see him. There is no passive formation of a "complex"; how could this drama be a cause of Genet's behavior since most delinquents *choose* to stay within the bonds of standard
morality, since, in their own way, they want to be good like the rest of
us. Genet, on the contrary, will yearn freely for evil, as hero and saint
yearn for the good.

In vain, of course. The Platonic ideas of Good and Evil which Genet
borrows from his foster parents are nothing but an effort at self-justifica-
tion; they are a product of society's self-righteousness or, in Sartrean
terms, of its *bad faith*. The bad Genet, like all of us good people, is a
comedian trying to convince himself he is not acting; but he is also
a *martyr* since he selected the part no one wants to play, since he fights
society single-handed, although with the wrong weapons.

The fight ends in a liberation or the hope of a liberation from the
false morality of essence which Sartre would like to see all of us abandon.
Genet, realizing the unreality of it all, the arbitrariness of his choice,
will become able to revoke it.

The benevolent analyst only helps along a process of ethical enlightenment in which the work of art plays an eminent part. The inclusion of
the aesthetic structure inside a larger one, the author's whole behavior,
does not mean that Sartre relegates the work of art to a subordinate
position. Nothing can be subordinate in a "totalitarian" interpretation
which does not distinguish between the man and his works. It is not art
as such but the whole of behavior which remains under suspicion as
long as *bad faith* subsists. But the liberation of Genet shows us that
artistic expression at its highest is endowed with an autopsychoanalytic
character which is one with the depth of its insight into ourselves and
our world.

Behind success lurks one danger: monotony. Mindful, perhaps, of the
objections to his sketchy *Baudelaire*, Sartre returns tirelessly to the same
fundamental themes with new illustrative variations of literary and
non-literary behavior. The careful reader, however, does not find the
book repetitious. Genet's liberation takes place in stages during which
dialectical possibilities of Good and Evil are successively tried and
rejected. One cannot fail to admire the virtuosity with which Sartre
unravels the maze, gathers up thread after thread in Genet's life, brings
order to chaos, finally manages to convince those who follow him to the

end that every incident in his author's life, every line he ever wrote is a new variation on the same leitmotif.

No student of the present critical trends in France can omit *Saint-Genêt* since this work offers, to this date, the most thorough illustration of phenomenology applied to literature. It is tempting, in view of Sartre's influence during the first postwar years, to consider the book as a model for all the young critics who have turned, if not to phenomenological description, at least to criticism in the phenomenological style.

This huge study, however, was not as passionately discussed as some of Sartre's previous works. The reasons usually invoked to account for this relative neglect—the impenetrable density of the demonstration and the scandalous nature of Genet's writings—have relevance only when the *grand public* is involved.[1] The truth is that Sartre has lost his monopoly on a certain type of analysis. The publication of *Saint-Genêt* was a literary event but only a literary event *among others.*

Sartre's system includes many elements which did not originate with him. Structural criticism was practiced in Germany and Central Europe before it was introduced in France. Like the Gestalt theory and phenomenology, it was part of the general reaction against the positivism of the early twentieth century. Sartre, strongly influenced by the early Heidegger, formulated a new and original synthesis. His ideas found an extremely favorable and almost virgin field of expansion in France. For a few years it was difficult to distinguish what was specifically Sartrean in the new approach to man which seemed, among other contributions, to offer the literary critic a third way between the pitfalls of disguised impressionism and pseudo-scientific imitation of experimental methods.

This period is over. The disciples are on their own. They can view phenomenology and existentialism with enough perspective to adopt or reject whatever fits their own inclinations. The new outlook, on the other hand, although its first systematizations were German, had literary antecedents in France. Seen in retrospect, some critical essays and reflexions on criticism by such writers as Valéry, Proust, Alain and by critics like Thibaudet and Jean Prévost appear as partial realizations or formulations of the new critical ideal.

The tendency, however, after having exaggerated it, is now to minimize Sartre's influence. If a rigidly orthodox "Sartrisme" is on the decline it is, partly, as a consequence of the diffusion of many original or adapted Sartrean ideas. Many critics, today, however different their style from the austere and rigidly geometrical patterns of *Saint-Genêt*, aim, like Sartre, at the explicit formulation of a meaning implicit in the work of art. They proceed, essentially, in the same circular fashion. From the comparison of significant details a hypothesis emerges as to their com-

---

[1] The reader's resistance to Genet is, of course, from a Sartrean point of view, a symptom of *mauvaise foi;* it gives added proof that this writer—correctly interpreted—is particularly fit to shock us out of our morality of essence.

mon denominator; this hypothesis is confirmed if it illuminates all aspects of the work just as a ray of light, placed at the right angle, is refracted from every facet of a diamond. The critic may not attempt to reach what Sartre calls the original choice, he may not even believe there is one single key to an entire existence, but his goal is still the unique structure of the work and, ultimately, of the author's existence. The final term in the process may not be named a project but it is still a dynamic attitude toward existence, at the same time fundamental and unique, of which the work of art is an actualization. And this attitude cannot be defined as a mixture of "sentiments" and "qualities" which appear more fundamental but are really less significant, since they apply to more and more individuals. The critic must tend toward the primordial, the irreducible, without losing the concrete richness of existence. His is primarily a search for singularity.

In this perspective, what Malraux calls *"la pointe extrême de l'œuvre,"* these works, usually later ones, in which a writer is most specifically himself, are likely to take precedence over universally acclaimed masterpieces. The tradition of "rediscovery" and "rehabilitation" of the great writers' neglected works is stronger than ever. Hugo's metaphysical poems of the exile period, for instance, have lost none of their fascination, whereas some critics—such as Pierre Schneider in *La Voix vive*—do not hide their indifference for the romantic of the Thirties. The Flaubert of the *Correspondence* is still preferred to the tortured novelist. Michelet the *visionnaire* and perhaps even Saint-Simon the fanatical nobleman push into the background the great historians who "resurrected the French past."

Even when they do not adopt Sartre's theories on committed literature, these critics do not view writing as an autonomous human activity and they do not believe in art for art's sake. Unlike the Anglo-Saxon New Critics, their distrust of literary history does not lead them to do away with history. They reject, indeed, the collateral facts intended to buttress the critic's position. Far from being neutral, such facts are already charged with a significance which is easily substituted for the significant structure the critic wants to bring out. History must not be a background provided by various specialists and arranged behind the author; this author has to be shown *facing* historical problems as he faces aesthetic problems. The attitudes are correlated; both can be read into the formal and stylistic characteristics of the work. The nature of this correlation, from Sartre's "Qu'est-ce que la littérature?" to Roland Barthes' *Le Degré zéro de l'écriture,* has been the object of many essays.

As in the Freudian or in the Marxist approach, the outside observer is better placed to reveal the objective meaning of the subject's behavior than the subject himself. But any attempt at causal reduction is rejected; the critic does not take refuge in a "complex" or in the "infrastructures of society." He does not want to talk around the work but about it.

How can the privileged position of the observer be justified without a causal link? Sartre's famous solution, bad faith, achieves this end: the project is of an easier access to the psychoanalyst than to the subject, who nevertheless remains free and responsible. Bad faith is delusion; it is neither hypocrisy—which implies, on the part of the subject, the knowledge of everything there is to know—nor the unpassable barrier erected by Freud or Marx between consciousness and reality. This Jansenist attitude, however, is especially hard to maintain when one deals with admired writers. But the problem is a theoretical one; the attitude of most critics is pragmatic: there is an objective dimension in the work of art which critical distance alone can reveal, just as there are laws in a language, invisible to the native speaker, which the most halting foreigner never fails to perceive.

Especially close to Sartre is Francis Jeanson, an essayist and the director of the critical collection *Écrivains de toujours*. To this collection he contributed a *Montaigne par lui-même* and, quite recently, a *Jean-Paul Sartre par lui-même* in which the disciple turns, rather discreetly, the psychoanalytical weapon against the master who armed his hand.

Besides Jeanson's, many critical works in this collection are representative of the new directions. Among the best are those of Roland Barthes, Jean-Marie Domenach, Jean Starobinski, Albert Béguin, Claude Roy, Gaëtan Picon. The title of these small volumes, *Barrès par lui-même*, *Montesquieu par lui-même*, is, in itself, a program. The core of the book is an essay which aims to reveal the writer through his works and the works through the writer. The excerpts which follow do not constitute an anthology; they are chosen for their self-revelatory value. Since actions and attitudes are as significant as the written word, illustrations and portraits abound; personal documents are reproduced. These are sometimes more likely to satisfy a superficial curiosity than to provide an added insight into the author's existence, but commercial exigencies are not allowed to take precedence.

The critic tries to look at the world through the eyes of the author; he becomes obsessed with his obsessions; he relives the genesis of the work of art. When in a radical mood, he attempts to substitute re-creation for interpretation. The critic may even mime the author for the benefit of his readers: he never misses a chance to use his favorite expressions; he adopts his linguistic and stylistic peculiarities, forcibly calling them to the reader's attention by borrowing the writer's voice when expected to use his own. All this deliberately, and not through some kind of literary osmosis. This dramatic character comes close to parody in some pages of Bastide's *Saint-Simon*. Existentialist moralists have not spoken in vain! Having renounced the part he was playing to himself the critic can now play, to a larger audience, the part of an *Écrivain de toujours*.

But there are as many styles as there are critics, since the critical approach to the work of art is the artist's approach to reality. As Michel Vinaver put it in *Les Lettres nouvelles* (June 1953), the critic "tries to create an image of the work just as the work tries to create an image of the world, in a word to raise the work to the second degree."

This new image differs, in one essential aspect, from the original one. What is revealed is the work of art as such: no longer a faithful reproduction of reality as the writer intended it but creation, human, all too human creation. When these critics are not psychoanalytical like Sartre and Jeanson they remain, in their majority, "demystifying." Truth has become the author's truth, not falsehood but mythology. Similarly, paintings and statues cease to incarnate the "absolute" when they enter Malraux's imaginary museum.

This type of description has a negative force which appears, at times, to threaten even the critic's particular version of truth, whether it be Sartrean or Christian existentialism, Marxism, etc. In his *Pascal par lui-même* Albert Béguin seems, in some passages, to shield his author from the destructive power of his own analysis. Phenomenological comprehension starts beyond the sphere of praise and condemnation, it is incompatible with any judgment depending on a system of reference alien to the work itself. It cannot, therefore, situate its object in a hierarchy of works of art, even within its genre, a category which has lost much of its significance.[2] Traditional aesthetic judgment had become rare, indeed, in the last decades, but the critic no longer feels guilty about his inability to compare. The more successful the critic the more incomparable the work of art is shown to be.

A new task, however, confronts the critic; he can try to judge the author from the author's point of view, he can view his achievements in the light of his technical intentions. This is what Roland Barthes attempts in his *Michelet par lui-même*. The critic registers the writer's failure which is, indeed, as Bernard Dort pointed out in *Critique* (1954, p. 731), the failure of language itself: "I am born of the people, I have the people in my heart. . . . But its language, its language was barred to me. I could not make the people speak."

The author is always interpreted through the very means he uses in his quest. His constant presence has, as its ideal counterpart, the total absence of the critic. This absence is not evasion; this silence is not facility, it represents a harsh conquest over our innate conviction that our senses and culture give us access to an absolute reality, an absolute

---

[2] The writings of Sartre which distinguish between genres or between poetry and prose are normative and not descriptive. These distinctions have no relevance in *Saint-Genêt*; a chapter dealing with prose works is significantly entitled: "Un mécanisme ayant du vers l'exacte rigueur. . . ." Jean Pouillon's *Temps et roman* constitutes, at least in some aspects, an effort to develop the dogmatic viewpoint of *littérature engagée* into a general theory of the novel.

beauty which the writer should attempt to imprison in his work. Self-criticism must precede criticism.

This amounts, one might say, to a renewed emphasis on an old truth: criticism is no better than the critic. But self-criticism must now be conceived along the lines of a psychoanalysis, Sartrean or other. Traditional suspension of belief is not enough, since the deeper the belief the more likely it is to present itself as "fact." The education of the critic must be defined in negative terms, by his ability to detach himself from his own experience, to uproot himself from whatever constitutes his native soil. It has little to do with the acquisition of skills and "methods," the manipulation of statistics and other devices purporting to guarantee accuracy of observation. "Scientific" precautions ultimately strengthen the subjective fallacy since they encourage the critic to "trust his own eyes" and view the work of art as an object in *his* world rather than himself as a potential object in the writer's world.

The exercise of this new methodical doubt has made it possible to assert the subjective and contingent character of certain dimensions of experience, the necessity and universality of which appeared formerly guaranteed by God or human nature.

One such dimension is our contact with material reality. There is no such a thing as pure, anonymous sensation. Even our apprehension of the elements is already charged with unformulated meaning and values. Gaston Bachelard, inaugurating a "psychoanalysis of matter," has studied elemental images in various writers. Influenced by these works, Jean-Pierre Richard, in *Littérature et sensation,* asserts his conviction that, at no level of experience, is there such a thing as objective perception. He shows how irreducibly personal is the poetical metamorphosis of every-day language.

A second dimension is time. In order to understand the very possibility of critical studies such as Georges Poulet's *Études sur le temps humain,* one must realize how far-reaching is the new conception of personality. Human time has little to do with the time of clocks, modeled after space and divisible in equal parts; it is an essential aspect of a strictly individual experience or, in Sartrean terms, of the individual *projet.* Georges Poulet infers from the text itself, which he always quotes abundantly, a fundamental attitude toward time which commands the genesis of the work of art. Here again, the critic is interested in a creative process which he attempts to retrace from "farther back" than was previously thought possible. New fields of investigation are open to the critic.

Another explorer of uncharted areas is Maurice Blanchot. A novelist and a brilliant critic of Sade, Lautréamont, and other writers, he has turned, in his monthly *chronique* for the *Nouvelle Revue Française,* toward the artistic project itself—unique project in so far as it is not directed toward the outside world but toward the subject and his experience. Writing is the experience of experience and, as such, it makes the renewal of the original experience impossible.

One recognizes, at this point, something akin to the autopsychoanalytical virtues which Sartre confers upon artistic expression at its greatest. But the consequences are not even remotely similar. For Sartre, the discarded project must give way to real ethical life and a new *engagement*. For Blanchot no new worldly project is possible. His, however, is not the casual nihilism of some of the young critics. What he discerns, behind the crumbling structures of our world, is a barren and desolate landscape where all human purposes and desires become meaningless, where silence, that silence which is the ultimate significance in the novels of a Kafka, is the only thing left to express. The fundamental structures of aesthetic experience as Blanchot sees them recall certain accounts of mystical experience, but the critic never lapses into theology or messianic romanticism.

With these writers the approach to the work of art is so original, the future is still so rich with promise that any attempt to cling to doctrinal labels seems futile. But the very terms in which Albert Béguin anticipates, in *Esprit* (March 1955), a new critical revolution suggest that existentialism and phenomenology gave the impulsion which makes new developments possible:

> It may be that at last, with the end of the period when the work was translated into a doctrine, with the end of any illusions about the historical view as about all psychological and sociological imperialism, it may be that today the moment has come to approach the literary work in its essential particularity. And this fact is of no slight importance, if it be true that in this fashion, at the origin of every literary transfiguration, we are in a position to discover a movement proceeding from the person, in its whole irreducible thusness—in what constitutes it, first of all, in the depths of its solitude, before there can be effected its opening out onto the world of others and onto the treasures of the community.

Literature and Poetry

by Guido Morpurgo-Tagliabue

. . . Sartre has very often turned his attention to problems of art, but always haphazardly and in different ways, spurred on by diverse interests. This is why it is difficult to delimit an aesthetic doctrine peculiar to him; on the other hand, it is not difficult to indicate the continuity of some of his general ideas.[1]

He begins with a simple and elementary distinction that comes to him from Mallarmé, I believe, but to which many theorists from Croce to the New Critics might adhere. He distinguishes a *literary* language and a *poetic* language, which to simplify matters he calls respectively *prose* and *poetry*. (Mallarmé called them *reportage* and *musique*.) The first is a semantic language—it gives the meaning of things, it is an instrument of the intellect, composed of significant symbols. The second is, one might say, asemantic: it "presents" things, it does not represent them; it unveils, as do painting and music, the *sense* of things; their immediate totality, both affective and emotive. (We can think of similar ideas already noted in Valéry, but also in I. A. Richards, Charles Morris, and Susanne K. Langer.) The first idea is linked to the conscious will, to the author's responsibility and morality; the second, to his unconscious and surreal world, to a dimension of his inner life that only metaphor and analogy can convey. The first has something to do with reality and the second with imagination. The pages of "Qu'est-ce que la littérature?" (1947), now collected in *Situations II*, and all those in general on *art engagé* form a copious documentation of the first concept. We find evidence of the second in the preface to Leibowitz's *L'Artiste et la conscience* (Paris: L'Arche, 1950) and in the study on Jean Genet (1952), and finally in certain pages of *Situations I* and *II*. This means, in short, a literature that is inclined toward "eloquence," and a poetry that tends toward "suggestion." Sartre could not be more French: a modern Frenchman,

"Literature and Poetry." From *L'Esthétique contemporaine: Une enquête*, by Guido Morpurgo-Tagliabue, translated by Sterling Haig. Copyright © 1960 by Marzorati-Editeur-Milan. Reprinted by permission of Marzorati-Editeur-Milan. The pages reprinted here are part of the chapter "L'Existentialisme et l'esthétique."

[1] For Sartre's aesthetic views up to 1950, see C. Rau, "Jean-Paul Sartre's Aesthetic," *Journal of Aesthetics and Art Criticism*, IX, No. 2, 1950. For Sartre as an artist, see C. Falconi, *J.-P. Sartre*, 1949; E. Paci, *Ancora sull'esistenzialismo* (Turin, 1956).

feeling fully the romantic impact that during the past century has become a poetic attitude, yet not renouncing his classical tradition which is both intellectual and rhetorical.

It is this last aspect that is most widely known. His apologetics for an *art engagé* is precisely in the classical tradition, that of art as a vehicle for moral principles, in accord with Horace's didactic and pedagogical conceptions. In Sartre's work, this ancient principle becomes the following thesis: literature unveils to readers their own situation in order that they themselves may assume its responsibility.[2] It is a social function in opposition to the other widespread ideal: of art for art's sake.[3] The best known text on this subject in his long essay entitled "Qu'est-ce que la littérature?"

Literature is action, practice: it unveils a situation in order to modify it. Croce would have quite accepted this definition, for from the beginning he placed literature in the genre of oratorical art or historiography, which in his opinion too is always a cognitive operation with an action in view. In his last years, Croce returned to this idea (*La Poésie*, 1936), to confirm it while lessening its rigidity. In turn, Sartre himself tends to attenuate the practical character of "literature" by defending its stylistic preoccupations[4] (which a surrealist would not have done). But at the same time he rejects the hybrid nature of "poetic prose"[5]—that is, he maintains the primacy of the practical in art where literature is concerned.

It is significant that Sartre, nurtured by so much surrealist experience, adopts a thoroughly relentless position against surrealism. Between surrealism and existentialism there is a relationship of continuity and opposition. It has been said that "existentialism was born from a critique of surrealism, from a meditation on its lack of success, from a reflection on its ambiguity."[6] But this supposes a common ideal. Sartre now blames surrealism for the means and methods that made it fail—in short, for its lack of moral seriousness. What authors does he value? Prévost, Bost, Champion, Aveline. By their "man's job" [*métier d'hommes*], by their

---

[2] See *Présentation des Temps modernes*, 1945, now in *Situations II*, 1948; also "Qu'est-ce que la littérature?" *ibid.*, Chap. I; cf. Chap. IV: "for us, to show the world is always to unveil it in the perspective of a possible change, . . . to reveal to the reader, in each concrete case, his power to make and unmake, in short, to act" (p. 311).

[3] On the theory of "art for art's sake," see A. Cassagne, *La Liberté de l'art pour l'art chez les derniers romantiques et les premiers réalistes* (Paris, 1906); R. Frances Egan, *The Genesis of the Theory of Art for Art's Sake in Germany and England*, Smith College Studies in Modern Languages, II, No. 4, 1921; G. Delfel, *L'Esthétique de Mallarmé.* (Paris: Flammarion, 1951); J. Wilcox, "L'Art pour l'art en France," *Revue d'Esthétique*, No. 1, 1953; M. Petrucciani, *L'estetica dell'Ermetismo* (Turin: Loescher, 1955).

[4] "Qu'est-ce que la littérature?" *Situations II*, Chap. I.

[5] *Ibid.*, p. 76.

[6] F. Alquié, "Humanisme, surréalisme, existentialisme," in *L'Homme, le monde, l'histoire* (Paris: Arthaud, 1948), p. 156.

remaining aloof from myths, by their "discreet humanism," and above all by their devotion to the public, they anticipate existentialism. For literature is "reading"; it amounts to a relationship between the writer and his public. On one hand, Sartre develops a magnificent phenomenology of this relationship from the Middle Ages to the twentieth century[7] and on the other he draws from that phenomenology a rule which is the literary version of his transcendental law of freedom. Literature is an appeal to the reader's freedom.[8] As in Kant, that law of freedom constitutes the final principle of history. It is only a question of making it explicit and conscious (as Kant did for moral freedom by means of legal freedom), of recognizing literature "as the permanent exercise of generosity," and—in the last analysis—as man's duty. Here Sartre reiterates a paralogism concerning literature that Kant used concerning the moral imperative. For literature cannot exist as "reading" without the reader's free collaboration, and the function of literary art must be to defend and encourage that freedom: the means become an end. In Kant, to be frank, all this is at once more radical and more coherent. Since morality is constituted by a formal will that has no other purpose outside itself, the defense of formal will itself—as an end for men—must become the content of that will. Thus, for Sartre, literature is a "freedom that has taken freedom as its end":[9] the *condition* of literature becomes its own *purpose*. And more than once he refers to Kant and his realm of ends.[10] This proves the moral dignity that Sartre attributes to literary art: its function is to clear up ambiguity, to point out bad faith, to arouse responsibility. On the other hand, even if it is strangely significant and weighs considerably on the recent politics of culture, the mission that he ascribes to literature in the present situation is less convincing. It draws its strength from the paralogism we have spoken of, and is its application. Since literary art is based on the reader's free collaboration, it must aim at the extension of that freedom: the man of letters must free himself from his dependence on élites, which are always engaged in a conservative way on the political level, and aim at reaching a larger public, at creating an art for the masses, and thus declare himself politically against any privilege. "Privilege" means restriction of the public, and consequently a shrinking of that sphere of freedom to which he appeals as a writer and which nourishes his art. In short, an enlarged public is equivalent to the creation of freedom. And it is known that this

---

[7] *Op. cit.,* Chap. III, "Pour qui écrit-on?"

[8] *Ibid.,* p. 154.

[9] *Op. cit.,* p. 110. See all of Chap. II, "Pourquoi écrire?" Such a paralogism is rather frequent. See also L. Tolstoy: art is the communication of feelings, therefore a brotherly activity: it must have fraternity as its object (that is, religious sentiments, that which survives in our time from Christianity). Or at least it must express universal feelings. The content is drawn from the form. See "Qu'est-ce que l'art?," Chaps. IV, XV, XVIII, and the conclusion.

[10] *Op. cit.,* pp. 110, 293.

concept does not remain theoretical or utopian for Sartre. He tries to realize it, as a matter of fact, in ways that are far from utopian. Indeed, on the basis of these presuppositions Sartre has tried, with his magazine *Les Temps modernes,* to make a group of lettered men the independent intermediary between an élite of technicians, the political party of the masses (the Communist Party), and a public chosen from the middle class which in turn was to serve as an intermediary for more numerous categories of the people. But it is clear that the freedom in question is not the reader's formal will, the free collaboration with the author, but *a certain* freedom with a specific content. The reasoning therefore seems to be a sophism.

In summarizing, we may state this as certain. The concept of "literature" corresponds to a morality of *generosity,* of sociality, of the recognition and promotion of freedom in other people's freedom: in short, a continuation and a confirmation of the principles of 1789.

The other conception of art as poetry is less evident and incisive, more problematic, but also more fertile in singular and disconcerting developments. It too is linked to a tradition, that of symbolism. Poetry is an entirely imaginary activity, gratuitous, beyond good and evil. Art is the *imaginative,* and the imaginative is a negation; it is the annihilation of the real. At first it appears to be the repetition of a concept or, as it seems to us, of an idealistic error: the ideal as opposed to the real, but transposed to a different level from the gnosiological level—to a level of existential psychology,[11] where it permits absolutely unforeseen results. Let us add that this form of pure art, though opposed to engaged literature, is itself not unknown to moral engagement. But is a morality in the imaginary world, outside the real, possible? This gives rise to complications. It must be a question of another form of morality—not social, but anarchistic, interhuman and yet individualistic—that Sartre frankly likens to martyrdom and saintliness. Until now he has written in the most paradoxical and disorderly manner on this subject, but one has the impression that he has not yet had his last say. What is totally lacking in Sartre's work is a dialectic between the two forms of art and morality. This is why the two concepts of literature and poetry are very often confounded, and the confusion is also promoted by the summary and convenient identification between literature and prose. (One is constantly faced with this problem in the essays we have quoted.)

If the value of the concept of *literature* is that it is linked, in the most recent writings, with the ideas of freedom, engagement, and responsibility, the concept of *poetry* as he deals with it orients us toward a different world—toward the world of the unconscious that psychoanalysis has tried to penetrate through the study of dreams, and that

---

[11] Sartre's thought is reduced to an "unavowed psychologism" by R. Cantoni in *Studi Filosofici,* No. 2, 1948. Cf. also E. Pesch, *L'Existentialisme* (Paris, 1946); G. Vaccari, *Filosofia dell'immaginario ed esistenzialismo* (Pavia, 1952).

surrealism believed to have been grasped through "automatic writing," a state of indifference between dreaming and waking. Sartre now indicates—but only indicates!—that he wants to penetrate this domain by means of an analysis of the characteristics, tendencies, idiosyncrasies, affinities, and repulsions of the individual in respect to things. This is what he calls "existential psychoanalysis." [12] Sympathy and repulsion reveal an individual's original attitude, his existential choice, what one would commonly call his "personality." Moreover, they bring to light an entirety of imaginative relationships which are the source of an artist's analogies, metaphors, vocabulary, and figurative choices. [13]

Poetry leads us on this road to another problem, that of the "myth" or the "mystification" of the modern artist. This is a question we have already met and in which the crisis of romantic and modern art reaches its apogee.

For Sartre, art, in the sense of poetry, means imagination: the world of the unreal, of the non-being. Sartre started his career as a philosopher in 1936 with the problem of the imagination. He took up this problem again in 1940 with a phenomenology of the imaginative world, and finally brought it to the aesthetic and moral level in 1952. [14] The imagination is defined phenomenologically by Sartre as the intentionality of an "unrealizing consciousness" [*conscience irréalisante*], completely different from memory, which is the consciousness of an existing (in the past) reality. Bergson's *memory* has thus been dethroned by Sartre's *imagination:* one was the authentic recovery of the real, the other is the "nihilation of the world in its essential structure." In principle, however, it is not a question of the poetic decomposition of the universe that Baudelaire wished for, nor of the nihilation of the concrete—that erosion of things that we owe to Mallarmé and thanks to which one should recognize the absolute as a void, as a lack, as a nothingness. Sartre's "imaginative" is something simpler, more basic: it is a gnosiological dimension, not the surrealists' automatism. It is a free act that posits

[12] Cf. *L'Être et le néant*, pp. 643-62; "Qu'est-ce que la littérature?"

[13] The inspiration for this idea of Sartre's was probably drawn from Bachelard's original works, which attempted to find the frame of reference for a poet's inspiration in his images, metaphors, and linguistic choices: the active dynamism of a Ducasse, Kafka's temporal regression and involution, Lautréamont's zoömorphic aggressiveness, the rapidity, the dissolution of Shelley, and so on; also for other poets such as Baudelaire, Mallarmé, Valéry, Rilke. See G. Bachelard, *La Psychanalyse du feu* (Paris, 1932); *L'Air et les songes* (1934); *Lautréamont* (1939); *L'Eau et les rêves* (1942); *La Dialectique de la durée* (1950); *La Poétique de l'espace* (1957). On Bachelard, see G. Dorfles, "Bachelard o l'immaginazione creatrice," *Aut-Aut*, No. 9, 1952; S. Breton, "Symbolisme et imagination de la matière," *Filosofia e simbolismo* (Rome: Archivio di Filosofia, 1956); J. Hyppolite, "G. Bachelard ou le romantisme de l'intelligence," *Revue philosophique de la France et de l'Étranger*, 1957; P. M. Schuhl, in *Revue philosophique*, No. 2, 1958.

[14] Jean-Paul Sartre, *L'Imagination* (Paris: 1936); *Esquisse d'une théorie des émotions* (Paris, 1939); *L'Imaginaire* (Paris, 1940); *Saint-Genêt, Comédien et martyr* (Paris, 1952).

beauty. The beautiful is always a suspension of the real, a disinterested contemplation of non-being, therefore an abstraction of existence. But non-being is evil and the aesthete is always evil. Here that moral indifference of art, that Sartre still stressed in *L'Imaginaire* and "Qu'est-ce que la littérature?" has been surpassed. Sartre arrives at these last conclusions by delving more deeply into and elaborating the phenomenology of the imagination in his commentary on Genet's life and works. The imaginative, the beautiful, is an "ought-to-be" [*devoir-être*] that does not take its place within being as the good does, but withdraws from it.

At first glance it might be surprising that beauty should be defined as evil,[15] but only to someone unfamiliar with decadent poetry, which has long since made this a commonplace from Baudelaire to Swinburne. Sartre has made this definition more profound by giving it a metaphysical foundation upon which he has based inexhaustible psychological analyses. The imaginative is evil because it is unreal, because it is only an appearance. Beauty is precisely this refusal of reality, to the extent that being is a form. For the moment let us pass over the hyperbolical psychology that makes this act a conscious destruction, and, as is the case for all perversion, a voluntary failure and consequently an abnegation, a sacrifice, a religious act by which the criminal can transform himself into a martyr and finally, into a saint.[16] The important thing is that if *literature* is the will to intervene in the real, and *poetry* the will to escape from it, neither of the two is contemplation: disinterestedness is also an interest, a value.

Paradoxically, it is even the only value. Values have two directions: the good and the beautiful. A value is *good* when it ends in reality; it is *beautiful* when it finds satisfaction in itself. A form that is isolated within itself is the traditional definition of beauty (it is no coincidence that for a century and a half theorists have been repeating the Kantian formula of taste):[17] this beautiful, as an unreality opposed to reality, is the opposite of good. This is why one cannot conceive of the artist's being *on this side* of good and evil (Croce). *On this side* is still evil. But one must add that there is not even a choice between two values, for evil is the *only value*. The good being the very structure of the real, it is a habit, a renunciation of liberty, a self-destructive virtue, a non-value—whether one interprets it as God or as a "social machine." "In doing good, I lose myself in Being. . . . And so in the good that attracts

---

[15] *Saint-Genêt*, p. 344. It is the contrary of Platonic beautiful-good or Kantian beautiful-sublime relationships, which have become traditional and meaningless: C. Levêque, ". . . it betters us to pour into our souls the delicious emotion of the beautiful," *La Science du beau*, Vol. 4, 1861, p. 14.

[16] *Ibid.*, pp. 155-225. The processes of this psychology are developed by contradictions, ambiguities, and necessary sophisms, as abstruse and twisting as Jaspers' are simple and banal. Sartre, without bias, calls them *tourniquets, farce-attrapes*, etc.

[17] Already in Aquinas: "pulchrum autem dicatur id cuius ipsa apprehensio placet," *Summa Theologica*, I^a, II^{ae}, q. 27, a. I, ad. 3^m.

me, there is an element which turns me from it: that is, it already is.
. . . And in the evil that horrifies me, there is an element that attracts
me, that is, it comes from myself. . . ." [18] But how can one wish for
evil? Whatever one wishes, one wishes for the positive, since the real is
completely positive. One has only to place oneself outside the real, in
appearance. "Evil is also simply called the imaginative." [19] We see the
importance of the equation: beautiful = evil = freedom.

From this we can arrive at least at a provisional conclusion. If the
"man of letters" enters into the fullness of the concrete, of the real—
and this can only be freedom (by non-contradiction, as we have seen)—
the "poet" on the other hand starts from an outside position (we do not
know yet if he will stay there). He starts from a state of de-realizing consciousness, of formal negation, of a refusal of the real and consequently
of society, in short from an abstract individualistic world that constitutes
the imaginative, the beautiful, and evil. To oversimplify: literature is
to social ethics what poetry is to individual ethics.

[18] (*Op. cit.*, pp. 152-53). This is even the sense of Goetz' choices in *Le Diable et le
bon Dieu*. He chooses evil because the good is "already done," it is in the order of
being. He wants freedom. When the priest, Heinrich, shows him that evil too is
God's order, then he chooses good. But this gratuitous good turns out to be *non en
situation*, an unrealizable, imaginary act, that is to say, evil. It is only when he is
enlightened by that experience that Goetz will truly be able to "choose," not as a
rebellious sinner or as a saint, but as a man; and man can only wish for a possible
order by destroying the established order, in this case by making war. All of Sartre's
dramas are apologues.
[19] *Ibid.*, p. 154.

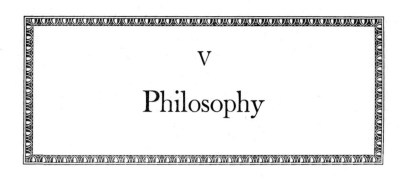

V

Philosophy

The New Empiricism

by John D. Wild

The existentialist philosophers accept the radical empiricism of Kierkegaard. They are not interested in artificial problems, nor in theoretical constructions. They are interested rather in the concrete data of immediate experience, and in describing these data so far as possible exactly as they are given. This is the phenomenological method. They have applied this method to many regions not previously explored, but especially to the pervasive data of existence, awareness, and human value which lie at the root of the disciplines of metaphysics, epistemology, and ethics. In all these fields, their descriptions have revealed certain facts which are quite at variance with major trends of modern thought and contemporary analytic philosophy.

Gabriel Marcel, for example, in his interesting intellectual biography, tells us how he found many of the problems of modern philosophy to be "of merely academic interest." [1] Among these last was "the problem of the reality of the outward world as it is stated in philosophical textbooks. None of the extremist forms of idealism which deny this reality ever seemed to me convincing: for to what more certain or more intimate

[1] *The Philosophy of Existence* (New York: Philosophical Library, 1949), p. 87.

experience could this reality be opposed?" [2] This is a characteristic comment. Before he read Kierkegaard, he said that "Hegelianism inspired me with a profound mistrust." [3] Reality as we live it cannot be squeezed within the framework of an *a priori* system. "It seemed to me," writes Marcel, "that there was a danger of making an illicit use of the idea of integration, and that the more one relied on the richest and most concrete data of experience, the less this idea appeared to be applicable to reality." [4]

There is no real reason why phenomenology should be restricted to human existence. Other modes of being can also be described and analyzed. Nevertheless, Kierkegaard held that he had reliable access only to his own existence. Hence he is primarily concerned with the task of describing moral choice as he finds it in himself, and the different ways of life to which it leads. [5] This attitude also has been taken over by his modern followers.

Jaspers and Marcel have been more interested in describing the perspectives and the acts of the individual person. Heidegger and Sartre, on the other hand, have gone a step further. They attempt to describe the existential structure of human experience as such, and thus to arrive at a general descriptive anthropology.

Human existence is maintained under certain conditions which are the same for all men everywhere. A primary aim of existentialist philosophy is to describe these constant conditions as they are found to be, and then the two ways, authentic and unauthentic, in which these conditions may be understood and faced by living men in the concrete. Thus Heidegger in the early pages of *Sein und Zeit*[6] has presented a phenomenological description of that being-in-the-world which belongs to all human existence.

He has recognized the vast richness of the world of immediate experience, and the presence of many pervasive structures to which modern "empiricism" has been oblivious. These phenomena lie beyond the range of the restricted sciences. The existentialists have at last embarked on the arduous task of describing them accurately as they are given.[7]

*　　*　　*

The oversimplified phenomenology of pan-objectivism reduces everything to an object, and that of pan-subjectivism reduces everything to a subject or some subjective state. It is clear from the account we have just given that such oversimplifications of the original data are rejected by the new empiricism. From this point of view it is pan-objectivism which is guilty of the worst error, for it ignores or reduces the existing subject,

[2] *Loc. cit.*　　　　　　　　　　　[3] *Ibid.*, p. 78.
[4] *Ibid.*, p. 94.　　　　　　　　　　[5] Cf. *ibid.*, ch. 4.
[6] Heidegger, *Sein und Zeit* (Halle: Niemeyer, 1931), pp. 52-89.
[7] *Ibid.*, pp. 27-39.

which surely lies at the very center of human experience. The existentialist literature is filled with attacks on this view, many of which are more detailed and exhaustive than that of Kierkegaard.

Jaspers, for example, in the first volume of his *Philosophie* [8] points out that pan-objectivism is an essential phase of positivism. He subjects it to a cogent criticism which brings out the internal inconsistencies resulting from its wanton reduction of empirical evidence. All the existentialists accept Kierkegaard's bitter attack on idealism, which flouts the empirical evidence by failing to distinguish between being and mental being,[9] by thinking of the free individual as absorbed in an organic whole,[10] and by ignoring time and history as they are given.[11]

The new empiricism has made an equally radical break with the Cartesian subjectivism which has so long dominated our conception of the immediate data of experience. According to this view, the mind is conceived as a passive container of subjective impressions which are immediately known, simply by being contained. External persons and things are known only through indirect inferences from these privileged internal data. This has led Lord Russell and others to speak of a private world of psychic impressions and a public world of physical things. This dualism is a figment of the logical mind, wholly unsupported by a careful study of the actual data. It is completely abandoned by the new empiricism.

I find myself not in two worlds, but in one. This ultimate horizon is not just spatial, but spatio-temporal in character. External events, internal feelings and acts, the theoretical objects of science, so far as these are verified, are all in one moving world horizon. I can think of myself alone. But this is a sheer abstraction. Being-in-the-world belongs to my very existence. No world, no subjective existence. Heidegger, Sartre, and Jaspers would all accept this formula.[12] Internal data have no special epistemological privilege. It is absurd to suppose that the carpenter knows his own act of hammering before he knows the instrument and the object he is hammering. He himself, his acts, his instruments, and their external objects are all known together as existing within the ultimate horizon.

Nor do I have to infer the existence of other "minds" from any more certain data. Being-with-others belongs to my own existence. I cannot be aware of the latter without being aware of the former. To feel alone is a privative mode of feeling-with, which is the more primitive phenomenon. Awareness is not being in a mind container; it is being towards something—a relation. Hence there is no reason why I cannot be directly aware of an external thing or an external person. As a matter of fact,

[8] Jaspers, *Philosophie* (Berlin: Springer, 1932), vol. 1, pp. 213-214.
[9] *Ibid.,* pp. 222-223.
[10] Marcel, *Metaphysical Journal* (Chicago: Regnery, 1952), pp. 9-12.
[11] Jaspers, *op. cit.,* pp. 229-230.
[12] Heidegger, *op. cit.,* p. 88; Sartre, *L'Être et le néant,* p. 149; Jaspers, *op. cit.,* p. 62.

I am. I am also immediately aware of my own body, a fact denied by the subjectivist. Hence Russell's fantastic assertion that he has to infer the existence of his own body. The new empiricism must reject this radically anti-empirical view, as Gabriel Marcel has shown with great clarity in his illuminating studies of the mind-body problem in the first volume of *The Mystery of Being*.[13] The body may not be physically contained in a mind thing. But nothing really is. Hence we may follow the evidence which indicates that, as against the Cartesians, I am not a mind thing cut off from my body, but that rather I am my body, and know it directly and immediately.

All awareness is intentional or relational, from a subjective pole to an object of some sort. My immediate experience always falls into a bipolar structure. Its center lies within my physical body. Around it lie various spatio-temporal fields which are terminated and replaced by others until the ultimate world horizon. The equilibrium between subject and object is very unstable and constantly ready to pass into a consistent pan-objective positivism or a pan-subjective idealism. Jaspers has given a brilliant exposition of this instability.[14] The subject is somehow a different thing from the object. He has inherited this substantive view of mind from Kant. And yet the subject leads us to the object and is somehow identified with it. So we try to identify one with the other, subjectivizing the object, and objectifying the subject. But this brings us to insuperable difficulties.[15] According to Jaspers, no stable solution is possible. "Only the passage from subjective to objective and *vice versa* is true." "Nur das Drängen vom Subjectiven zum Objectiven und umgekehrt ist wahr." *Philosophie*, Vol. 2, p. 342.

Heidegger and Sartre have broken more radically with the presuppositions of past empiricism. They cannot rest with such a confused dialectical tension. They have more clearly grasped the peculiar intentional structure of human awareness. Thus, according to Heidegger, we should not think of the mind as a thing that is simply there.[16] It has a peculiar relational structure of its own, being always of something real that it understands in the light of being, which is somehow present to it. For Sartre, all awareness is a pure relation of identity. He even goes so far as to say that it is relation as such.[17] The *pour soi* is the thing in itself (*en soi*) which it knows. The one cannot be reduced to the other. The world of experience is bipolarized. These two poles cannot be confused without distortion of the data.

The more advanced existentialist thought has also rejected the Kantian notion of the appearance or phenomenon as another entity separated from the thing as it really is, as an effect is separated from its cause. No existentialist defends this purely causal theory of awareness. The thing

---

[13] Marcel, *The Mystery of Being* (Chicago: Regnery, 1950), vol. 1, pp. 92ff.
[14] *Philosophie*, vol. 2, ch. 10.   [15] *Ibid.*, pp. 336ff.
[16] *Sein und Zeit*, p. 159.   [17] *L'Être et le néant*, p. 429.

does not produce its appearance in something else which also helps to cause it. It is the thing itself which appears. The mind does not *make* its objects. It apprehends them by a relational act. If my act created the appearance or helped to produce it, it would at least in part belong to me. I should say that part of the appearance is *my* appearing, as part of a joint book is *my* writing. But we make no such claim with reference to an appearance. It is not I who am appearing, but the thing. I may make it possible for something to appear, but the precise determination of that which appears is not due to me. As we say, it is the thing which appears.

Thus someone might provide the funds for my book to appear. But in this case he would not claim that the book was his. In the same way it is the thing itself which appears, not my sense organs or brain or any part of me. Hence while some aspects of Sartre's analysis are less sound, he is surely right in maintaining that it is reality itself which appears, though not the thing in its entirety. This last unfortunately is a mistake.[18] But reality does exist apart from my knowing it, and may be described as it is. Phenomenalism is a misreading of the original data. Existence is given. Hence a phenomenological ontology is possible.[19]

*   *   *

The revival of philosophy in Europe is largely due to such a reawakening of phenomenological interest. The existentialist philosophers are once more turning to the data. They have shown beyond all doubt that these data, as given, are not restricted to a small number of clear and distinct atomic *qualia*. They are rich in variety, manifold in order, and jumbled together in vast confusions. As Gabriel Marcel remarks: "What is given to me beyond all possible doubt is the confused and global experience of the world inasmuch as it is existent."[20] No man has ever sensed a red patch. He grasps this by sense and reason together, each apprehending the object in its own proper way. What is given to both in the first place is a blurred confusion. "What is given us to start with is a sort of unnamed and unnamable confusion where abstractions not yet elaborated are like so many little unseparated clots of matter."[21]

Clarity does not come all at once in an instant. It requires patient brooding and analysis. "It is only by going through and beyond the process of scientific abstraction that the concrete can be regrasped and reconquered."[22] All the important existentialist philosophers would agree with this recognition of vagueness and confusion as ever-present factors

[18] Cf. *ibid.*, pp. 12-13.
[19] "In the first place let us remind ourselves that today there can be no philosophy worth considering that will not involve an analysis of a phenomenological type bearing on the fundamental situation of man." (G. Marcel, *Man Against Mass Society* [Chicago: Regnery, 1952], p. 90.) Cf. *ibid.*, p. 12.
[20] *Metaphysical Journal*, p. 322.
[21] *Man Against Mass Society*, p. 119.
[22] *Loc. cit.*

in experience. Reason is an apprehensive power. As such, it is able to make guesses and inferences on the basis of what it already knows. But its primary function is to clarify the original data of experience, which are certain but very confused. This task can be achieved only by phenomenological description and analysis. The existentialist thinkers have already made many important contributions to this essential phase of the philosophical enterprise.

Existentialism as a Philosophy

by John D. Wild

Of all the existentialist thinkers, Sartre has gone the furthest in try-ing to clarify his basic ontological principles, and to relate them together in a coherent manner. In trying to perform this difficult task, he has sometimes made dubious assumptions of his own. But his thought is existentialist in the sense that he accepts the central ideas we have been tracing. Furthermore, he is thoroughly familiar with the work of Heideg-ger, the most disciplined of all the existentialist writers and the sharpest observer of empirical evidence. His attempt to clarify the basic concepts presupposed by this body of fact and doctrine, and to fit them together into a systematic structure is, therefore, of great interest. Strong points as well as basic weaknesses are bound to be revealed in a much brighter light. What sort of total view of being and man is implied by the central core of existentialism? Sartre has devoted his energies to giving us pre-cisely such a total view.

Like other existentialists, Sartre is primarily interested in the concrete data of experience as they actually appear. Like them, he claims to follow a purely descriptive or phenomenological method. His major work bears the subtitle, *Essai d'ontologie phénoménologique,* an *Essay on Phenom-enological Ontology.* This descriptive method is common to all members of the school. But he has gone farther in trying to clarify what this description must involve, and what *phenomena* really are. We may charac-terize his explanation as an extreme reaction to idealism.

. . . Sartre is especially anxious to reject the Kantian conception of a thing in itself behind the phenomena, and separated from them by an impassable gulf. This is correct, for it is surely the thing which appears. But he goes too far when he asserts not only that the phenomena are real but that they exhaust *all* positive reality. The appearance is an aspect of reality, not all there is. It does not distort being. But neither does it comprehend this being in its totality. Other aspects are also there to be revealed in other ways. This identification of being with the succession

"Existentialism as a Philosophy." From *The Challenge of Existentialism* by John D. Wild. Copyright © 1955 by the Indiana University Press, Bloomington, Indiana. Reprinted by permission of the Indiana University Press. The pages reprinted here are parts of Chapter VI. (The footnotes have been renumbered.)

of its finished appearances has important consequences in the Sartrean ontology.

For one thing, it leads to the strange conception of the *en soi* [In-itself] as an absolute plenum with no potency, and indeed no real relations to anything beyond. In itself, the appearance is complete. It is supplemented only by other appearances, each of which is fixed and finished. The way is thus prepared for a view of being in itself (*en soi*) as a finished continuum fully in act, and lacking all power and potency. Heidegger suggests such a view by his conception of subhuman existence as a determinate being-on-hand (*Vorhandensein*), something finished and simply there, in violent contrast to the unfinished potentiality of *Dasein*. In Sartre, this contrast between a subhuman *en soi* that is fully in act, and a human *pour soi* [For-itself] that is a purely potential nothingness, is magnified to an exaggerated opposition that warps his whole ontology.

If being is a dense field without distinction, there is no place in it for determinate structure or finite difference. One thing cannot be distinguished from another. All such distinctions then have to be referred to the projects of the *pour soi* which literally makes its world. If this expanse of being is fully in act, it cannot be deprived of anything it requires. Hence negation and privation have no ground in reality. They, too, must be referred to the negativity of human existence. Sartre does not use his phenomenological method to test these basic principles. He simply assumes them without argument.[1] Had he tried to examine them in the light of the evidence, he could hardly have failed to see their empirical inadequacy. The cloud in the sky before me is not an airplane. Each finite structure has limits which are the ontological ground for negative judgments. Nor is the cloud fully in act. It can pass away, or turn into rain. These potencies are not nothing, but they are marked by an absence of realization. Without a recognition of them, the fact of physical change becomes unintelligible.

This denial of physical potency also leads him to follow Heidegger in adopting an even more subjective interpretation of the principle of sufficient reason. The *en soi* has no internal structure nor causal powers. Hence it cannot act nor be the *ground* of anything. Action seems to be restricted to man. In fact, the whole idea of a ground lacks any real basis beyond the processes of human freedom. Things cannot be otherwise than they are. But the *pour soi* is free. It always might choose otherwise. This is the meaning of the question *why*. But the only answer is to be found in an arbitrary choice of some kind, which has no intelligible grounds. Hence in the last analysis, everything, both the *en soi* which is simply there, and the *pour soi* with its caprices, is ungrounded.

Sartre recognizes this consequence, and emphasizes what he calls the radical contingency of our world, which lacks any reason for being. Every-

[1] For an illuminating discussion of Sartre's procedure, cf. Régis Jolivet, *Les Doctrines existentialistes* (Paris: Fontenelle, 1948), pp. 155-156, including note 20, and p. 165, n. 37.

thing is absurd. This he states as a truth that really holds of all being.[2] At this point, he recognizes the principle of sufficient reason as something more than a peculiar habit of the *pour soi*. Things really need a ground, but such grounds are absent. This is inconsistent with subjectivism. On the other hand, if sufficient reason is not really required, to assert that the universe is absurd is quite meaningless. Sartre's views here are either inconsistent or unintelligible.

His account of the constitutive structure of human existence is full of interesting and often penetrating psychological observations, though the question is legitimately raised as to whether these observations have anything more than a limited personal significance. His analysis follows Heidegger very closely, but differs from it in one fundamental respect. Sartre complains that his predecessor has restricted himself too much to the level of pure description, and has failed to give an intelligible ontological explanation of these phenomena.[3] This objection is certainly striking, coming as it does from a thinker who also asserts that everything is ultimately absurd and inexplicable. Nevertheless, it does express a weakness in Heidegger's anthropology, which is admittedly only a descriptive fragment rather than a full-fledged theory of being. Sartre's attempt to complete this theory is important not only as an exercise in basic ontology, but also as revealing certain further weaknesses in the structure of existentialist thought.

We have already noted the characteristic tendency to minimize theoretical reflection and the determinate structure (essence) which is its object. In Sartre, this baldly emerges in the statement that man has no common nature or essence. He makes himself into what he is by the projects which he chooses. Heidegger is somewhat vague on this issue, but the drift of his thought is in the same direction. Sartre states it in such a way that the error becomes quite clear.[4] It is so clear, in fact, that Sartre himself is forced to correct it at certain points where he refers to common "conditions" which always apply to human life.[5] Man, for example, is condemned to freedom. Whether he likes it or not, he must choose. He also desires to be *en soi*. Such statements certainly imply the presence of that common structure which has previously been called *essence* or *nature*. Existence is never found without such structure. To slur over its presence in man is to commit a serious error.

Heidegger gives no ontological explanation of the basic cognitive act to which he refers descriptively as *disclosing*. He gives us no careful analysis of this intentional outstretching of the mind towards its object. On the other hand, as we have seen, he devotes many pages to the temporal ecstasies, or ways in which our *practical* activities are stretched

---

[2] *L'Être et le néant*, pp. 34, 124.   [3] *Ibid.*, pp. 53ff.
[4] *Ibid.*, p. 655; cf. *Existentialism* (New York: Philosophical Library, 1947), p. 18.
[5] *Existentialism*, pp. 45ff.

out into the future and the past. He finally seems to conclude that the former is reducible to the latter, and that all cognition is, therefore, subjectively centered and practical. Sartre follows this in the main. But there are certain points at which he makes significant departures.

First of all, he insists that cognitive disclosure must be carefully analyzed and explained, and devotes many pages to this topic. The cognitive act of disclosing is itself ecstatic, stretched out towards something other that transcends it. His explanation in terms of the *pour soi* as *nothing* is indefensible if taken literally. But, as we have seen, if taken as a capacity first empty but then reaching objective fulfilment, it is suggestive and probably sound.[6]

In the second place, while he follows Heidegger's illuminating account of the ecstasies of time,[7] he never tries to explain cognition in terms of these. Both modes of stretching are characteristic of the *pour soi*, but they are clearly distinguished.[8] This is an important modification which shows at least some recognition of the independence of theory from practice. The fact that cognition is dealt with first of all, as necessarily involved in the whole phenomenological method, would seem to suggest a certain priority of the theoretical over the practical, though this is more dubious.

In his analysis of action, Sartre follows Heidegger quite closely. I *am* the past that I have been, and I am always projected ahead of myself in the future. The ecstasies cannot be separated. They constitute an integrated order of transformation. The future is ever becoming the future perfect; this is becoming present; and the present is turning into the past. Human care always follows this pattern, and cannot be divided into an authentic and an unauthentic mode of temporalization. Human action is not a mode of being at all, but rather a mode of negativity. It is a totality always pursuing itself, but never achieving unity.[9] Instead of being filled with final choice, the moment is always refused. Choice itself is viewed as a flight from the present into the future. No sooner is any aim realized, than it must be rejected to preserve the fluid negativity of the *pour soi*, which can never rest. This doctrine of personal nothingness is a basic departure from Heidegger and other existentialists, certainly for the worse both systematically and phenomenologically. Whatever he may be, the human self, with its knowledge and acts, is not literally annihilating nothingness.

Nevertheless, Sartre's analysis reveals three weaknesses of the existentialist theory of man in striking clarity. The first of these is the supposed arbitrariness of human choice, and the lack of any firm grounds. For Sartre, the whole effort to justify an act is a cowardly abandonment of freedom and responsibility, the turning of myself into a thing. Whether I decide to die for justice or drink at a bar, the matter is indifferent. As

---

[6] Cf. pp. 90-95.   [7] *L'Être et le néant*, pp. 150-218.
[8] *Ibid.*, pp. 201-218.   [9] *Ibid.*, pp. 185-196.

Heidegger also maintains, in either case I am necessarily and equally guilty. This may be an account of something we may call metaphysical guilt. But the phenomena of moral guilt and justification are never focused.

The second weakness is an almost exclusive emphasis on what we may call *subjective time*. It may be true that human existence temporalizes itself through an integral order of the ecstasies. But surely this is not the only time with which we are concerned. There is a flux of world-time also which is sweeping the stars, the planets, and my own life in a single irreversible direction. Sartre recognizes this more clearly than Heidegger. According to him, my past sinks back into this world-time, but not my present and future.[10] This answer is not satisfactory. Unless it is wholly fantastic, my projected future must take account of world-time, and my very act of projecting it must occur within this universal flux. We cannot follow Heidegger in dismissing it as an unauthentic expression of human time.

Finally, the third and most evident phenomenological weakness of the existentialist theory of man is its failure to account for human communication. According to Heidegger, my ordinary mode of being with others is impersonal, debased, and unauthentic. He briefly refers to the possibility of authentic communication between persons, but nowhere explains how this is possible or even reconcilable with his picture of the genuine person who has broken from his fellows to live alone with himself in a world of his own choice. The more authentic we become, the more isolated we seem to be. Jaspers has struggled with this problem, but his rejection of universal concepts and judgments makes an intelligible solution impossible. In Sartre, this weakness emerges with brutal clarity.[11] When two persons meet, each tries to absorb the other as an object into his world. Communication is thus restricted to conflict. Love, friendship, and devoted cooperation for common ends are excluded *a priori*. This must seem dubious to any careful empiricist.

Sartre has not yet written his book on man and human ethics.[12] But what men ought to do depends on what they are. My ethics will be determined by my view of human existence. This is clear to all the existentialist thinkers. The basic value is really to exist. Hence their anthropological descriptions are constantly passing over into moral suggestions and recommendations. This is also true of Sartre. Unless he changes his whole philosophy, the existentialist ethics he must defend is already clear in outline.

We may describe this as an ethics of pure freedom: man has no stable nature; he possesses no constant tendencies. There are no changeless norms to which he can look for the guidance of his conduct. To set up

---

[10] *Ibid.*, pp. 255-268.   [11] Cf. *ibid.*, pp. 477ff.
[12] *Ibid.*, pp. 720-722.

such norms is merely to rationalize choices that have already been made. Liberty itself is the only stable norm. To maintain this is always good. To stifle it, especially in myself, is always evil. What is this freedom? For Heidegger, with his positive view of human existence, it is a freedom *for* final commitment-unto-death. For Sartre, with his negative view, it is rather a freedom *from* any such commitment, save to the principle of having no final commitments at all.

Accordingly, the free man chooses his motives and reasons as the situation demands. But he never gives himself wholly to any of them. Retaining the negative mobility that he essentially is, he constantly places his past behind him, and steps into a creative future. No sooner does this appear on the scene than it too is rejected. Men cannot help but imagine stable states of realization in which they might stay satisfied with their mobility intact. But such a union of the *pour soi* with the *en soi* is impossible. Those only become maximally free who train themselves to dispense with such illusions. They therefore flow lightly (with no viscosity or hardening) over the surface of things and retain their negativity. On such an individualistic basis, there is no place for social ethics at all. Sartre has flirted with many political theories and movements, last of all Marxism. But the connection between existentialist thought and any definite political philosophy, as it is now presented to us, is wholly arbitrary and unstable.

Sartre does not care for the terms authentic and unauthentic. But the same notion appears in other language, and underlies all those moral suggestions and insinuations with which his works are filled. The free man lives out his existential nothingness, and becomes what he really is, i.e., what he is not. He is dynamic, fluid, and ever creative. The non-free person, on the other hand, is ceaselessly trying in bad faith to become something fixed and affirmative which he is not. Such people adopt fixed principles, and have a firm and serious sense of duty. They are the conformists who make up the masses. Above all they are the serious people who move slowly and heavily,[13] giving many reasons for the immediate policies to which they rigidly adhere, but falling into mythical Utopianism when questioned concerning the ultimate end.

Such bad faith takes two distinguishable forms—*les lâches,* the cowards who hide themselves behind their norms and reasons, and the *salauds* (an untranslatable term), who use them as weapons for aggressive self-assertion.[14] They never succeed in making themselves into solid things, for the restless negativity, which they are, turns every achievement into bitter ashes. They never remain satisfied. The most they can achieve is to become viscous and sticky, like a slimy stream, or a smile that, as we say, becomes frozen on the lips.[15]

---

[13] *Ibid.,* p. 669. [14] *Existentialism,* p. 55.
[15] Cf. *L'Être et le néant,* pp. 701-702.

This cannot be identified with the ethics of existentialism. Nevertheless, it singles out a dominant note of this ethics, the note of pure freedom, and thinks it through with a wealth of concrete illustration and a ruthless consistency. Sartre is profoundly sensitive to ontological problems, a master of dialectic, and a really great psychologist.

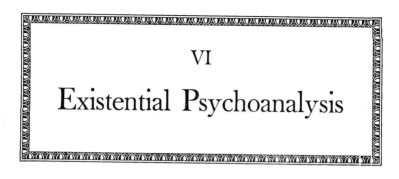

VI

Existential Psychoanalysis

Humanistic Existentialism and Contemporary Psychoanalysis

by Hazel E. Barnes

. . . Sartre has scrupulously indicated the relation between his ideas and those of psychologists to whom he is indebted or with whom he sharply disagrees. The list includes the early psychologists, of course (Freud, Adler, Janet), and many of the later ones (*e.g.,* Stekel, Lewin, Dembo, Piaget, Alain, and especially Bachelard). My purpose, however, is not to trace influences either upon or from Sartre, nor am I attempting a technical appraisal of his psychology as compared with that of his contemporaries. Rather I should like to show what is possibly a purely coincidental parallel between Sartre and certain psychologists now influential in America and to indicate briefly Sartre's relation to those continental psychologists who may be loosely grouped as phenomenological psychiatrists or existential psychologists. . . .

For significant parallels in fundamental outlook (along with important disagreements) we may consider the work of Erich Fromm and Karen Horney. As far as I have been able to discover, Sartre has never men-

tioned either Fromm or Horney. Fromm makes one interesting reference
to Sartre in a footnote in his *Man for Himself,* which was published
four years after *Being and Nothingness.*

> I have used this term *existential* without reference to the terminology of
> existentialism. During the revision of the manuscript I became acquainted
> with Jean-Paul Sartre's *Flies* and his *Existentialism Is a Humanism.* I do not
> feel that any changes or additions are warranted. Although there are certain
> points in common, I cannot judge the degree of agreement since I have had
> as yet no access to Sartre's main philosophical opus. (p. 41) [1]

In *The Sane Society* (1955) Fromm paralleled Sartrean terminology still
more closely; but if he had read more of Sartre's work in the meantime,
he has not seen fit to mention the fact. On the other hand, there is at
least one indication of possible influence in the other direction—or else
of use of a common source. Fromm and Sartre both choose to illustrate
a person's first awareness of individual self-consciousness by an example
taken from Richard Hughes' *A High Wind in Jamaica;* Fromm in *Escape
from Freedom* (1941)[2] and Sartre in *Baudelaire* (1947).[3] Aside from all
question of influence and dependence upon similar authorities, the comparison between Sartre on the one hand and Fromm and Horney on
the other is particularly appropriate for several reasons. All three have
written books addressed to the general public as well as to specialists in
their own field. All are concerned with the particular area in which
philosophy and psychology are inextricably interwoven. Sartre as a
philosopher has laid the basis for a new psychological method; Fromm
and Horney as psychologists have developed the philosophical implications of their views and offered a new interpretation of man. All three
hold that psychology must not be divorced from ethical considerations,
that it may properly be concerned with the normative as well as the
descriptive. All question the concept of mere "adjustment" as the legitimate goal for the analyst and feel that there is such a thing as a
"pathology of normalcy." All emphasize sociological rather than biological conditioning and are greatly concerned with what Sullivan calls the
"psychology of interpersonal relationships." [4] We may sum up all this
by saying that the Fromm-Horney school proposes a study of the human
being in situation—which is precisely the central focus of existentialism.

Turning specifically to Fromm, I find a most striking parallel with
Sartre in Fromm's concept of man's alienation from nature and the

---

[1] Erich Fromm, *Man for Himself* (New York: Holt, Rinehart, & Winston, 1947).

[2] Erich Fromm, *Escape from Freedom* (New York: Holt, Rinehart, & Winston, 1941),
p. 27.

[3] Jean-Paul Sartre, *Baudelaire,* translated by Martin Turnell (Norfolk: New Directions, 1950).

[4] The work of Harry Stack Sullivan . . . would be interesting to examine from the
point of view of existentialism. . . .

related view of the ambivalent character of freedom. In *Escape from Freedom* Fromm had already declared that "human existence and freedom are from the beginning inseparable," and he pointed out that as in the Biblical myth of the Garden of Eden, human history began with an act of choice. Man's first encounter with freedom is negative; it is "freedom from," not "freedom to." Man's expulsion from Paradise was in truth the beginning of his war with nature. He was free *from* complete subordination of nature, but not yet free *to* use his powers so as to live well apart from her. For by his self-consciousness, which is identical with his power to choose, man is removed from the oneness with nature which the other animals enjoy. He lacks their instinctual guarantees; he must determine his own destiny both as an individual and as a species. His grandeur is at the same time his crushing fate. Freedom is opportunity, responsibility, insecurity. Lacking the courage to struggle to develop their inner resources in new ways, or prevented by society from developing the potentialities which they recognize in themselves, most men find the burden of freedom intolerable and seek to lose their individuality by submersion in systems developed by others and passed off as absolute (Sartre's Serious World). Later, in *The Sane Society*, Fromm speaks of birth in negative terms.

> The fact that man's birth is primarily a negative act, that of being thrown out of the original oneness with nature, that he cannot return to where he came from, implies that the process of birth is by no means an easy one. (p. 27) [5]

Meanwhile in *Man for Himself* Fromm had related man's anguish before freedom to a dichotomy in his nature, and he pointed out that man's intellectual and scientific progress as well as his loneliness were to be explained in terms of man's "filling in" the lack which he felt in himself.

> He is driven to overcome this inner split, tormented by a craving for "absoluteness," for another kind of harmony which can lift the curse by which he was separated from nature, from his fellow men, and from himself. (p. 41)

Only the word "Nothingness" or "For-itself" is necessary to make this passage veritably Sartrean. Fromm goes on to develop as "existential dichotomies" what Sartre would call components of the human condition. These are three paradoxes which have all one way or another received special attention from the existentialists. There is first the fact that man's life is inalterably permeated with the idea that he must die, and yet death is not compatible with or intelligible to the experience of living. Second, there is the discrepancy between man's infinite poten-

---

[5] Erich Fromm, *The Sane Society* (New York: Holt, Rinehart, & Winston, 1955).

tialities and the finitude which from the start confines his actualities within an infinitesimal compass. Finally, Fromm stresses the paradox inherent in man's ultimate isolation and solitude and his need for relatedness. For Fromm, as for humanistic existentialists, there is never full communication between men; yet no man can come to know himself apart from other men nor develop his powers without them. In contrast to the "existential dichotomies," Fromm adds the "historical dichotomies." These are not contradictions inherent in the human condition, but rather those contradictions in men's existence which are man-made and potentially solvable. . . .

These ideas all imply a certain view of human nature. Here Fromm is closer to the existentialists in theory than in practice. He denies that there is such a thing as a fixed human nature in the Hegelian sense or even in the common sense of the maxim, "You can't change human nature." At the same time he denies that human nature is infinitely malleable, for he recognizes that such an admission would be equivalent to saying that men can be manipulated without limit, which would be to deny all human freedom. This is exactly the existentialist position. There are many occasions, however, when Fromm in spite of his theory implies that there are certain human values which are absolute, and such a view demands that human nature also must be in some way fixed. Here he is closer to Camus than to Sartre. Yet it must be admitted that Sartre and de Beauvoir too assume a sameness of human reactions to certain basic needs even though they do not postulate it as part of their theory.

Fromm's famous "orientations" have no specific, one-for-one equivalents in existentialism, but the general idea back of them is certainly comparable to the formulated theories of Sartre and de Beauvoir. Fromm contrasts his view with Freud's by saying,

> The fundamental basis of character is not seen in various types of libido organization but in specific kinds of a person's relatedness to the world. In the process of living, man relates himself to the world (1) by acquiring and assimilating things, and (2) by relating himself to people (and himself). p. 58) [6]

Sartre says the same thing in other words by stressing the idea that man comes to know himself and makes himself by means of the way in which he organizes the things of the world into a kind of instrumental hierarchy with himself as center of reference, and by the particular pattern of subject-object relations which he adopts with regard to other people. The specific orientations which Fromm discusses (receptive, hoarding, exploitative, marketing, and—in contrast to the others—the productive), in so far as they are *total* life-adaptations, come close to the existential-

---

[6] Erich Fromm, *Man for Himself.*

ist original choice of being. Though one should not press the parallel too closely, it is not inaccurate to say that the nonproductive orientations are similar to patterns of bad faith and that the productive resembles "good faith." The productive orientation demands that one adopt a truthful and rational outlook and that one spontaneously develop his own unique potentialities rather than conform to external authoritarian standards, this process being limited, however, by the recognition of the right of other persons to do the same thing. Similarly, existentialist good faith requires that a man assume full responsibility for his life, recognizing his freedom to make of it what he will, relentlessly rejecting self-illusion and wishful thinking, and, once more, voluntarily restricting the external scope of his free acts by respecting the freedom of others. Especially interesting in this connection is Fromm's "market personality" (not identical with, but reminding one of, the "outer-directed person" of *The Lonely Crowd*). The man with the "market personality" lives "as you desire me," always trying to make himself into the semblance which he feels his associates expect and admire, changing from group to group almost with the shifting styles of the season. Fromm's sketch of such persons is exactly equivalent to Sartre's description of those who try to be their Self-for-others instead of accepting the responsibilities of Being-for-itself. There is also the moving passage in *Being and Nothingness* in which Sartre discusses society's inclination to try to imprison men within the social roles which they have chosen, to make of a waiter only a waiter rather than a man who waits on tables, a soldier only a soldier, and so on. And most men, Sartre says, are only too happy to *be* the part they play . . .

In *The Sane Society* Fromm brings his brand of humanism still closer to that of existentialism by pointing out that man's greatest needs and passions do not spring from his biology but from "the very peculiarity of his existence." "There lies also the key to humanistic psychoanalysis. . . . The most powerful forces motivating man's behavior stem from the condition of his existence, the 'human situation.' " (p. 28) . . .

Turning now to Karen Horney, I think we need not make a completely separate case, since many points of similarity between her views and existential psychoanalysis are those which she shares with Fromm. But we may note certain parallels peculiar to her theory. Jack L. Rubins in 1954, in a review of the English translation of *Existential Psychoanalysis*, pointed out a general similarity between Horney and Sartre. Stressing especially a similarity in their notions about the nature of the Self, he says quite rightly that bad faith may be considered as a theoretical explanation of "the clinical concept of duplicity and alienation." . . .

There are four other general resemblances between Sartre and Horney. First, Horney, more than most psychiatrists working in the Freudian tradition, recognizes the impossibility of genuine detachment on the part of the analyst; she urges that since the analyst will not be perfectly objective under any circumstances, he should be willing to make some self-commitment in his effort to help the patient. (Obviously Horney would never allow this to go to the point of deliberate manipulation without respect for the patient's right to self-determination.) Sartre and all existentialists would agree here, for the impossibility of an impersonal, totally objective point of view is one of the most fundamental of existentialist principles. Second, the neurotic trends of which Horney speaks may be contradictory to one another, although taken together they constitute what seems to the subject a "safe" orientation toward the world. Similarly . . . in his biographies of Baudelaire and Genet, Sartre too maintains that the basic choice of being may involve an impossible contradiction though this does not prevent the person's making of it a *modus vivendi* throughout most or all of a lifetime. Third, Horney in her psychoanalysis gives far greater attention to the ego than is traditional with Freudians. She refuses to see the ego either as the mere servant of the id or as its detached supervisor. Whereas the Freudian analyst will largely limit himself to helping the ego become aware of repressed material, Horney insists that to help the patient change the attitudes of the ego itself is part of the essential task of the therapist. This position is at least an advance in the direction of Sartre's insistence that we must consider man to be wholly conscious, though Horney's position is by no means as radical a departure from the hypothesis of the unconscious as is Sartre's. Finally, Horney criticizes Freud's concept of transference as being too "mechanistic-evolutionistic." [7] She feels that the patient's attitude toward the analyst is seldom if ever the simple result of the patient's substituting the analyst for whatever person had served to polarize the infantile reactions responsible for the later disturbance. Horney holds that the transference is merely one manifestation among many of the subject's basic orientation toward the world, that his attitude toward the analyst will probably be more intense because the analysand feels that his whole way of life is brought into question; but for that very reason his conduct in relation to the analyst will bring into play exactly that behavior which he is accustomed to manifest in all of his personal relations. This is precisely the position of existential psychoanalysis, which views every act and attitude, however trivial, as part of the complex symbolic structure which makes concrete the underlying choice of being.

Nevertheless I do not wish to stress unduly the parallel between the Fromm-Horney theories and existential psychoanalysis. In the first place, there are vast areas in which there is no overlapping even by way of disagreement. Sartre says nothing about the many strictly clinical prob-

[7] Karen Horney, *New Ways in Psychoanalysis* (New York: Norton, 1939), p. 156. This book contains Horney's own comparison of her theory with that of Freud.

lems which interest the other two, and this is as it should be, since Sartre is a philosopher and theoretical psychologist. On the other hand, Fromm and Horney are uninterested in the purely philosophical speculations which make up such a large part of Sartre's work. . . .

While it seems to me that the existentialists may be profitably compared with Fromm and Horney in their general view of man and society, existential psychoanalysis in its technical aspect is most closely affiliated with phenomenological psychiatry. In part this close relation is due to common intellectual ancestry, for both these psychiatrists and Sartre have been profoundly influenced not only by Freud but by the ideas of Edmund Husserl, the founder of the school of phenomenology, particularly as interpreted and given an existentialist twist by Martin Heidegger. The phenomenological psychiatrists, however, owe a great deal also to the work of Karl Jaspers, whereas Sartre is not very sympathetic to Jaspers. Moreover Sartre has developed a concept of consciousness which orthodox phenomenologists would never accept. The question of influence, however, is a complicated one; Sartre has borrowed from individual phenomenologists, and the phenomenological psychiatrists, especially during the last decade, have been considerably influenced by Sartre. On the whole, this type of psychology has until very recently been prevalent chiefly in Europe, so much so that in 1954 Ulrich Sonnemann, formerly of the New School of Social Research, wrote a book with the express purpose of introducing this new theory to American psychiatrists. Unfortunately Sonnemann's work, *Existence and Therapy: An Introduction to Phenomenological Psychology and Existential Analysis,* is so abstract and so frequently almost unintelligible that it is not really informative. He does, however, give an admirable summing up of the existentialist (and phenomenologist) approach.

We may say that it decidedly steers away from positivism, functionalism, instrumentalism, pragmatism, and operationalism, and toward a rediscovery of *spontaneous man in his world.* . . . Existentialism, to sum up, uncovers and questions exactly those constant and implicit assumptions of the functionalistic theories of man which to the functionalists themselves have become so completely self-evident that they are hardly aware of them, let alone of their aprioristic nature. (p. ix) [8]

As Sonnemann indicates in his title, there are two different groups which share in common a peculiar emphasis on "existence." There are the phenomenological psychiatrists proper—of whom Eugene Minkowski, V. E. von Gebsattel, and Erwin Straus are probably the best known— and there are the existential analysts working in the tradition established

[8] Ulrich Sonnemann, *Existence and Therapy* (New York: Grune and Stratton, 1954).

by Ludwig Binswanger and continued by Medard Boss and Roland Kuhn.[9] The dividing line is not too clear. A man such as Franz Fischer might well be put on either side or both. In any case there is little point in listing names, and any attempt at examination of the theories of the individual psychiatrists would be inappropriate to our enterprise. What would be both pertinent and profitable, however, would be for us to consider briefly a book by the Dutch psychologist, J. H. Van Den Berg, *The Phenomenological Approach to Psychiatry.*[10] Van Den Berg, who is himself a follower of Binswanger, uses the term "phenomenological" to cover all these "psychiatrists of existence." What he has done is to point out what he believes to be the most crucial differences between their approach and traditional Freudian psychoanalysis, refraining from urging his own personal point of view and emphasizing only those positions which phenomenological psychiatrists hold in common. Although he is aware of Sartre's importance, he is by no means a follower of his and uses examples from Sartre chiefly to illustrate principles drawn from the clinical observations of phenomenologists.

Van Den Berg begins his book by introducing a hypothetical patient and describing his disturbed symptoms. The traditional psychoanalyst, he says, will treat this patient by making use of four fundamental concepts, each of which the phenomenologist will radically modify: *projection,* which involves the patient's attitude toward the world (and in part towards society); *conversion,* which is a manifestation of his relation to his own body; *transference,* which is a special example of his attitude toward other people and in particular toward the analyst; and *mythification,* which is his subjective remaking of his own experiences (implying a particular attitude toward time). . . .

All of this we have met already in the work of Sartre—though not specifically related to the problem of conducting an analysis. Sartre's basic definition of consciousness implies Van Den Berg's position. Consciousness is always consciousness *of* something, a never-ending active relationship between consciousness and the world, a world which has meaning only *for a consciousness.* Man experiences the external world as a complex network or hierarchy of instruments through which he may realize his potentialities. In his rational approach to reality he observes exclusively those relations between himself and the environment which

---

[9] In 1958 considerable excitement was evoked in this country by the appearance of *Existence: A New Dimension in Psychiatry and Psychology,* edited by Rollo May, Ernest Angel, and Henri F. Ellenberger (New York: Basic Books, 1958). This includes introductory essays by May and Ellenberger and translations of selected works by the phenomenologists (Minkowski, Straus, von Gebsattel) and by the existential analysts (Binswanger and Kuhn). . . .

[10] J. H. Van Den Berg, *The Phenomenological Approach to Psychiatry* (Springfield, Ill.: Thomas, 1955). I am indebted to Dr. Harold Kelman, editor of the *American Journal of Psychoanalysis,* for introducing me to Van Den Berg's book. . . .

he observes are sustained by all other people and which offer no inconsistency as he moves from one enterprise to another. But in his emotions man effects a magical organization of the world wherein he is content with a world which is responsive to his present impulses. Sartre's point (and Van Den Berg's) is not that the environment does not have any fixed physical structure, but that with the possible exception of artificial scientific investigation, one never sees everyday objects for what they are physically in themselves. One transcends them toward their subjectively established possibilities. Thus to a prisoner a gate may seem tremendous in size and strength, the central focus of the whole environment. To a visitor it may be only one architectural section among others of an imposing building. De Beauvoir's novels are particularly rich in passages illustrating these sudden subjective modifications of the environment. . . .

Next we may consider the problem of *conversion*. The patient claims that he suffers from ailments which medical examination cannot discern. The traditional theory explains this situation by saying that the patient "converts" his psychic illness into physical; he transfers the pains from his mind into his bodily organs. Here Van Den Berg argues that there is a hidden tendency to objectivize all the respective parts—pains and psyche as well as body—and that the theory quite openly presupposes a distinction between psyche and body as in the old soul-body dualism. But the idea that something nonspatial can be inside or outside anything, that man has a soul *and* a body, "is not comprehensible to anybody." Actually, says Van Den Berg, all that we know in so-called "conversion" cases is that psychiatrically disturbed patients frequently have physical complaints. . . .

It is particularly interesting that both Van Den Berg and Sartre mention nausea as the physical manifestation of man's psychological (one might almost say his metaphysical) orientation. Van Den Berg remarks that the patient "often localizes his fear in the cardiac region; his general dissatisfaction with life is identified with a bad taste in his mouth and with a sensation of nausea in his throat" (p. 19). Sartre claims that "a dull and inescapable nausea perpetually reveals my body to my consciousness." This nausea, this flat, insipid taste is always present as the background of all my experiences; it is the indication to my consciousness of its contingency and its facticity.

> We must not take the term *nausea* as a metaphor derived from our physiological disgust. On the contrary, we must realize that it is on the foundation of this nausea that all concrete and empirical nauseas (nausea caused by spoiled meat, fresh blood, excrement, etc.) are produced and make us vomit.[11]

[11] *Being and Nothingness*, pp. 338-339.

Van Den Berg proceeds next to the question of *transference*. The standard theory assumes that the patient's feelings of hostility or dependency, which had originally been directed toward a dominating father or mother or the like, are now *transferred* to the analyst, although he has done nothing on his own to merit the excessive love or hate which is suddenly bestowed upon him. Van Den Berg objects that the theory treats emotions as if they were things which could be carried from one place to another. But hate and love are inseparable from their objects; they exist only as the hate or love of particular persons and things; they cannot be "transferred." What we must look for in the patient is not some half-forgotten episode in the past but a clue to his present orientation, so that we may see why he chooses to relate himself to *all* people through hostility rather than friendliness, or separation rather than communication. . . .

Finally, Van Den Berg discusses the concept of *mythification*.[12] As often happens, Van Den Berg's hypothetical patient gives a bad account of his youth. Yet the psychotherapist investigating finds that the past as the patient describes it does not jibe with the record of the past as confirmed by numerous other witnesses. Are we to conclude, as most psychoanalysts would, that the patient's neurosis has led him to effect a "mythification of his past"? He does not deliberately falsify, and Van Den Berg insists that the patient is in good faith. Yet our subject will resist evidence which would certainly be convincing to him if he were dealing with unemotional, factual memories. According to Van Den Berg the doctrine of "mythification" contains an error analogous to that which we saw apropos of the patient and "the world"; it assumes the existence of a past which is wholly neutral, a succession of absolute, nonsignifying events against which the "mythification" can be measured. But "this 'impartial' past never and nowhere occurs within the scope of human existence." The patient may or may not be accurate in describing the past as he has lived it, but even this is not of major importance. What is significant is how the past appears to the patient in the present. The task of the analyst is not to free the patient from the psychotraumata of the past but to liberate him from the meaning of these psychotraumata as they even now exist for him.

Van Den Berg's view of man's situation in respect to time is for all practical purposes identical with Sartre's, and both men are heavily indebted to Martin Heidegger. The position is essentially this: The past as lived is not a series of finished events; it depends upon the present, for we are continually remaking the past as we decide anew the meaning it will have in our present enterprises. But inasmuch as our present acts are determined by our projects of what is about to be, this means that the past comes to meet us from the future. Van Den Berg complains that

[12] In speaking of the patient's "mythification of his past," Van Den Berg is following specifically the French psychiatrist Dupré.

psychoanalysts have given too little importance to the future, and he points out that it is frequently the patient's fear of the way his past will come to him out of the future which brings the patient to the analyst. Van Den Berg combines this emphasis on the future with the idea that the essence of man is choice. In words which might easily have come out of *Being and Nothingness* he writes,

> Man chooses the form in which he throws his past before him, he chooses the form in which he places himself in the future. He chooses a similar aspect of the future, that it becomes possible for him to live *on*. (p. 75)

And again,

> The patient learns to choose differently. . . . The patient changes his past and in doing so gives a new aspect to the future, from which, as we know, this past continually comes to meet him. (pp. 81-82)

The two most fundamental and most distinctive principles of existential psychoanalysis are the belief that man is free and the rejection of the unconscious. How does phenomenological psychiatry (at least as interpreted by Van Den Berg) stand on these? It would seem that in all of Van Den Berg's discussion of projection, conversion, transference, and mythification, the individual's freedom is necessarily implied. Man is presented as free to choose the meaning of his past, free to determine his own future. Unfortunately Van Den Berg never quite states his position in unmistakable terms. At one point he seems to make a reservation. Speaking of another hypothetical patient, one who must decide "how to place his broken leg in the future," he says, "He is—not quite— forced into a—not quite—*free* choice (Sartre, p. 77)." Does this mean that Van Den Berg feels that Sartre's position is too extreme and must be modified? Or that he simply interprets Sartre's concept of facticity as being itself a factual limit of freedom which does not actually affect freedom as a psychological capacity? I suspect the latter, but one cannot be sure.

With regard to the unconscious there is no question as to Van Den Berg's position. Early in his book he suggests that the hypothesis of the unconscious is maintained because it makes it easier for the psychoanalyst to explain the processes of projection, conversion, etc., which would be difficult to accept without it. He asks, "For is not the unconscious defined as exactly that which eludes our attention? The unconscious is never experienced, so in an appeal to experience there is no sense at all" (p. 26). Toward the end of his discussion he points out that the approach which he has been presenting has been outlined with no recourse to *the unconscious*. There is no objection, he says, to our applying the adjective "unconscious" to those things which have escaped our attention (Sartre's

levels of awareness or reflection), but we must not assume "an" unconscious "which would be supposed to exist as a second reality behind the
phantoms of healthy and of neurotic life. There is but one reality: that
of life as it is lived." The Freudian unconscious, Van Den Berg believes,
is "the product of a premature cessation of the psychological analysis of
human existence" (p. 93).[13]

Phenomenological psychiatry is certainly close to existential psychoanalysis—so, in fact, that the comparison may very well result in
our crediting Sartre with less originality than at first seemed due him.
We must remember, however, that Van Den Berg is friendly enough to
Sartre so that he has tended to stress parallels and even to modify his
presentation under Sartre's influence. In any case, what should concern
us here is primarily the question of whether there is any support for
Sartre's psychology in the empirical work of practicing psychiatrists. If
Van Den Berg's presentation of the phenomenological—and existential
—approach is (as surely we must assume that it is) the result of com-
paring the case histories and reports of the psychiatrists whom he men-
tions, then we are justified, I believe, in saying that there is clinical
evidence to support at least some of the claims of existential psychoanalysis. While it would be more satisfactory if Sartre had been in a
position to offer his own empirical corroboration, at least we need not
keep existential psychoanalysis wholly isolated in a vacuum while it
awaits the coming of its Freud.

[13] Since the problem of the unconscious is so vital to any psychoanalysis, I should like
to refer the reader to Sonnemann's chapter on this subject. That his position is
essentially that of Van Den Berg's can be seen from his opening paragraph. "The
unconscious *per se* can be inferred from any experience of the emergence of our minds
into a state of awareness, because the phenomenality of *emergence* as an event implies
it: that state from which our minds emerge, relative to their subsequent states, is one
of unconsciousness. It becomes evident that 'awareness' as we used it as well as 'unconsciousness' as we used it both require qualifications in the form of a genetive
[genitive?], linking them with a content *of* which the subject is aware or of which he
is unconscious; the habit of conceptual reification (*the* conscious, *the* unconscious),
which is a convenience of thoughtlessness unless the reification stays aware of that
requirement, became possible only at a moment in history when language, as was its
specific fate during the nineteenth century, had sufficiently been flattened out—ab-
stractified—to dim its phenomenal references so much that the tacit but constitutive
'of what' inherent in both concepts ('aware' and 'unconscious') could become relatively
invisible." (p. 191)

VII

Politics

Neo-Marxism and

Criticism of Dialectical Reasoning

by René Marill-Albérès

Since 1947 Sartre's major writings have been political essays directly related to the contemporary scene. Whether writing about [French] Indo-China, Algeria, American politics, or the Negro problem, he has never denied that for him the only possible system of analysis and line of conduct in the field of action is the Marxist. But the points of departure of historical materialism are not the same as those of Sartre's original philosophy. Marxism takes as its prime datum the biological and social condition of man, whose consciousness is but a "superstructure."

In *Nausea* and in *Being and Nothingness* Jean-Paul Sartre started as did the ancient "idealists" (though he stated the problem differently) from the interiority of consciousness. Marxism starts from something *external* to consciousness—the biological and social datum of the human collectivity and its class structure. There was therefore a rigid philosophical opposition between the Marxist system and Sartre's. Far from concealing this opposition, Sartre still acknowledges it, even after fifteen years of apprenticeship:

We were *at the same time* convinced that historical materialism provided
the only valid interpretation of history, and that existentialism constituted
the only concrete approach to reality.[1]

The phrase "at the same time" (the italics are Sartre's) shows the
dilemma which he faced for years: convinced that he was right in his
analysis of man's situation and that the Communists were right in their
analysis of history, he was tormented by the fact that the Marxist interpretation of history was grounded on a principle which he could not
accept. In the preface to his *Criticism of Dialectical Reasoning* (first
published in 1957 as *Question of Method*), he affirms without tergiversa-
tion that in its present form Communism has become a sterile, com-
pulsory doctrine, that through neglect even its fountainhead remains
obstructed:

> After attracting us as the moon attracts the tide, after transforming all our
> ideas, after effacing in us the categories of bourgeois thought, Marxism
> suddenly left us on a plateau; it failed to satisfy our need to understand;
> it no longer had anything to teach us, for it had stopped.[2]

Are we to believe that Sartre is challenging, rejecting, and attacking
historical materialism? No. He continues to believe that it affords the
only effective instruments for influencing the course of history. But
its truth is practical and empirical; its philosophical bases are not solid:

> Why are we not simply Marxists? Because we look upon the statements
> made by Engels and by Garaudy as *guiding principles,* as suggestions for
> action, as statements of problems, and not as *concrete truths.*[3]

In other words, Communism never errs *in the sphere of action,* but
Communism as a political system has developed at the expense of the
philosophy of communism. Here as well as in the doctrine of action, self-
criticism should be given free reign:

> It ought to be allowed to take root and develop as free criticism of itself
> and at the same time as the development of History and knowledge. That
> is something that has not yet been done; it has been checked by dogmatism.[4]

In his *Criticism of Dialectical Reasoning* Sartre proposes to enrich the
philosophical substrata of dialectical materialism, whose *practical* truth
he finds incontestable. Contemporary Marxist theory is nothing more
than "empirical anthropology,[5] and what is needed is "a dynamic

---

[1] *Critique de la raison dialectique,* p. 24.
[2] *Ibid.,* p. 25.   [3] *Ibid.,* p. 33.
[4] *Ibid.,* p. 120.   [5] *Ibid.,* p. 117.

Marxism which will incorporate the disciplines that still remain outside it." [6] These disciplines can all be reduced to phenomenology, which studies the structures of existence and discovers that the primary datum is not the social one but rather the datum of consciousness. In contrast to Marxism, which has as its starting point cosmic, biological, and social elements, Sartre starts from *human experience,* from consciousness, from the individual—even if the individual is the victim of the social conditions under which he lives:

> We refuse to confuse the alienated (oppressed) man with a thing or his alienation with the physical laws governing external conditions. *We affirm the specific nature of the human act,* which cuts through the social structure even as it preserves determinism. [7]

Putting it another way, Sartre will not look upon man as the simple resultant of the material, biological, and social conditions in which he finds himself. Man is rather a *project* fashioned in his or their *consciousness* by an individual or a group exposed to certain conditions. This is a restatement of the theory of freedom and responsibility expressed earlier in *Being and Nothingness* and in *The Flies.*

The problem is to reconcile Marxism, which explains the individual in terms of his social conditions, and Sartre's philosophy, which cannot avoid giving first place to *what is actually experienced by the individual.* From Marxism Sartre borrows the notion of the dialectic, that is, the development of a reality through several stages and through several forms, each more complex than the one that preceded. But in his *Criticism of Dialectical Reasoning,* the Marxist dialectic ceases to be a social mechanism and becomes instead something experienced by the individual.

Naturally, the experience is not lived through in solitude. In earlier works Sartre had clearly shown that each individual is free and independent *within a situation;* the individual is influenced by his situation, but he can accept it, modify it, or transcend it. In his *Criticism of Dialectical Reasoning,* he points up this basic fact: Marxism posits the lived, individual experience as the reflex of a social phenomenon; analysis of structures (those of the individual consciousness as well as social structure) reveals that this experience is on the contrary the dynamic, concrete, and—this bears repetition—"lived" aspect of the general and social statistical fact to which Marxism attributes the movement of history.

The problem of reconciliation confronting Sartre is therefore what he calls "totalization," or passing from the individual to the group, from consciousness to history. In this process, are individual experiences and actions "totalized" to yield the collective phenomena studied by Marxism?

The problem, for us, is one of classification. Given individuals, *who* or *what* is to be totalized? [8]

To resolve the issue, Sartre transports "dialectical movement" from the collectivity to the individual and, in contrast to Marxism, sees in consciousness the source of the collectivity; it is the individual that experiences social realities, reacts, develops dialectically, and creates the social dialectic:

There would be no trace of even partial totalization if the individual were not *himself* totalizing. *The whole structure of the historical dialectic rests on individual praxis insofar as it is already dialectical.*[9]

Thus the historical movement originates in the individual, not through any magical or statistical operation, but because in themselves individuals, in the normal dialectic of their lives, manifest the need for "totalization" which creates the collective phenomenon.

Sartre therefore studies in the individual, from the onset of consciousness, the movement that creates history. The titles of the first two parts of his *Criticism* are revealing. In "From Individual *Praxis* to Inert *Praxis*" he shows that man is by nature committed to the (economic) *praxis* on which Marxism is based. This *praxis* is inert so long as it is not historical action; it becomes historical action in the second part, "From the Group to History." And Volume II of his *Criticism* will carry this evolution to its completion.

That is how Sartre reconciles the lived experience (the basis of his philosophy) and the Marxist movement of history, on the one hand, and on the other, freedom and necessity. For every stage through which the individual creates the social "totalization" that will acquire a historical meaning represents a conflict between the necessity that constrains him and freedom that enables him to resist and "transcend" his "situation":

Freedom and necessity are one and the same. . . . It is an individual construction whose sole agents are individual men carrying out their functions as free activities.[10]

That is also how he recreates Marxism and explains it in terms of human freedoms.

In 1960 Sartre appears as the creator of a *neo-Marxism,* or as one who would adapt orthodox Marxism to the necessities of not abandoning, in

---

[8] *Ibid.,* p. 165.   [9] *Ibid.,* p. 165. Italics are Sartre's.
[10] *Ibid.,* p. 377.

favor of the inexorable social mechanism of history, the lived individual experience, and with it the notions of freedom, responsibility, and independence. His able brief is convincing, even if understandable only to other philosophers; for the simple fact is that it was not written for the public at large.

Jean-Paul Sartre, the philosopher and advocate of neo-Marxism in 1960, bears scant resemblance to the author of *Nausea* in 1938. Still, the evolution from one to the other is quite obvious and easily explained. Coming on the heels of the generation that had, independently of the prewar tradition, focused attention on the total freedom of the individual, Sartre emphasized the emptiness of human freedom, the individual's terror in the face of his freedom.

The only answer to the emptiness of freedom is responsibility. In Bernanos, who is after all one of Sartre's contemporaries, it is a spiritual responsibility. In Malraux, it is man's affirmation of himself as a mortal and eternal being. Sartre had chosen, between *Nausea* and *The Flies,* man's *historical* responsibility, and this led him first to Marxism, then to what is rightly termed neo-Marxism. His theory is developed in a work in which the "militant intellectual" and the philosopher win out over the simple man of letters. His more recent works are less seductive than those produced between 1938 and 1947; they are also less accessible to nonmilitants. It is possible that Sartre deliberately sacrificed his talent and his success as a writer to his historical mission. For his talent has not vanished: a play like *Les Séquestrés d'Altona,* in which the bourgeoisie is subjected to self-criticism, still attracts middle-class audiences whose average age is past fifty. This is one more proof of his talent. In his *Criticism of Dialectical Reasoning,* he seems to disdain talent and to prefer instead difficult, pedantic analyses which, though they reach but a limited public, are of supreme interest to him. There is an element of nobility in his mission and in his near renunciation of "literature."

Anguished Responsibility

by H. J. Blackham

Existentialists are commonly ridiculed for dramatizing the ordinary.
Sensible people accept the contingency of the world and get on with
the job of living in it. Existentialists moan in anguish to find themselves gratuitous and derelict in a possibly impossible world, shelterless
orphans deprived of the mother comfort of reason and necessity. Everybody solemnly quotes the saying of Plato that to be astonished is the
truly philosophical feeling. What else but a first-hand recovery of wonder
is this nausea and all its related affects? Plato's philosophical wonder
is excited by the vision of an intelligible system of being, a rational
harmony repeated in the virtuous man, the ideal republic, and the
organic cosmos. The philosophical wonder inaugurated by nausea is excited by the sense of a different type of order. The discovery of the world
as gratuitous and absurd (its acceptance as given, in unemotional words)
is not disillusionment, nor wild grief that God is dead, nor stoical resignation, nor anything of the sort; it is, above all, the context which brings
out the meaning of man's separation from himself and from the world,
which is the existential root of all philosophies and the foundation of all
foundations in existential philosophies. If the speculative fantasies of
the classical rationalist philosophies were true in principle, and the individual could be assigned an appointed place in a system, man as man
would not exist. Man's separation is a malaise, but it is not nostalgia for
the great chain of being; it is a disorder which founds and refounds the
human order of possibilities which are temporal and modest and never
final. In this order, the existing individual has no refuge from continuous
responsibility. But why the anguished responsibility of the existentialist?
A certain anxiety in carrying out given tasks and duties, a fear of not
being equal to the demands, is understandable enough; and normal
people feel acute anxiety in the midst of the uncertainties which beset an
original decision: but these are only echoes of the primordial anxiety
felt by the man who knows that at every moment in absolute solitariness

he is responsible for the fate of man. This absolute responsibility of the individual can be treated as a platitude, or it may be held to be the fundamental truth about the individual which he is most reluctant to face and accept although he is only authentically man in so far as he lives and acts in the full consciousness of it. When there is prevailing confidence in established values and authorities, the primordial, absolute and solitary responsibility of the individual is regarded either as a meaningless platitude or as a dangerous thought; in less settled times, it may come vividly home to some as a sharp and searching truth, and when they exhibit it dramatically they are not (as it has been said) beating their breasts in a vain and stupid lament that values are not objective in the same sense as scientific knowledge. They are acutely aware that only the solitariness of decision discharges the responsibility responsibly. The case of Sartre exemplifies this.

Marcel, with the most emphatic disapproval, quotes the following from Sartre:

> My freedom is the unique foundation of values. And since I am the being by virtue of whom values exist, nothing—absolutely nothing—can justify me in adopting this or that value or scale of values. As the unique basis of the existence of values, I am totally unjustifiable. And my freedom is in anguish at finding that it is the baseless basis of values.

On humanist assumptions, values are human valuations; and the public values of a society or a civilization are contributed and upheld by private individual choice. Sartre puts the being of man in his not-being, his negative capability, his power and right to secede, and therefore the individual is not relieved of his responsibility to choose for himself all over again, and stands in primitive isolation even though he is bound in place by the demands and pressures of modern industrial society. This view of the relation of individual valuations to social valuations is an intellectual myth of our time, like the social contract of earlier generations, both true and false. Rationalism, emancipation, enlightenment, education for change, these are the progressive influences that have encouraged detachment and scepticism, freedom from ties and traditions as well as from prejudices and superstitions. Such is the modern evacuated condition of Orestes in *Les Mouches* and of Mathieu in *Les Chemins de la liberté*. Sartre himself is in revolt (with reservations) against the values of bourgeois society. His revolt, however, is not an inverted acceptance, a fear of freedom, such as he supposes Baudelaire's to have been—the type of the rebel intellectual; it is a revolt which accepts and rejoices in and trembles under the burden of responsibility for a new order. Sartre makes total responsibility the obverse of the power to secede which man is: they belong together inseparably. This puts him with Nietzsche, makes him an existentialist and not, for example, a surrealist. But why not a Marxist, since it is precisely Marxism which attacks bourgeois society and proposes to replace it? Indeed, that is the capital question to ask about Sartre, for he fully accepts the Marxist analysis of capitalism. We know what the Marxist answer is, for Sartre and his school have been much engaged in controversy with Communists in France; and there is the elaborate examination of existentialism by the Hungarian Marxist Professor Lukács, who treats it as the last vain effort of bourgeois intellectuals to find a third way beyond materialism and a bankrupt idealism, an effort to remain in the metaphysical world of ideas and ideals in order to escape having to accept historical socialism as it exists in concrete reality in the Soviet Union—as eighteenth century philosophers invented a conceptual Deism to make a third way between atheism and positive historical or mystical religion, and to oppose the Church. Sartre, indeed, does oppose metaphysics to history in putting the being of man in the power to secede, as a metaphysical absolute independent of historical conditions. In *L'Être et le néant,* he condemns the spirit of literal seriousness which attributes greater reality to the world than to oneself, or attributes reality to oneself in so far as one belongs to the world. Seriousness in this sense, he says, is the abdication of human presence in favour of the world, and the serious person buries his consciousness of his liberty at the bottom of himself. He adds: "Marx posed the chief dogma of seriousness when he affirmed the priority of the object over the subject, and man is serious when he takes himself for an object." Dialectical materialism makes good and evil vanish conjointly, for it abolishes their source.

Sartre, therefore, cannot be a Marxist because Marx, like Hegel, missed the permanent meaning of man's separation from himself and from the world and Marxist theory deprives man of his real being. But Sartre's own actual secession and total responsibility involves him in political action, reinforced in theory and in practice by his experience of the resistance movement in France during the German occupation. In those extreme circumstances, the isolation of the existing individual, his original and solitary responsibility for the essence and the fate of man, was not merely a moral platitude nor a metaphysical idea, but was the visible personal presence of men.

For political realism as for philosophical idealism Evil was not a very serious matter.

We have been taught to take it seriously. It is neither our fault nor our merit if we lived in a time when torture was a daily fact. Châteaubriand, Oradour, the Rue des Saussaies, Dachau, and Auschwitz have all demonstrated to us that Evil is not an appearance, that knowing its cause does not dispel it, that it is not opposed to Good as a confused idea is to a clear one, that it is not the effects of passions which might be cured, of a fear which might be overcome, of a passing aberration which might be excused, of an ignorance which might be enlightened, that it can in no way be diverted, brought back, reduced, and incorporated into idealistic humanism, like that shade of which Leibnitz has written that it is necessary for the glare of daylight. . . .

Perhaps a day will come when a happy age, looking back at the past, will see in this suffering and shame one of the paths which led to peace. But we are not on the side of history already made. We were, as I have said, *situated* in such a way that every lived minute seemed to us like something irreducible. Therefore, in spite of ourselves, we came to this conclusion, which will seem shocking to lofty souls: Evil cannot be redeemed.

But, on the other hand, most of the resisters, though beaten, burned, blinded, and broken, did not speak. They broke the circle of Evil and reaffirmed the human—for themselves, for us, and for their very torturers. They did it without witness, without help, without hope, often even without faith. For them it was not a matter of believing in man but of wanting to. Everything conspired to discourage them: so many indications everywhere about them, those faces bent over them, that misery within them. Everything concurred in making them believe that they were only insects, that man is the impossible dream of spies and squealers, and that they would awaken as vermin like everybody else.

This man had to be invented with their martyrized flesh, with their hunted thoughts which were already betraying them—invented on the basis of nothing, for nothing, in absolute gratuitousness. For it is within the human that one can distinguish means and ends, values and preferences, but they were still at the creation of the world and they had only to decide in sovereign fashion whether there would be anything more than the reign of the animal within it. They remained silent and man was born of their silence. We knew that every moment of the day, in the four corners of Paris, man was a hundred times destroyed and reaffirmed. . . .

Five years. We lived entranced and as we did not take our profession of writer lightly, this state of trance is still reflected in our writings. We have undertaken to create a literature of extreme situations. . . .

Therefore, we are Jansenists because the age has made us such, and in so far as it has made us touch our limits I shall say that we are all metaphysical writers. . . . For metaphysics is not a sterile discussion about abstract notions which have nothing to do with experience. It is a living effort to embrace from within the human condition in its totality.

Forced by circumstances to discover the pressure of history, as Torricelli discovered atmospheric pressure, and tossed by the cruelty of the time into that forlornness from where we can see our condition as man to the very limit, to the absurd, to the night of unknowingness, we have a task for which we may not be strong enough (this is not the first time that an age, for want of talents, has lacked its art and its philosophy). It is to create a literature which unites and reconciles the metaphysical absolute and the relativity of the historical fact. . . . It is not a question for us of escaping into the eternal or of abdicating in the face of what the unspeakable Mr. Zaslavsky calls in *Pravda* the "historical process." ("Qu'est-ce que la littérature?," pp. 246-51)

There is rhetoric in these extracts, but they are not rhetoric. As Hobbes's state of nature before the social contract is sometimes realized historically in the anarchy of national sovereign states, so in these extreme situations the source of civilization in the absolute will of the isolated individual was not merely a metaphysical myth. It is Kierkegaard's vision of political events forcing the individual back into his ethical isolation or dissipating him in the dust of nonentity. Again, it is Kierkegaard's figure of that sister of Destiny who cuts the thread when the quantitative individual decision has spread itself about and imposes itself as a new quality—an objective value. The individual in virtue of his human transcendence is a concrete universal. All I think, decide, and do separates me from the solid ground of what is there, and this is to universalize myself as man, to give man an essence by my existence— which is quite different from making myself a particular realization of a universal already given.

The relation of individual and universal is the central persistent theme of philosophical debate. The concrete historical universal of Hegel or the abstract rational universal of Kant owes nothing to personal decision. If the universal is once truly valid it does not need to be willed, it requires to be obeyed; the all-important thing is not the liberty of the individual in face of it, but the fertilization and development of the individual under its regime, not the assent of the person but the expansion and expense of the personality in its name. Therefore, it is frivolous to force the person to choose in ethical isolation, because what matters to him and to all is to bring him out on the right side, so that everything works out well. The answer of the existentialist is that man cannot be simply and finally brought under and identified with any law, whether it be promulgated as the law of his nature or as the law of the universe; the rule cannot justify the act nor the person, for only the act justifies the rule, as the paint not the school justifies the painter. In rejecting the view that personality gets whatever dignity and value it has from the universals which it adopts or to which it submits, existentialism does not hold that personality has a moral dignity or mystic value of its own which it communicates to whatever it adheres to; the rejection is based on an appreciation of the structure of personal being and universal being: man cannot be man and be bound, even by himself, and the world is open and cannot be circumvallated by universals and kept snug and safe. The individual act is always absolute and never final: this is the uncompromising theme of existentialist meditation. Of course the function of universals as information is not affected by the criticism of them as absolutes. Indeed, the point just is that they have their source in experience and not in the structure of man nor in the structure of the universe.

The violence and fantastic abstractness of some of Sartre's ethical pronouncements, then, must be read in the light of the extreme situations and radical issues of the present phase in human affairs. Even a theory founded upon a metaphysical absolute—the eternal situation of man—is not to be taken out of its context in the existing historical situation. Not the least virtue of this existentialist theory or affirmation at this time is the leaven of tolerance which it introduces. The liberty of all is implied by and is necessary to the liberty of each. The concern is to awaken each to his liberty, not to convert him to a doctrine. "The very maximum of what one human being can do for another in relation to that wherein each man has to do solely with himself, is to inspire him with concern and unrest" (Kierkegaard). Communication is promoted and the poison of moralism eliminated. It is not the tolerance of easy-going indifference, for in rejecting the fanatical or intransigent either-or aimed at the life of the other it espouses the either-or within the self of personal decision and absolute responsibility. Thus it is an ethic of human solidarity, without crying peace, peace, where there is no peace—where there is the degradation of man to a thing. . . .

Chronology of Important Dates

1905, June 21	Jean-Paul Sartre born in Paris.
1907	His father dies.
	His first studies at the Lycée Henri IV.
1916	His mother, *née* Anne-Marie Schweitzer, remarries.
1917-1919	Studies at the Lycée de la Rochelle.
1924-1928	Studies at the École Normale Supérieur.
1929	Receives *agrégation* in Philosophy.
1929-1931	Military service.
1931	Appointed Professor of Philosophy at the Lycée of Le Havre, where he remains for two years.
1933-1934	Resident at the Institut Français in Berlin.
1934-1936	Professor of Philosophy at the Lycée of Le Havre.
1936-1937	Professor of Philosophy at the Lycée of Laon.
1937-1939	Professor of Philosophy at the Lycée Pasteur.
1939	Drafted.
1940-1941	Prisoner of war.
1941-1944	Professor of Philosophy at the Lycée Condorcet.
1944	Gives up teaching to devote his time to writing.
1945	Founds and edits *Les Temps modernes*.
	Travels throughout his career in Egypt, Greece, Italy, the United States, and Russia.

Notes on the Editor and Authors

EDITH KERN, editor of this volume, is author of a book on French literary criticism in the seventeenth century. She has published many articles on comparative and contemporary literary criticism, dealing particularly with such writers as Beckett and Brecht. She is a professor of French at St. John's University, New York, and has recently been Visiting Professor of Comparative Literature at the University of California at Los Angeles.

RENÉ MARILL-ALBÉRÈS, well-known French novelist, critic, and teacher, is intimately acquainted with the intellectual climate that produced the man Sartre and his works. He is the author of a volume on Jean-Paul Sartre.

HAZEL E. BARNES is author of *The Literature of Possibility* and has translated Sartre's fundamental work *L'Être et le néant* (*Being and Nothingness*), providing it with an illuminating introduction. She is a Professor of Classics at the University of Colorado and has contributed many articles to scholarly periodicals.

ERIC BENTLEY, outstanding drama critic, author of books on theatrical criticism, and translator of Brecht, is Professor of Dramatic Literature at Columbia University. He has directed plays on well-known American as well as European stages and personally assisted Brecht in the direction of his own plays.

H. J. BLACKHAM is an English philosopher, writer, and editor with a special talent for presenting the complexities of thought in a simple manner. He is the author of *Six Existentialist Thinkers; The Human Tradition;* and *Political Discipline in a Free Society;* as well as editor of a humanist journal.

ROBERT CHAMPIGNY, author of *Stages on Sartre's Way* and a study of Camus entitled *Sur un héros païen,* is a French critic, philosopher, and poet, now teaching at Indiana University.

KENNETH DOUGLAS is a Professor of French at Yale University. He is editor of *Yale French Studies,* co-editor of an *Anthology of World Masterpieces,* and is author of the *Critical Bibliography of Existentialism* and many critical essays on Valéry, Sartre, and other contemporary writers.

RENÉ GIRARD, the author of *Mensonge romantique et vérité romanesque* and editor of *Proust,* a volume in Prentice-Hall's Twentieth Century Views series. He has contributed to French and American journals on topics of literary criticism and the history of ideas. He is a Professor of French at Johns Hopkins University.

JACQUES GUICHARNAUD became an admirer and friend of Sartre, Beauvoir, and Camus, whose intellectual influence and leadership during the French Resistance he deeply appreciated as a young student in wartime France. He has since established himself as playwright, teacher, and critic, and has recently published a volume on *Modern French Theatre from Giraudoux to Beckett*. He is a Professor of French at Yale University.

FREDRIC JAMESON teaches French at Harvard University. He is author of the first large-scale stylistic study of Sartre, entitled *Sartre: The Origins of a Style*.

CLAUDE-EDMONDE MAGNY, French critic, writer, and teacher, is one of the most perceptive observers and interpreters of the contemporary literary scene in France and the United States. She has published brilliant studies of the modern novel.

GUIDO MORPURGO-TAGLIABUE is a well-known Italian philosopher and author of numerous books on aesthetics and stylistics. He is a Professor at the University of Milan.

HENRI PEYRE, outstanding French scholar, writer, critic, and brilliant commentator on the cultural climate of our times, is head of the Romance Language Department at Yale University.

ORESTE PUCCIANI is author of *The French Theatre Since 1930* and Chairman of the French Department at the University of California at Los Angeles. He has personally interviewed Sartre concerning the play on which he comments here, and has enthusiastically and searchingly interpreted existentialist literature to specialized as well as general audiences through essays, lectures, and presentations of Sartre's plays.

THEOPHIL SPOERRI, until 1956 Professor of French and Italian Literature (and for two years Rector) at the University of Zürich, is an author of world-renown and a profound and sensitive critic.

JOHN D. WILD is a Professor of Philosophy at Harvard University and has written a number of books, giving expression to the manifold interests in his field. As a Guggenheim Fellow he studied for a year with Martin Heidegger at Freiburg.

EDMUND WILSON, one of the most versatile minds on the American literary scene, has distinguished himself as book reviewer and author of novels and plays as well as of books in the fields of economics, history and, above all, literary criticism.

Bibliography of Works by Sartre

PHILOSOPHY

1936   *L'Imagination* (Paris: Presses Universitaires). Trans.: *Psychology and Imagination* (New York: Philosophical Library, 1948)

1936-
1937   "La Transcendance de l'Égo," *Recherches Philosophiques*, VI. Trans.: *The Transcendence of the Ego* (New York: The Noonday Press, 1957)

1939   *Esquisse d'une théorie des émotions* (Paris: Hermann). Trans.: *The Emotions, Outline of a Theory* (New York: Philosophical Library, 1948)

1940   *L'Imaginaire, psychologie phénoménologique de l'imagination* (Paris: Gallimard). Trans.: *The Psychology of the Imagination* (New York: Rider, 1951)

1943   *L'Être et le néant* (Paris: Gallimard). Trans.: *Being and Nothingness* (New York: Philosophical Library, 1956)

1960   *Critique de la raison dialectique*, I (Paris: Gallimard)

NOVELS AND SHORT STORIES

1938   *La Nausée* (Paris: Gallimard). Trans.: *Nausea* (New York: New Directions, 1949)

1939   *Le Mur* (Paris: Gallimard). Trans.: *The Wall and Other Stories* (New York: New Directions, 1948)

1945-
1949   *Les Chemins de la liberté*: I, *L'Âge de raison;* II, *Le Sursis;* III. *La Mort dans l'âme* (Paris: Gallimard). Trans.: *Roads to Freedom:* I, *Age of Reason* (1947); II, *The Reprieve* (1947); III, *Troubled Sleep* (1951) (New York: Knopf)

THEATER

1943   *Les Mouches* (Paris: Gallimard). Trans.: *The Flies* (New York: Knopf, 1947)

1944   *Huis-clos* (Paris: Gallimard). Trans.: *No Exit* (New York: Knopf, 1947)

1946   *Morts sans sépulture, Théâtre I* (Paris: Gallimard). Trans.: *The Victors: Three Plays* (New York: Knopf, 1949)

1946   *La Putain respectueuse* (Paris: Nagel). Trans.: *The Respectful Prostitute, Art and Action* (New York: Twice A Year Press, 1949)

1948   *Les Mains sales* (Paris: Gallimard). Trans.: *Dirty Hands: Three Plays* (New York: Knopf, 1949)

1951   *Le Diable et le bon Dieu* (Paris: Gallimard). Trans.: *The Devil and the Good Lord and Two Other Plays* (New York: Knopf, 1960). Trans. (England): *Lucifer and the Good Lord* (London: Hamilton, 1952)

1954   *Kean* (Paris: Gallimard). Trans.: *Kean, The Devil and the Good Lord and Two Other Plays* (New York: Knopf, 1960)

1955   *Nekrassov* (Paris: Gallimard)

1960   *Les Séquestrés d'Altona* (Paris: Gallimard). Trans.: *The Condemned of Altona* (New York: Knopf, 1961)

LITERARY CRITICISM AND POLITICS

1946   *L'Existentialisme est un humanisme* (Paris: Nagel). Trans.: *Existentialism* (New York: Philosophical Library, 1947)

1947   "Qu'est-ce que la littérature?" *Les Temps modernes,* II:18-III:22. Trans.: *What is Literature?* (New York: Philosophical Library, 1949)

1947   *Situation I* (Paris: Gallimard). Partly translated in: *Literary and Philosophical Essays* (New York: Philosophical Library, 1957)

1947   *Baudelaire* (Paris: Gallimard). Trans.: *Baudelaire* (Norfolk: New Directions, 1950)

1948   *Situation II* (Paris: Gallimard). Contains "Qu'est-ce que la littérature?"

1949   *Situation III* (Paris: Gallimard). Partly translated in *Literary and Philosophical Essays* (New York: Philosophical Library, 1957)

1952   *Saint-Genêt: comédien et martyr* (Paris: Gallimard)

Selected Critical Bibliography of Works on Sartre

Bibliography

Douglas, Kenneth. *A Critical Bibliography of Existentialism* (The Paris School). *Yale French Studies,* Monograph No. 1 (New Haven, 1950). This carefully organized work lists Sartre's publications and contains a critical bibliography of books and articles on the author up to the date of publication. Extremely useful.

Biographical

Beauvoir, Simone de. *La Force de l'âge* (Paris: Gallimard, 1960). Intelligent, anecdotal. Throws light on the origin and development of some of Sartre's ideas. Many references to collaboration and friendship between the two authors.

Chapsal, Madeleine. "Jean-Paul Sartre," *Les Écrivains en personne* (Paris: Julliard, 1960). Interesting personal interview.

Jeanson, Francis. *Sartre par lui-même* (Paris: Editions du Seuil, 1955). Applies Sartrean procedure of seeing the writer and his work as the synthesis of an original choice. Instructive and interesting, but often biased.

Philosophy

Barnes, Hazel E. "Introduction," *Being and Nothingness by Jean-Paul Sartre* (New York: Philosophical Library, 1956). Comments on and illuminates Sartrean thought as expressed in *Being and Nothingness* and previous writings.

Beauvoir, Simone de. *The Ethics of Ambiguity.* Trans. Bernard Frechtman (New York: Philosophical Library, 1948). Interesting though perhaps misleading interweaving of her own and Sartre's views on existentialist Ethics.

Blackham, H. J. *Six Existentialist Thinkers* (New York: The Macmillan Company, 1952). Admirably concise and clear presentation of existential thought, establishing differences and similarities between its best-known representatives.

Campbell, Robert. *Sartre ou une littérature philosophique* (Paris: Ardent, 1945). Still eminently valid for its intelligent emphasis on the psychological and literary aspects of Sartre's philosophy.

Collins, James. *The Existentialists: A Critical Study* (Chicago: Regnery, 1952). Intelligently and objectively presents the Catholic point of view.

Desan, Wilfrid. *The Tragic Finale: An Essay on the Philosophy of Jean-Paul Sartre* (Cambridge: Harvard University Press, 1954). Reprinted in paperback by Harper Torchbooks, 1960. A good survey of the various facets of Sartrean thought, including Sartre's views on psychoanalysis. Often dissenting and pointing out inconsistencies.

Dutt, K. Guru. *Existentialism and Indian Thought* (New York: 1960). Brief presentation of Hindu philosophy and its contacts with existentialism.

Grene, Marjorie. *Existentialism* (Chicago: University of Chicago Press, 1960). First published as *Dreadful Freedom* (1948). Penetrating introduction to existential thought, although the author admits need for revision in the light of her later studies. Dissenting.

Heidegger, Martin. *Über den Humanismus* (Frankfurt am Main: Vittorio Klostermann, 1947). Of special interest because of controversial discussion of Sartre's *Existentialism*.

Holz, Hans Heinz, *Jean-Paul Sartre: Darstellung und Kritik seiner Philosophie* (Meisenheim: Westkulturverlag, 1951). Intelligent and faithful presentation of Sartre's philosophy against the background of German philosophical thought.

Jeanson, Francis. *Le problème moral de la pensée de Sartre* (Paris: Eds. du Myrthe, 1947). Praised by Sartre as the best presentation of his Ethics.

Moeller, Joseph. *Absurdes Sein: Eine Auseinandersetzung mit der Ontologie Jean-Paul Sartres* (Stuttgart: Kohlhammer, 1959). A critical evaluation of Sartrean thought and an attempt to "surpass" it. Valuable for its comprehensive bibliography, which lists German titles of Sartre's works.

Murdoch, Iris. *Sartre: Romantic Rationalist* (New Haven: Yale University Press, 1953). A brief general survey of the man and his work with spots of profound insight.

Wahl, Jean. *A Short History of Existentialism.* Trans. F. Williams and S. Maron (New York: Philosophical Library, 1949). Contains thumbnail definitions of existential thought.

Wild, John D. *The Challenge of Existentialism* (Bloomington: Indiana University Press, 1959). A thorough and comprehensible introduction to existential thought and thinkers.

Literature

Some issues of periodicals entirely dedicated to Existentialism:

Existentialism. Yale French Studies, I: 1 (1948)

Foray Through Existentialism, Yale French Studies, XVI (Winter 1955-56)

The Theatre of Jean-Paul Sartre, The Tulane Drama Review, V (Spring 1961)

Albérès, René Marill. *Jean-Paul Sartre: Philosopher Without Faith.* Trans. Wade Baskin (New York: Philosophical Library, 1961). Good, brief, general introduction to Sartre's work.

Barnes, Hazel E. *The Literature of Possibility: A Study in Humanistic Existentialism* (Lincoln: University of Nebraska Press, 1959). Sartre's literary work seen particularly from philosophical, psychological, and sociological points of view.

Bentley, Eric. *The Playwright as Thinker* (New York: Noonday Press, 1955). First published in 1945, it represents an early but still valid view of Sartre as playwright.

Brombert, Victor. *The Intellectual Hero; Studies in the French Novel, 1880-1955* (Philadelphia: Lippincott, 1961). Contains a brilliant chapter on the "impossible heroes" of Sartre.

Champigny, Robert. *Stages on Sartre's Way* (Bloomington: Indiana University

Press, 1959). Sartre's work considered as stages of an unfinished itinerary. Emphasis on aesthetics. Ethical concepts derived from Sartre's fiction.

Guicharnaud, Jacques, *Modern French Theatre from Giraudoux to Beckett* (New Haven: Yale University Press, 1961). Has a chapter discussing the role of Sartre and Camus in modern French theater. Practical aspects of the theater are also illumined. Very useful.

Jameson, Fredric. *Sartre: The Origins of a Style* (New Haven: Yale University Press, 1961). First full-scale study of Sartre's style. Searching, perceptive, profound.

Magny, Claude-Edmonde. *Les Sandales d'Empédocle* (Neufchâtel. La Baconnière, 1945). Contains an excellent chapter on Sartre's short stories and on *Nausea*.

Koefoed, Oleg. "L'Oeuvre littéraire de Sartre," *Orbis Litterarum*, VI (1948), pp. 209-72 and VII (1949), pp. 61-141. Major Danish article, a thorough and comprehensive study of Sartre's literary work. Especially good interpretations of the short stories.

Peyre, Henri. *The Contemporary French Novel* (New York: Oxford University Press, 1955). Contains a brilliant and highly informative chapter on Sartre's novels.

Spoerri, Theophil. *Die Struktur der Existenz: Einführung in die Kunst der Interpretation* (Zürich: Speer-Verlag, 1951). Imaginative and stimulating interpretation of literature and life in terms of their common existential structure.

Criticism

Morpurgo-Tagliabue, Guido. *L'Esthétique contemporaine* (Milan: Marzorati, 1960). Places Sartre's literary criticism in the wider frame of existential and phenomenological aesthetics. Critical, scholarly investigation. Some brilliant insights.

Psychoanalysis

American Journal of Psychoanalysis, passim.

Fromm, Erich. *Escape From Freedom* (New York: Rinehart, 1941); *Man For Himself: An Inquiry into the Psychology of Ethics* (New York: Rinehart, 1947); *Psychoanalysis and Religion* (New Haven: Yale University Press, 1950); *The Sane Society* (New York: Rinehart, 1955). All these works contain many ideas parallel to Sartrean thought.

Horney, Karen. *New Ways in Psychoanalysis* (New York: Norton, 1939). Interesting parallels to existentialist thinking.

Kelman, Harold. "Life History as Therapy," *American Journal of Psychoanalysis,* a series of articles starting with XV, No. 2 (1955).

May, Rollo, Ernst Angel, and Henri F. Ellenberger. *Existence: A New Dimension in Psychiatry and Psychology* (New York: Basic Books, 1958). Though it takes issue with "existential psychoanalysis," it utilizes Sartre's work.

Sonnemann, Ulrich. *Existence and Therapy: An Introduction to Phenomenological Psychology and Existential Analysis* (New York: Grune and Stratton, 1954). In spite of a promising title, this proves too involved for the non-specialist.

Van Den Berg, J. H. *The Phenomenological Approach to Psychiatry: An Introduction to Recent Phenomenological Psychopathology* (Springfield: Thomas, 1955). Hazel Barnes points out many parallels and references to Sartre's work.

TWENTIETH CENTURY VIEWS

S-TC-1   CAMUS, edited by Germaine Brée

S-TC-2   T. S. ELIOT, edited by Hugh Kenner

S-TC-3   ROBERT FROST, edited by James M. Cox

S-TC-4   PROUST, edited by René Girard

S-TC-5   WHITMAN, edited by Roy Harvey Pearce

S-TC-6   SINCLAIR LEWIS, edited by Mark Schorer

S-TC-7   STENDAHL, edited by Victor Brombert

S-TC-8   HEMINGWAY, edited by Robert P. Weeks

S-TC-9   FIELDING, edited by Ronald Paulson

S-TC-10   THOREAU, edited by Sherman Paul

S-TC-11   BRECHT, edited by Peter Demetz

S-TC-12   EMERSON, edited by Milton R. Konvitz and Stephen E. Whicher

S-TC-13   MELVILLE, edited by Richard Chase

S-TC-14   LORCA, edited by Manuel Duran

S-TC-15   Homer, edited by George Steiner and Robert Fagles

S-TC-16   DOSTOEVSKY, edited by René Wellek

S-TC-17   KAFKA, edited by Ronald Gray

S-TC-18   BAUDELAIRE, edited by Henri Peyre

S-TC-19   JOHN DONNE, edited by Helen Gardner

S-TC-20   EDITH WHARTON, edited by Irving Howe

S-TC-21   SARTRE, edited by Edith Kern

S-TC-22   BEN JONSON, edited by Jonas A. Barish

S-TC-23   YEATS, edited by John Unterecker

Future Titles

JANE AUSTEN, edited by Ian Watt

BLAKE, edited by Northrop Frye

EMILY DICKINSON, edited by Richard B. Sewall

DRYDEN, edited by Bernard Schilling

FAULKNER, edited by Robert Penn Warren

FITZGERALD, edited by Arthur Mizener

HARDY, edited by Albert J. Guerard

HOPKINS, edited by John Hollander

HENRY JAMES, edited by Leon Edel

JOYCE, edited by Cleanth Brooks

LAWRENCE, edited by Mark Spilka

MALRAUX, edited by R. W. B. Lewis

MILTON, edited by Louis Martz

POE, edited by Harrison Hayford

POUND, edited by Walter Sutton

STEVENS, edited by Marie Borroff

SWIFT, edited by Ernest Tuveson

MARK TWAIN, edited by Henry Nash Smith

WORDSWORTH, edited by M. H. Abrams

DATE DUE

JAN 10 '66	JAN 8 '71		
MAR 28 '66	OCT 1 '71		
MAY 11 '66	FEB 8 '72		
MAY 19 '66	MAR 17 '72		
MAR 6 '67	JAN 3 '73		
MAY 4 '67	JUN 12 1974		
MAY 15 '67	MAY 20 '75		
MAY 30 '67	MAR 18 '76		
APR 4 '68	NOV 3 '76		
APR 26 '68	NOV 17 '76		
MAY 10 '68	AUG 5 '81		
MAY 31 '68	DEC 29 '81		
JUL 11 '68			
Jul 22 '68			
DEC 16 '68			
JAN 6 '69			
APR 29 '69			
MAY 1 '70			
GAYLORD			PRINTED IN U.S.A.